Memoirs of an Intelligence Sapper

Memoirs of an Intelligence Sapper

by

Lt General Sir David Willison

The Memoir Club

© Sir David Willison 2007

First published in 2007 by
The Memoir Club
Stanhope Old Hall
Stanhope
Weardale
County Durham

All rights reserved.
Unauthorised duplication
contravenes existing laws.

British Library Cataloguing in
Publication Data.
A catalogue record for this book
is available from the
British Library

ISBN: 978-1-84104-073-8

Typeset by TW Typesetting, Plymouth, Devon
Printed by CPI Bath

Contents

List of Illustrations vii
Foreword ix

Chapter 1   1919–1939 1
Chapter 2   Wartime days 10
Chapter 3   Post-war period (1945–1950) 33
Chapter 4   To Egypt and Berlin (1950–1955) 50
Chapter 5   Camberley and Aden (1955–1960) 64
Chapter 6   Command in Ripon (1960–1963) 84
Chapter 7   London (1963–1966) Colonel MI4 98
Chapter 8   London and Germany (1967–1971) BGS
            (Intelligence) 113
Chapter 9   London (1971–1975) DS (Int) then Deputy Chief
            of Defence Staff (Intelligence) 133
Chapter 10 MoD London (1975–1978) Director General
            Intelligence 157
Chapter 11 Lymington: 1978 onwards 178

Index 196

List of Illustrations

My term at the 'Shop', RMA Woolwich, 1939	8
Inspecting a dual carriageway Bailey built at the SME Ripon, 1943	16
Plaque recording 17 Fd Coy Bridge over the Orne Canal that disappeared soon after the death of M. Gondrée	19
HQ 1 Indian Infantry Brigade in Java, 1946	35
Topping-out Ceremony, British HQ Berlin, 1953	59
My mother and father, 1952	67
Appletree Cottage, Charlton, Andover, 1964	70
With Betty, Janet and Robin at the OBE Presentation at Buckingham Palace, 1961	78
Commanding 38 Corps Engineer Regiment at Ripon, 1962	85
Inspecting the Guard of Honour with the Mayor before the Cathedral Service, Ripon Square, 1977	87
Hurricane Hattie, British Honduras, 1962, with George Price, Chief Minister	92
Tour of Congo, 1965	103
Commissioning of Jeremy Nittle into the US Navy at Philadelphia Naval Base, 1969	124
Deputy Chief of Defence Staff (Intelligence), 1972–75	139
Cruising with Betty, 1980	141
As Chief Royal Engineer at Old Comrades Parade at Chatham, 1980	166
Farewell visit to Washington as Director General Intelligence MOD with Director of DIA, 1978	173
Freedom of Nienburg Procession, 1979	179

Chard presentation, Hatch Beauchamp, 1981 181

Visit by Prime Minister Gibraltar to Gibraltar Barracks Minley with Governor General Sir William Jackson GCB, KBE, MC (late RE), 1981 183

With David Kern at Nat West, 1982 185

Freedom of the City of London, 1979 186

Unveiling of Royal Engineers Memorial, Arromanches, 1994 ... 193

Foreword

By Major-General L Scott-Bowden CBE, DSO, MC

I have known David Willison for over seventy-two years, having met him at the Royal Military Academy Woolwich. Our paths have crossed frequently. In Normandy he was very severely wounded late on D-Day 6 June 1944 when 'as senior officer on the spot' he was giving orders to an officer in a tank, for an immediate attack by his sappers of the 17th (Nova Scotia) Field Company Royal Engineers, which had burnt down the White House, and destroyed part of the Navy Yard in Washington in 1912 in a previous contretemps! The tank was hit by a shot from a German antitank gun. A large splinter from the shot hit David in the back of his neck; he was fortunate not to have been killed.

After four months' hospitalisation, he was determined to get back to 3rd Divisional Engineers and returned to replace Nigel Gell, who had just been wounded, to command 246 (Welsh) Field Company. Casualties in the 3rd British Infantry Division were indeed heavy, particularly in the Engineers and Infantry, who had led the initial assault on the beaches. David found in subsequent researches when he was the Chief Royal Engineer, that a third of the British troops on shore by the end of D-Day were Royal Engineers!

David's early years were spent in Egypt. He came home to preparatory school in England, then went to Wellington College, and finally on to the Royal Military Academy Woolwich, from which he passed in and out top of his term. In 1942 he married Elizabeth (Betty) Bates who was charming, delightful, very attractive and also a good sailor. Later, they were unbeatable in the Sunday morning races at the Aden Yacht Club in 1960 to 1962. They had three children, Celia, Janet (to whom I am Godfather) and Robin. Betty died in 1989 and David was lucky enough to marry Trisha Clitherow in 1994. Trisha is quite delightful and a great help to him in his old age. Her first husband died of a heart attack in 1977. She has two children by this first marriage and five grandchildren.

David had attended the Staff College Course at Camberley, immediately after the war, and was then sent to the Far East as Brigade Major, First Indian Infantry Brigade, later holding a sector around Batavia (Jakarta) against Sukarno's forces, who were opposing the reoccupation of Java by 'Imperialistic' forces. The Dutch, who were recovering from German occupation, had unfortunately sent out their SS Brigade, which had fought in Russia against the allies, and were very unsuitable as immediate neighbours. They killed nine of the Seaforth Highlanders who had gone through one of their road blocks at night. The Seaforts were about to retaliate, and David was concerned in stopping another 'local war'.

After his Far Eastern tour, he returned to the Staff College as an instructor, commanded an engineer regiment and was assigned to an important post on the intelligence staff in the War Office, where full use was made of his talents. In due course he progressed to the top military appointment of Deputy Chief of Defence Staff (Intelligence) from 1973 to 1976, latterly as adviser to Field Marshal Lord Carver, the Chief of Defence Staff. On retirement from the Army he continued working in the MOD as Director General Intelligence from 1976 to 1978 and as intelligence adviser to the Minister of Defence. At times, he briefed the Prime Minister and other members of the Cabinet. He has produced a fascinating memoir of great personal interest and historical value.

Chapter 1

1919–1939

As a soldier I was always taught to define my aim. The aim is the most difficult part of any appreciation, and more thought should go into analysing what you are trying to achieve than into the rest of the work. First and foremost, then, I want to record for my family how my life has developed down the years. Secondly, there is the need to produce a saleable commodity. This entails introducing views on some people and policies within which my life has run its course. With these two strands in mind, my personal recollections are marshalled in the book.

Many years as an intelligence staff officer inclined me to practise what I preached by not retaining any papers. I have felt this failure acutely in preparing this account. Added to this, my father burned his house down around his ears in 1966. All family records and a unique collection of penny black stamps perished as a result, as did he. So memory has had to be my main guide.

I entered this life on Christmas Day, 1919 in Camberley, Surrey. My mother, Hyacinth D'Arcy Vigors, came from a Huguenot family who were settled in Ireland by the English soon after the revocation of the Edict of Nantes in 1690 and the resulting outflow of Protestants from France. My mother, born in 1896 to Hyacinth D'Arcy and Major Phillip Urban Vigors, met my father while nursing in a hospital in St Omer in 1917. My father was Arthur Cecil Willison who was commissioned from Sandhurst into the Sherwood Foresters in early 1915. He survived as an infantry officer throughout the rest of the war in France, collecting a DSO and two Military Crosses while doing so. Typical of his generation, he never said a word to me about the circumstances of these awards for bravery. My parents married in 1918; my father was part of the garrison of Schleswig Holstein during the Plebiscite there in 1919 and by Christmas 1919 was stationed at Blackdown near Camberley.

My father came from a typical Victorian family. The eldest son, William, was destined for the church and became a pastor in the Indian Army. The two daughters, Queenie and Mary, spent their lives looking after their parents. The youngest son, Arthur, went to the Imperial Services College and entered Sandhurst in 1913. My grandfather came from North Yorkshire, where he was born in 1861. He married a rich heiress called Pollard, whose family owned a large house called Scar Hall in Bradford. The site is now a housing estate, I believe. Their family solicitor escaped to America in 1912, taking virtually all my grandparents' money. When I first remember them, they were living in a small house in Southsea. My grandfather had been an insurance salesman but by then was retired. My grandmother can only be described as 'formidable' and ruled them all with a rod of iron. She died in the early thirties and the family then moved to Havant, where my paternal grandfather died in 1947.

My Uncle William led a roving life; after he retired as a pastor from the Indian Army he became a resident priest to the British community at Le Zoute in Belgium. By then he had married. He and his wife were evacuated to England in 1940, after which he took up a living outside Whitby in Yorkshire. After the war he went to Tangiers in the same capacity as he had held at Le Zoute. After retirement he settled in the outskirts of Torquay, where he married the daughter of an Admiral of the Fleet called Forbes, soon after the death of his first wife. He and I last met at my Aunt Queenie's funeral at Parracombe, North Devon, where she had looked after my father for several years. During the burial, Uncle William sidled up to me and said that, as my father would provide for me, he intended to leave me nothing. He was as good as his word. He left it all to the RSPCA, including family silver and memorabilia.

My mother's family also had their foibles. Her father had won a DSO during the South African War at the turn of the twentieth century. She grew up at Whimple near Exeter, where her father was stationed at the depot of the Devonshire Regiment. He had retired to Ireland by the First World War and my first memory of my grandparents was in the early twenties when they lived in a house in Rathmines, a suburb of Dublin, looking out over the harbour.

My maternal grandmother became a Christian Scientist in Dublin, and both my mother and her younger sister Evelyn were brought up as Christian Scientists, I suspect against my grandfather's wishes. He and my grandmother parted and he took up residence in a private hotel in the Cromwell Road in London. Every year he would go to Ireland to fish, basing himself on the house of the O'Gradys, the lady of the house being a Vigors. The O'Grady sons, Gerald and Phillip, were at Wellington College, where I was also educated. Phillip overlapped me there by two years, whilst Gerald was somewhat older.

Gerald became 'the' O'Grady on the death of his father, who was a Colonel in the Indian Army medical corps. Phillip became a gunner and I had contact with him later in my life at Camberley, where he was at the Royal Military Academy and I was teaching at the Staff College.

My mother's father died in 1938. I used to visit him for lunch at his hotel in the middle of the late thirties but never established a live relationship. My grandmother will reappear in my life as my tale unfolds.

My first recollections as a boy were of Bovington Camp, home to the newly-formed Royal Tank Regiment. My father was a founder member of the Regiment in 1922 on transfer from the Sherwood Foresters. He was known as 'The Ant' from much service with the Hampshire Regiment in the First World War. I recall climbing over a First War tank that was still in service in the twenties, thus providing a foretaste of things to come in the Defence weapons field. I remember vividly camping and swimming at Arishmel Gap camp on the coast below the tank firing ranges and also at Durdle Daw, an unusual rock formation on the shore towards Weymouth. In later years I have often sailed along this coast in my own boat with grandchildren aboard. I have bored them, no doubt, with stories of ancient times along this superb Dorset coast line.

In 1927 my father was given command of the armoured car squadron based on the Citadel in Cairo. On at least one occasion he was ordered to motor down furiously to the Musqué area to confront hostile crowds, in support of the Egyptian Police, but did not have to open fire. For me, Cairo meant going to school for the first time, after ministrations by governesses in England. I joined the English School in Cairo, which was then located in an ancient building adjacent to the Kasr el Nil Barracks in the heart of the city. The headmaster was called Mr Gross, a strict disciplinarian who ran an efficient and good school, and as a day-boy I learned a great deal.

In Cairo we lived in a pleasant flat in Dar el Shifa, a road in the Garden City, not far from the British Embassy and no great distance from my school. My parents had a wide circle of friends, including the Dempsters, long settled in Alexandria, and Dr Reisener, an American who was excavating in the Step Pyramid area, and who gave me a small relic of ancient Egypt: a scarab which I still retain. We often used to drive out to the Mena House Hotel to swim. The three great pyramids and the Sphinx were well known to us, as was the Step Pyramid at Saqquara. The Tutankhamen treasure was already on display at the Cairo Museum, a remarkable sight. The Gezira club was another favourite haunt. I learned to swim in its pool. Another memory is of staying with the Dempsters near the Nile Barrage where they had a farm. We saw the first trickle of the annual Nile flood entering their land – an unforgettable sight.

In the autumn of 1929, aged nearly 10, I started school in England at St Michael's Preparatory School in Uckfield, under Mr Hockey as headmaster. This was the only Christian Science-based school in

England. It had been started under the auspices of Lady Nancy Astor. Her two sons were sent there, one of whom, Jake, was a little older than me. Teaching standards were not brilliant and when I came to take the Common Entrance exam for Wellington in 1933, I barely scraped through and was placed in the Middle Fourth on arrival.

I have no very distinct memories of my four years at Uckfield. In the holidays I had to live with my maternal grandmother at Panswood, a house about two miles south of Farnham. For one summer holiday we both went out to Egypt to stay with my parents. In 1931 my father became a student at the Staff College at Camberley and we lived there until 1933 in a charming little house parallel to the railway line. I have fond memories of the garden, as I developed a painful mastoid in the summer of 1932 and spent much of the summer resting as best I could in the open air. My father used to ride in the Staff College Drag Hunt regularly; he was also gardens member of his year. In this he was ably supported by my mother, another keen gardener. By this time she had become a practitioner of the Christian Science Church and was much in demand as a faith healer. There was a local Christian Science church to which we went each Sunday. But I am afraid that little of the teaching of Mary Baker Eddy rubbed off on me. I remained a sceptic about the efficacy of faith healing, not least after my mastoid experience.

1933 saw me installed in the Blücher dormitory at Wellington, the same year that my parents set out for India. My father, still a captain, was sent initially to Razmak on the North West Frontier and then became G3 staff officer, Intelligence, to General Carslake at Western Command in Quetta. My parents were in Quetta at the time of the appalling earthquake in that area. My father, from personal observation, wrote the citation for the Albert Medal won by Captain John Cowley of the Royal Engineers for his bravery in rescuing many local people from their collapsed homes. (John Cowley was later my company commander at the Royal Military Academy at Woolwich and rose to the rank of Lieutenant General, Master General of the Ordnance, in the post-war period.) My mother, who was a trained nurse, went to Kohat to help with the large number of injured people. She was awarded the Kaiser-e-Hind gold medal for her work. My father became a major in 1937 and spent the rest of his time in India as Deputy Assistant Adjutant and Quartermaster (DAAQ) in Deccan District in Hyderabad, a princely state, not officially part of British India.

I returned to spending my holidays with my grandmother in Farnham. My Aunt Evelyn, who had married V.S. Pritchett, the well-known author, invited me on two occasions to sail on the Broads in a hired craft.

V.S.P. was a charming and cultivated man. Evelyn was left wing and had not progressed intellectually in step with her husband. I enjoyed both trips on the tranquil waters of the Broads in their company, but I was not surprised to hear that they had divorced in 1936. I suspect that failure to produce any children was a prime source of discord. Both did so on re-marriage. My aunt took up with a man half her age called Maxwell and produced three illegitimate children before eventually they conformed by getting married.

Wellington under headmaster Malim was a strange place. Homosexuality was rife in my dormitory amongst those mostly a bit older than the intake of 1933. Malim was a classicist who had been put in by the Board of Governors to leaven the mass of an essentially Army background school. He refused to have any dealings with those, like myself, who went either to Woolwich or to Sandhurst, the army then maintaining two training establishments for its future officers. He imported left-wing elements to the staff of whom the most notorious was Francis Worsley, my tutor in the Blücher. He was a self-confessed member of the Communist Party of Great Britain. As the menace of Germany became more and more apparent, opinions began to change. Worsley left College in 1936 and was succeeded by Mr Denbigh, who gassed himself in his study soon after the war ended.

Teaching was good at Wellington. I owe much to Mr MacDermott who taught me mathematics in the run-up to taking the entrance examination for the Royal Military Academy at Woolwich. Physics and chemistry were also well taught and helped me to pass the Higher Certificate in three subjects. In addition, I learned quite a useful amount of German, which I also managed to pass at Higher Certificate level. My last year was spent in the Army Sixth and led to my passing in first in the order of merit to enter Woolwich. The only man to ignore this result was my headmaster. I suppose he could not bring himself to speak to a militarist, as no doubt he regarded all those in the Army sixth form. Only classicists were acceptable.

Sport was naturally well supported at Wellington. I played three times for the rugby first team but was eventually pipped at the post by a taller and heavier character by the name of Coleman and had to settle for second fifteen colours. I was in the swimming eight for my last two years, mostly as a diver. Tennis was good fun, as were fives and squash.

I accompanied my maternal grandmother on several holiday trips to Ireland in the late thirties. She wanted to see a number of D'Arcy and Vigors relatives. We visited the main house of the Vigors clan at Burgage near Carlow, while staying with the O'Gradys near Kilkenny. Edward

Vigors, at that time clerk to the House of Lords, lived in the house. We also went to see his estranged wife Mary in Kerry. We met briefly Ashmead Vigors, who was Edward's brother. We spent a night in Deirdre Welsford's mother's family house. We also visited the Copes in Northern Ireland; they lived near Armagh. Their daughter Diana was about my age but, unfortunately, she already had a boyfriend.

I had contact with Desmond Vigors, who came to Wellington about two years after me. A D'Arcy relative was also there. I stayed with his family once in Guernsey during the summer holidays, where his father commanded a company of the Hampshire Regiment. Tim Vigors went to Cranwell at the same time as I went to Woolwich. I used to see quite a bit of him in London before the war. He escaped from Singapore and after retirement pioneered moving racehorses by air.

Another, even grander residence that my parents and I stayed at was Newcastle Lyons, about twenty miles west of Dublin. Kathleen Lawless, daughter of Lord Cloncurry, had been a close friend of my mother since they met as VAD nurses in 1918. Newcastle Lyons was a huge house and the estate included a large well-stocked deer park. The butler, Brett by name, took me out stalking the deer and taught me to row on the lake within the park.

Despite being a closed-up boy who did not make friends easily, I made a number of lifelong friends in the Blücher. These included Malcolm Younger, Richard Bremner and Jamie Laing, to whose son I became godfather. I fear I failed in my duties to my godchild. All three sets of parents were most kind and generous to me while my parents were in India, and we went on skiing holidays to the Alps each winter before the outbreak of the Second World War. Malcolm and Richard became gunners and Jamie a sapper like myself.

In the summer of 1938 my parents paid for me to visit Secunderabad, where my father had become DAAG Deccan District. I took a train to Marseilles, joined a P & O liner and sailed to India amongst a group of young officers returning from leave at home. On arrival in Bombay I caught a train through Poona to Secunderabad. Life there was most pleasant. My parents had their own horses and we went riding every day. I met a number of young, newly-commissioned Indian officers, including Cariappa, later Chief of Staff of the Indian Army after independence. I remember the jewels in the palace of the Maharaja of Hyderabad and also the beautiful Turkish wife of his eldest son.

The return journey was even more exciting. From Bombay I went by ship to Karachi. There I boarded an Imperial Airways Dakota that had just begun a weekly service to India. We spent two and a half days on the journey, spending nights at Bahrain and Athens en route.

One of the main discussion points at Wellington amongst my contemporaries was whether or not to go into the Army. Some decided to go to university in the hope of finishing their degrees before war came. Others, myself among them, decided to get in on the ground floor of the Army because we felt in our bones that war was coming. Munich was regarded as a turning-point for the onset of war in the not so distant future. And so it was that I started training at the RMA Woolwich in January 1938. I passed out in June 1939, the last course to complete the full eighteen months' curriculum before the Second War.

The 'Shop' at Woolwich was in many ways an old-fashioned establishment. Military training amounted to little more than infantry tactics with a red flag to represent the section machine gun. Drill was a major factor culminating in a ceremonial passing-out parade on the large parade ground on the east front of the Shop buildings. This took place every six months as each intake was commissioned. Those at or near the top of the passing-out list became sappers. Many more became gunners and signallers, with the odd one going into the Royal Tank Regiment.

The great social event was the six-monthly ball following each passing-out parade. Since my last days at Wellington I had taken a great interest in girls. My earliest girlfriend was Deirdre Welsford. In the summer of 1932 my parents took a house in Mull which they shared with Deirdre's mother. On one occasion we took a dinghy out in perfect weather and covered about three miles on the open sea. On return we both got into hot water with our parents for a foolhardy escapade. Thereafter we kept in touch and Deirdre was my first guest at the Woolwich Ball. She repelled my ardour and I then took up with Pam Stewart, a blonde as against a brunette. We used to meet at my great aunt's house in 18 Alexander Place opposite the Victoria & Albert Museum. She became my second Ball guest.

In 1939 my parents came back from India via the Pacific and the Panama Canal. My father was posted as Second in Command, 5th Battalion Royal Tank Regiment at Perham Down near Tidworth. As the Commanding Officer was unmarried, my parents took over the CO's married quarters – Cambria House. They had an old friend in Weyhill, and there I met my future wife, Betty Vernon Bates, whose parents lived near-by: her father was a Group Captain in RAF Maintenance Command. Betty and I took to each other at once, and I began to see quite a bit of her. She worked in London as a secretary in the Shell Oil Company. She became my third guest at my passing-out ball in June 1939.

Before this event all those destined to become sappers had taken the Cambridge inter B.Sc. examination. I passed with flying colours and then

My term at the 'Shop', RMA Woolwich, 1939

learned that I was destined for Magdalen College, Cambridge, in October 1939. Having passed in first in the Army examination to enter Woolwich, I passed out first and was awarded the Pollock Gold Medal for so doing. On 1 July my term were commissioned into the Royal Engineers with orders to report for young officer training at the School of Military Engineering at Chatham later that month. We were fourteen strong from Woolwich and at Chatham we joined up with two university-entry officers and two Canadians from the Canadian Military Academy at Kingston to make eighteen in all. My career in the Army had begun.

CHAPTER 2

Wartime days

This chapter deals with my Second World War experiences and ends with attendance on the first post-war Staff College course at Camberley.

I REPORTED TO THE School of Military Engineering at Chatham in early July 1939. My commission was dated 1 July of that year and signed by King George VI. The term below mine was commissioned on 3 July, so both lots were in training as young officers together. Particular friends for life were Tommy Cochrane, Jack Gatford, Scotty Scott-Bowden and 'Dopey' Cowtan. My parents had kindly presented me with a Morris 8 Tourer at about the time of my final passing-out parade at 'The Shop'. So at Chatham I had wheels, a great advantage in getting both to London and to my father and mother at Perham Down.

At Chatham we young officers came under the beady eyes of the Brigade Major of the School and of the Adjutant, an incredibly well-turned-out Captain Foster. Our instructors included well-known characters in the Corps of Royal Engineers, such as Frank Simpson and 'Hindy' Caldwell, whom I later met as my Chief Engineer in 1941.

On Sunday 3 September we all went to the Garrison Church for morning service. As we came out the sirens sounded for an air raid warning, the first of the war. We trooped down to the cellars below the Headquarters Mess and waited in sepulchral silence for the bombing to begin. None was forthcoming. Some days later we were told that our course was to be telescoped so that we would be posted to units in February 1940. During that winter we were worked hard at the full gamut of engineer activities, both field and works services. Training culminated in 'wet' bridging at Wouldham during the bitter winter of January 1940 when we had to break the ice each morning to get the pontoons to move. On the Thames Estuary the sea along the shore froze solid.

Mess life went on as pre-war. We young officers had to be passed through the lower tier of the gauge while others beat us with rolled newspapers, as an initiation ritual. Weekends, however, were still ours to enjoy. I saw a lot of Betty Bates in London. My father had been posted on the outbreak of war as commanding officer of 40 Battalion Royal

Tank Regiment, a London TA Unit. My mother bought a charming house in Charlton, a mile north of Andover, to provide a family base. Sixty Six, as it was called, played a big part in our lives until 1947.

In January 1940, I received my first posting order. To my fury, it was not active service but in training. As top of my Batch I was sentenced to go to 141 Royal Engineers Officer Cadet Training Unit to help train young officers for the Corps. I reported for duty under Lt. Col. Binney at Malta Barracks, Aldershot, as a Class Officer in charge of thirty cadets. Most of my contemporaries at Chatham joined units in Belgium and were evacuated through Dunkerque in May, less several who had been killed or taken prisoner.

Once German bombing started soon after Dunkerque, the Sappers were ordered to set up a bomb disposal organisation. As an interim measure, a Captain Hawkins was designated as our unit bomb disposal officer. He co-opted me; together we went and looked at various holes in the ground where unexploded bombs were thought to lie. Of course, we had little knowledge of what to do and lacked any specialist equipment – that was still being developed. An abiding memory is of being called out to an Ordnance Depot at Thatcham near Newbury. I can still see in my mind's eye a huge warehouse full of picks and shovels, tied in bundles. A bomb had fallen through the roof and gone off amongst them. All the remaining roof trusses were festooned with bundles of picks and shovels!

On another occasion we were assembled in the Officers' Mess for tea when the air raid sirens sounded. Soon we heard the rumble of approaching German Heinkels. Led by Colonel Binney, we filed out onto the lawn and soon saw bombs actually falling from bomb bays onto Farnborough Airfield, which lay across the main road from where we were standing. Such was our innocence in those days.

At weekends I used to go to London to see Betty, whose office had moved from the City to Lensbury, alongside the Thames opposite Teddington. At night we went to the brightest and best places to dine and dance, particularly Hatchetts in Piccadilly. On the pay of 2/Lt. plus a grant of £50 a year to go with my Pollock Medal, I could afford to run a car, pay my mess bill and do all the things I wanted to do in London. Happy days indeed, while prices were still so cheap.

In September I reported to Havant as a Section Officer in 59 Field Company, 4th Divisional Engineers. In 1940 a Company consisted of 240 officers and men, and was divided into sections. (Now the figure for a Squadron is nearly a hundred lower but with much more machine power to support the sappers.)

My Section consisted of nearly sixty men with the excellent Sergeant Alexander as my prop and support. Two-thirds of 4th Divisional Engineers (who would now be called a Regiment of Royal Engineers) were still regular pre-war soldiers and 59 Field Company was no exception. Our Commander Royal Engineers (CRE) was Lt. Col. Coxwell-Rogers, a well-known horseman whose life pre-war had been bound up with a field squadron of horsed engineers in support of cavalry. He was a great character and a great man to work for. The Division had fought in France in the early summer and mostly had escaped from Dunkerque and beaches with little else other than clothes and personal weapons. After being re-equipped and made up to strength, the Division was allotted the sector from Chichester Harbour to Southampton to defend against the expected German sea-borne attack.

On arrival I found 59 Company ensconced in requisitioned houses and buildings in Havant. Jobs came thick and fast in the way of laying wire and mines as defences. My most vivid memory is of laying a tubular scaffolding obstacle across the bar at the mouth of Chichester Harbour. At high water we went out in boats and dropped tubular scaffolding over the side. At low water we went back, recovered our stores, and assembled them into a substantial obstacle to boatloads of German troops. One day we were so engaged when Stuka fighter-bombers came over us and dived to attack Tangmere airfield close by. I can assure my readers that runnels of sand give minimal protection even to a horizontal body! In all this work I was, of course, a learner driver and I could not have got by without the willing support of my Section Sergeant, the other NCOs and above all the sappers themselves. Many of them had up to ten years of service – in India as well as England. I learnt fast how to get on with them all, experience I sorely needed at the start of my career with soldiers.

Major Cowie, my company commander, was a very senior officer who remained aloof as I settled into the company community, but kindly towards us all. After the pressures on us diminished during the autumn of 1940 as a result of the success of the RAF in the Battle of Britain, he took up with a local barmaid and progressively absented himself from the Company. Our second-in-command was an intellectual but ineffective captain who seemed unable to cope with this untoward situation. We three section commanders were therefore thrust into the unenviable position of trying to cover up for our commander, whose absences steadily became longer.

The day came when our Colonel, based in Winchester, demanded to speak to Major Cowie. He was not with us so the Colonel demanded that he report to him early the following morning. I was deputed to go to the pub, find Major Cowie and tell him that his presence was demanded early the next day. I strode into the pub and demanded to see Major Cowie. The barmaid indicated that he was not there. I retorted that his career depended upon his attendance before the Colonel next morning. She relented and I was led upstairs where I found Major Cowie in bed and much the worse for wear. I explained what was required of him and said I would be round to collect him first thing in the morning. This I did and he was able to keep his end up with the Colonel next day. Things improved for the next few weeks, but then declined. We three subalterns decided that we had no alternative but to report to Winchester and tell our story. Colonel Coxwell-Rogers was quite unperturbed. He acted at once in suspending Major Cowie, who had previously been court-martialled for drinking – as the Colonel knew, and we did not. A new OC, Major Winkfield, arrived rapidly. Cowie was forced to retire and the last we heard of him was that he had become a fireman fighting the Blitz in London.

In the middle of the winter, the Company was ordered to move to Northwood House close to Sparsholt near Winchester. On one occasion, I was ordered to dispose of 2,000 pounds of weeping gelignite by blowing it up. We had a demolition training ground nearby, so I first of all ordered my Section to dig a shallow hole and very gingerly lifted out the weeping gelignite and put some into the hole. Having arranged alternative firing circuits as in our training, I pushed down the handle of the exploder. A most satisfactory bang resulted, plus a substantial hole in the ground. Progressively, I put more and more explosive in the hole that got steadily wider and deeper. I finished off with putting 500 pounds of dynamite in the crater. An appalling explosion took place and out of the crater rose a pressure ring of blast from which came a banshee howl. It screamed up into the sky and eventually disintegrated. My sappers were quite delighted as we made our way back to Northwood House.

In the early Spring of 1941, I was posted to Headquarters Royal Engineers as a Field Engineer on the Colonel's staff. Soon after we went on the first divisional exercise since Dunkerque. HQ was set up in a small village near Weymouth, with requisitioned houses as offices and messes. We junior folk in 'B' Mess watched agog as the senior officers' mess set itself up in a small house with only two bedrooms. One bedroom was obviously intended for the divisional commander and the other for the chief gunner, a brigadier. Next morning our chief, a half colonel, was in the bedroom and the brigadier was in the corridor. Need one say more about the personality of the Commander Royal Engineers? I think not!

In the late summer I was sent back to 59 Field Company as second-in-command, becoming a temporary captain, carrying out the administration for the Company and also still commanding a troop. We carried out a number of bridging exercises, including one to cross the River Thames near Goring. Two notable events occurred during the evening and early next morning. Firstly, we were visited by General Auchinleck, who was General Officer Commanding in Chief (GOC in C) Southern Command before going out to Egypt where my father came under his command. Secondly, I spent the night in unexpected company. When I went off duty a nurse conducted me to a bed in a house near the river. I fell asleep among recumbent forms – and woke up to find myself surrounded by gibbering lunatics! The house was an asylum, and no one had told me. I have never dressed myself so quickly in my life.

My father had been sent to Egypt in early 1941 with his regiment. After a brief spell as a staff officer in GHQ he was promoted Brigadier commanding 32 Army Tank Brigade with Matilda tanks and two pre-war regular battalions of his Regiment. His first assignment was to be put by sea into Tobruk to support the Australian division that garrisoned the port. When the break-out battles started in support of the main thrust by the 8th Army from the Egyptian border area, my father occupied the El Duda ridge south of Tobruk and withstood repeated attacks from the African Corps under Rommel. On at least one occasion the 7th Armoured Division took shelter behind his Matilda tanks in hull-down positions on reverse slopes, where his inferior guns supported by artillery were able to knock out the superior German tanks. He was awarded a bar to his DSO for this operation to add to his two MCs.

Subsequently, he supported the two British divisions in their defensive position between Bir Hakim and the coast against the Africa Corps assault that led to the second siege of Tobruk. After five weeks he was reduced to only twenty-five serviceable tanks when the order came to withdraw to the Alamein position covering Alexandria. General Auchinleck ordered him to withdraw into Tobruk to support the South African division because of his previous experience in the first siege. Early next morning my father was woken by his staff to say that the German attack was lapping around them, as two whole South African brigades under General Kloppa were surrendering with little or no resistance on their part.

My father ordered all remaining tanks to be immobilised and the remnants of the brigade to escape on their feet. He himself managed to get as far as Bardia on the Egyptian frontier when they were picked up by an Italian patrol and made prisoners. When Rommel heard that he had been captured, he sent for him and had a talk about recent battles before releasing him to the Italians who sent him to Italy to the senior officers' camp where other British generals taken in the desert battles were incarcerated.

Apart from a rising curve of learning about regimental soldiering, I retained my interest in current affairs that I first acquired in my later years at Wellington. I continued to take the De Courcey newsletter regularly. This interest continued throughout my life and led eventually to my many years in Defence Intelligence.

In the autumn of 1941 we were suddenly told that the Third Division was to acquire winter warfare equipment, including thick parkas. Subsequently, we learned that Churchill had offered our Division to the Russians to garrison Murmansk. Perhaps luckily, this did not occur. Betty and I discussed in depth how best our ever closer relationship should evolve. By this time she had given up her job at Lensbury and had taken one at Ludgersall at the Ordnance Depot there. She was living with my mother at 66 Charlton. We decided to get married before I sailed for Murmansk, although I was not yet 22 years of age and she was only six months older. We fixed on Andover Parish Church to be married, with a reception afterwards at my mother's house. Came the great day on 8 November 1941. Barny Barnikel, a fellow sapper and section commander whom I still see, was best man. Betty's parents came down from London where my father-in-law was at the Air Ministry. My father, of course, was in the desert. The honeymoon was to be a few days in the Dorchester Hotel in London which we reached that evening, quite exhausted. We tried to make love but, as both of us were virgins, we had a problem. Betty solved this next day by seeking out the house doctor. With his advice all was well.

I went back to Northwood House and Betty to her job in Ludgersall, based on my mother in Charlton. Within weeks came momentous news. My Colonel had been promoted Brigadier commanding the School of Military Engineering, now in Ripon in Yorkshire. I was to join him – and married accommodation was available! In January Betty and I were able to set up our first abode together in Ripon. 1942 clearly augured well for our married life together, which was to be broken only by her sudden death from two heart attacks in July 1989.

Meanwhile, I was now assistant instructor in bridging and came under a delightful man called Major George Harby, with whom I taught the Royal Engineers to use the Bailey Bridge. Donald Bailey at the Corps Experimental Establishment at Christchurch designed the remarkable bridge that was named after him. This wonderfully simple bridge of panels, special connecting pins and cross-girders to take the decking, was

Inspecting a dual carriageway Bailey built at the SME Ripon, 1943

a real war winner. Even in the twenty-first century a version of the original bridge is still being built in various parts of the world as an emergency structure. We set about teaching it not only to sappers but also to classes of officers up to lieutenant colonel, as the equipment was soon put into mass production not only in the UK but also in the US. I was supported by quartermaster sergeant instructors and sergeants in teaching bridging to students. These were senior soldiers with battle experience and I could not have got by without them. Together we evolved the drills for building Bailey bridges of various shapes and sizes. The largest single spans were triple double, that is two storeys each side of the bridge, each with three trusses. Later we got onto piers for multispan bridges. That summer Major Harby carried out the final troop trials of the Bailey pontoon bridge on a lake in the park surrounding Fountains Abbey. A single tank had to cross the bridge endlessly for hundreds of crossings before the bridge could be accepted for service as thoroughly sound. So life at work complemented the idyllic circumstances of newlyweds setting up house for the first time.

That autumn the invasion of North Africa was planned and executed. Brigadier Coxwell-Rogers was appointed Chief Engineer of the forces destined to land in Algeria and Tunisia. To my chagrin he failed to take me with him. I was left to carry on instruction in bridging. His successor, Brigadier Harrison, did not seem to take to me, nor me to him and those he brought with him to the School of Military Engineering.

My time came to an end and I was posted as Adjutant Royal Engineers to the 59th Division, then in Northern Ireland. My old Division had by then left for North Africa. Later they took part in the Italian campaign. Early in 1942 I had had to part with my excellent Morris 8 Tourer because petrol rationing had made private motoring virtually impossible. My fox terrier that I had acquired in 1939 also had to stay permanently with my mother until he died. So Betty and I had a miserable parting; she to live once again with my mother at 66 Charlton, I to go to Northern Ireland. Both of us left in opposite directions by train in early 1943; both of us wondered when we should be together again.

HQ of 59th Division was in Armagh. I reported there and met my new master, Lt. Col. MacKinley CRE of the Divisional Engineers. Fortunately we got on well, though he had recently returned to soldiering from a staff appointment and I had no background other than regimental service and teaching bridging. 59th Division was a second line TA Division that had been made up to strength and re-equipped fairly recently. We carried out a series of exercises that summer to train the Division for as yet unknown overseas service. There was no sign of IRA activity and the threat of German machinations, not least in Southern Ireland, had gone. But the great news for me was that Betty was pregnant and our first child was due to be born in September 1943. She was due to produce in Winchester Hospital and I was on tenterhooks as to what leave I could get, and when. In the event, my mother got her into hospital in good time and Celia Mary was born on 27 September. I arrived soon afterwards and found mother and child in good shape, despite wartime shortages. My mother had taken to keeping a goat, so fresh milk was assured for Betty and Celia on their return home. This fierce creature and I fell out, whenever my mother went to feed or milk it, the goat took a run at me with horns down. I used to pin it to the ground by its horns, much to its rage. Releasing it required the full skills of a Royal Engineer!

I managed to produce some acceptable operation orders for my colonel to govern what the divisional engineers got up to on exercise, thereby consolidating my position as adjutant. That autumn we received orders to move the Division to Kent. We were given to understand that we would be a follow-up Division for landings in France in 1944. I had to organise our move to Canterbury, which fortunately went off without a hitch. Our presence was put over to the Germans as part of the build-up for a landing in the Pas de Calais. This convinced Hitler that no major landings would occur in Normandy and led to his fatal decision not to move troops from the Pas de Calais to Normandy immediately after the landing there on 6 June 1944.

In March 1944 I was suddenly posted to command 17 Field Company in 3rd Division Engineers in the temporary rank of major. So I became lieutenant, temporary captain, then temporary major in the period from 1941 to 1944, still not having had battle experience. However, 3rd Division was to land on D-Day in Normandy, a fact that was given to me in secure briefing in Scotland soon after I took over. We were to land on Sword Beach on a front some miles to the west of Ouistreham at the mouth of the River Orne. My particular task was to land with a substantial quantity of folding boat equipment to produce Class 9 (nine ton) ferries over both the Orne Canal and the River Orne at Benouville, should 6th Airborne have failed to take both bridges intact. Our training in Scotland and subsequently in Southern England was focussed on preparation to execute this plan.

I found 17 Field Company at Old Meldrum, a small town inland from Aberdeen. 3rd Division Headquarters was in the Old Castle at Inverness. Soon after my arrival, we took part in a full-scale landing exercise at Lossiemouth. I embarked in the same LCT (Landing Craft Tank) that I should use to land in France. 3rd Division had its own fleet of landing ships by that time, mostly manned by Americans. A Rear Admiral in one of the escorting destroyers commanded our fleet. Most of my soldiers had landed over beaches up to fifteen times by the time that we hit the Normandy beaches. The Division had moved to Inverary in late 1941 and had been on continuous Combined Operations Training since then.

On that particular exercise I loaded my Scout Car with driver on the LCT in the afternoon near Inverness and we sailed north-east up the coast of Caithness. Darkness fell and the sea was full of ships around us. At dawn I went up on the bridge to find that our LCT was leading seven others, still sailing north-east with no one else in sight. A dot appeared on the horizon that rapidly grew into a destroyer. This ship screamed to a halt alongside and the bull voice of Admiral Talbot rang out with a tirade of obscenities against my unfortunate American skipper – who had failed to change course to southward to land on the beaches at Lossiemouth. We changed course sharply and put on full speed to the south. We were a bit late in landing, but then completed our Folding Boat (FBE) exercise ashore.

My CRE was Tiger Urquhart, a fiery officer of well-known reputation. Fortunately we got on well from the start, as I did with my fellow squadron commanders of 246 Field Company (Rodney Maude) and 253 Field Company (John Asher), both first line Territorial Army companies from the Cardiff area. Our divisional commander was General Rennie, an experienced officer who had seen much service in North

Plaque recording 17 Fd Coy Bridge over the Orne Canal that disappeared soon after the death of M. Gondrée

Africa. 17 Field Company supported 185 Brigade, but, because of our special role after landing on the beaches, I saw little of them before the landing.

After the exercise described above, we received orders to move to Southern England in preparation for the landing in Normandy. Southern England was one huge armed camp with many divisions from the UK and USA assembled under tight security measures to ensure secrecy. There was occasional night bombing by the Germans but by day the combined air forces reigned supreme. We moved to Littlehampton to occupy a delightful hotel overlooking the sea. The company occupied requisitioned houses nearby. Our attendant landing ships anchored at Shoreham after coming down from Scotland through the Straits of Dover. Detailed briefing for the landing took place under tight security at Divisional Headquarters near Winchester. I was able to slip home to Charlton for fleeting visits to my family, though I was, of course, unable even to hint at what we were planning to do – quite a strain on both sides.

We carried out one more landing exercise on the south coast, thereby showing once again how impotent the Germans had become. Again with hindsight, the landing was on beaches west of Beachy Head to give the impression to the Germans that we were aiming to land in the Pas de Calais. After landing, we built our Folding Boat Ferries over the River Arun above Arundel. This took place by night, fortunately a dry one.

Luckily, Tiger Urquhart was pleased with our performance, although the site was a difficult one for ferries and the current ran strongly in a tidal estuary.

D-Day was originally set for 5 June. As our Brigade was so far east, we had to embark much earlier than the rest of the Division that went on board in Spithead. So we duly loaded onto our ships at Shoreham on the morning of 4 June and turned westward to our turning point off Portsmouth for the run to the coast of Normandy. Wind and sea got steadily worse as we ground our way westward. Off the Isle of Wight, just as we were about to turn south for the beaches, an order came through the ship's radio to turn about and head back to Shoreham as the landing had been postponed. So back we went, this time with a following wind and sea, but landing craft tanks roll horribly and many soldiers were seasick on both legs of the course. Personally I do not worry about rough seas and felt fit throughout. That evening we disembarked and drove back to Littlehampton. Early next morning we were told that D-Day was to be at 0700 hours on 6 June. We re-embarked that morning, reached our turning point in rather better weather conditions and turned south with all the ships that were to land at H + 4 hours – 11 o'clock local time. On both days local people turned out in force en route to Shoreham to cheer us on our way. This was much appreciated.

That night we slept fitfully, if at all. After midnight a huge stream of aircraft passed over us heading for Normandy. This was 6th Airborne Division plus the infantry in gliders that were scheduled to take the Orne bridges on the way to Caen, amongst other objectives. As it began to get light we were able to see the vast armada of ships and escorting naval vessels all heading south. At 0700, the time for the initial landing, we were still perhaps twenty miles from land that was not yet visible other than high ground behind the beaches. As we got closer we could see battle ships, cruisers and destroyers firing their guns at targets ashore. The most awe-inspiring sight was converted landing-craft rocket ships discharging their full load of two hundred or so rockets in ripple fire. As the morning advanced we got steadily closer to Sword Beach at Luc-sur-Mer, where we were destined to beach.

As the landing-craft approached Sword Beach, shells could be seen falling along the road at the back of the beach and on the beaches themselves. In the foreground were many beached landing-craft, small assault craft and larger landing-craft, some of them wrecked by shell fire. The American Captain spotted a gap between them and drove his ship on to the beach. Infantry poured ashore, rapidly followed by vehicles, including my own Scout Car. All vehicles had been waterproofed for four feet depth of water; we, in fact, landed in about three feet depth. On both sides we could see beach defences partially cleared by lanes prepared by sappers on their feet and in engineer tanks that had landed with the swimmers in the surf. By this time the tide had receded a long way on the gently shelving sands, so the debris of battle was fully visible. Directed by the naval beach detachments, we made our way up onto the road at the back of the beach. Many houses were burning or shell-damaged. A few French people had emerged from the wreckage and were watching the landing apathetically, regardless of the odd German shell burst. The road verges were mined and taped off by those who had landed earlier. The Scout Car turned inland following a well-marked route. We came to embryo Divisional Headquarters, where we met Dacre Craven, a sapper officer on the staff, incidentally in my old post with 4th Division in Hampshire in 1940.

The Germans had a large underground and concrete gun position called Hillman on the ridge south of where we stopped. This was still in action, and naval and artillery shells were falling around it. Our route lay south-east skirting this position. We passed through our own infantry facing Hillman, who told us that they had seen or heard nothing on the road to Benouville. We therefore carried on alone on the same route that those who landed at H+2 hours must have followed. After an eerie ten minutes we came to the outskirts of Benouville and then to the road junction leading to Pegasus Bridge.

We saw some sleeping Parachute infantry as we approached the junction and there in a hollow, just short of the junction, were my advance party. Two reconnaissance officers had been wounded already, they told me, when trying to get down to the canal bank to look at our initial ferry site. German infantry had occupied a pillbox within 200 yards of Pegasus Bridge and had surrounded a Company of 6th Airborne parachutists around the Chateau de Benouville to the south. I went to see the Parachute Battalion commander, Lt. Col. Pine-Coffin, who confirmed the situation and said that he was in touch with his Brigade Headquarters, which was established on the east side of the bridge over the River Orne, about six hundred yards beyond Pegasus Bridge. I decided to go over both bridges to see the form.

Taking a good run, we sped across Pegasus Bridge, despite the German-held pillbox on the canal bank. I soon spotted a large clump of German bridging equipment and pontoons that had been dumped there for use in replacing both bridges in the event of destruction bombing. Wandering round this mass of equipment was thought-provoking, and I wondered if we could use it. The Scout Car took me on across the Orne

River bridge, guarded by more parachutists, and I soon came to Brigadier Nigel Poet's headquarters.

I returned to my company detachment that was growing by the hour as more elements reached Benouville from the beaches. More and more 3-ton trucks carrying Folding Boat Equipment and driven by Royal Army Service Corps soldiers kept piling in. Then some swimming tanks of 13th/18th Hussars arrived from Ouistreham where they had swum ashore in support of the Commando Brigade commanded by Lord Lovat. They followed Lord Lovat in person who led his Commando column of infantry through Pegasus Bridge and over to join 6th Airborne Division on the east bank of the Orne. By this time the local parachutists had cleared the offending pillbox of Germans. As the Commandos passed Benouville Church, they halted and fired everything they had at the top of the church tower. This surprised us, as we had not had any trouble from a German observation post in the tower.

I had a second Field Company under command that day. 71 Field Company arrived that afternoon, having landed at H+6 hours. So by then we had five hundred or so sappers, a mass of Royal Army Service Corps drivers and three or four tanks from 13th/18th Hussars. Colonel Pine-Coffin asked me to mount a counter-attack into south Benouville to relieve his company which was cut off there. I agreed to do so and consulted with the tank commander standing on the road junction leading to the Orne crossings. Looking up at the tank commander, I suddenly felt myself double up and fall into oblivion.

I came to about an hour later to find myself on a stretcher in the Regimental Aid Post in the main room of the Café Gondrée, right next to Pegasus Bridge. I remember Madame Gondrée coming to see me on several occasions when I regained consciousness. (On battlefield tours some years after the war I got to know her and her husband well.)

What had happened to me? Forty years later, my daughter Celia gave me a book for Christmas that consisted of accounts by officers and men from both sides of their experiences on D-Day. On leafing through the German section, I came upon the account of an Oberleutenant of the 21st Panzer Division who had commanded an anti-tank platoon, armed with an 88 mm anti-tank gun. His battle group had been stationed just south of Caen. Late morning they received orders to move north to try and recapture Pegasus Bridge. On reaching Benouville they clashed with 6th Airborne parachutists and succeeded in encircling a company in the Chateau de Benouville. As flank guard, his anti-tank platoon was put under cover about five hundred yards from the road junction leading to Pegasus Bridge. Through his field glasses he watched what went on there. Late afternoon he saw a tank stop at the road junction and the commander leaning out of his turret talking, as he recorded it, to a number of civilians – in practice, me. He wheeled his gun out of cover, fired one shot that knocked out the tank and rapidly pulled the gun back into cover without being detected. Return fire resulted but none in his particular direction. He survived the war and lived to record his tale. So did I: but for forty years I was left in ignorance of how, and by whom, I had been wounded.

My regimental medical officer, Dr Gibson, examined me on my stretcher and I was evacuated by ambulance to a beach medical station, where I received little attention as my records only showed that I had been grazed by a bullet. In fact, a large piece of shell or tank armour had entered my neck and slithered down to above my spine, where it lodged without breaking the skin of my back; but this was not yet known. Most of D+1 I lay on my stretcher, only conscious part of the time. German aircraft bombed us occasionally during that day, and my excellent second-in-command, Captain Watty Watkinson, together with Dacre Craven from HQRE were both killed by a random German bomb. My Field Company had therefore lost its commander, second-in-command and two reconnaissance officers in the first twenty-four hours of Operation Overland – a high proportion of seven officers. My old friend Scotty Scott-Bowden, who had reconnoitred Omaha Beach from a submarine about Christmas 1943, led in the American Division onto this beach, where they endured much punishment. Having survived this ordeal, he took over my job on D+2.

As the day was ending I and a number of others lying on stretchers were loaded into an amphibious truck and entered the sea, as the artificial smoke that covered the ships by night against German bombing was just being initiated. We approached several big landing-ships with their doors closed, but were turned away. As it was getting dark, at last a landing-ship opened its doors and we climbed up into the belly of the beast.

Next morning we were taken ashore to Haslar Hospital in Portsmouth. There I was X-rayed, but only down as far as the base of the neck, and then had an operation to tidy up the wound below my ear. Soon my wife and my mother appeared to see me, having been informed by telephone where I was. Within days I was told I was to be moved to a convalescent hospital in Sussex. Still on a stretcher, I was moved by train to Sussex, arriving by night. On the journey a big lump began to rise on my upper back and caused me some discomfort. On arrival at the new hospital I drew attention to this. Once again I was X-rayed and a large lump of metal showed above my spine. The metal piece had entered below my ear, plunged along through my neck and come to rest along my spine without breaking the skin. A second operation was rapidly organised to take it out. I heard afterwards that early signs of gangrene had caused the swelling, so a lot of tissue had to be removed with the metal object that I keep to this day. As another memento I still carry a big indented scar on my back. A further effect is that certain neck muscles were damaged, leaving me with a neck twitch that has persisted ever since. In later years this led to my not so close friends in the Ministry of Defence saddling me with the nickname 'Noddy'.

After a few days to recover from the second operation, I was moved by train to the Queen Elizabeth Hospital in Birmingham. This was an excellent establishment and I found myself very well cared for in a bright and airy ward. There I remained for about a month to regather my strength. My wife and my mother came to visit me several times. They stayed with a First War friend of my father's who had recently been Lord Mayor of Birmingham and who lived in Edgbaston. Celia Mary was left with friends in Andover.

Hospital gave me time to reflect on many topics. I had retained my interest in current affairs and now had an opportunity to read newspapers and magazines. Subject, of course, to censorship, there was much war coverage, not least of progress, or lack of it, in Normandy. Instinctively, there was a general trust in our war leadership, though individual actions were more suspect. I thought back to before D-Day and remembered a visit by Montgomery to my brigade. We formed up in a hollow square to be addressed. No sooner had Monty mounted the dais than he invited us to break ranks and gather round him. This did not go down well with our old soldiers who had not fought in the desert under Monty. It left a slight feeling of distrust amongst us. So criticism of the conduct of operations in Normandy did not altogether surprise me. In Italy, Anglo-American forces had made a lot of progress northwards. Only in the Pacific was the picture less bright, although the US Navy had had many victories and the threat to Australia had been thrown back. Nevertheless, I remained confident that we would defeat both Hitler and the Japanese.

From the family angle much had gone well. My father had managed to convince the International Red Cross Board that visited his camp to allow him to be repatriated as a medical case. After some months at home, he succeeded in being passed fit for general service other than against the Germans. By the time I was wounded he had been sent out to India, still in his substantive rank of lieutenant colonel, despite having been a temporary brigadier in command of an armoured brigade. I felt that his affair with a fellow officer's wife at Perham Down in 1939/40 had not been forgotten by the powers that be. But he was alive and kicking, as was I: so the load upon my mother had been partially lifted. Betty had a job at Ludgersall, while my mother looked after Celia by the day. In early August I was released from hospital on sick leave. Later that month I went before a medical grading board in London and was passed fit for active service. Betty and I celebrated by staying at Grosvenor House once again. Here we heard the first V2 go off in London. V1s were also audible occasionally, and it was a relief to get back to the peace of Charlton.

In no time I had to report for a draft of officers to be sent to Holland. Fortunately for me a visiting engineer staff officer from HQ Second Army recognised me and took me back with him to Eindhoven to live with Army HQ until a vacancy for squadron commander should arise. Nigel Gell, OC 246 Field Company in my old 3rd Division Engineers, was reported wounded, and so in early October I found myself back in the saddle in the aftermath of the Battle of Overloon. 3rd Division had taken most of the town of Venrai after a severe battle. 246 had been busy providing crossings over the Molenbeck, a small river obstacle covering the town, and my predecessor had been wounded by a German wooden anti-personnel mine called a Schûmine. German artillery still shelled the town at intervals, and the whole area was full of anti-tank Regel mines and Schûmines – we reckoned subsequently that up to a quarter of a million mines had been sown in our divisional area.

My first task was to cut down masses of fir trees and build a wooden causeway from Overloon, a distance of several miles. This took the best part of my first week in action after D-Day in Normandy. I reckoned that I had had a pretty miserable war so far, but it was good to be back amongst people I knew. Dr Gibson was still our Regimental Medical Officer, so I pulled his leg in a big way. My Brigade Commander was a well-decorated officer from the war in the desert called 'Copper' Cass. He was a fearless man who loved to get around in areas still thick with mines. On several occasions he contacted me to go with him into a new area now clear of Germans, but I agreed only for those tracks that I knew were cleared of mines. One day I had a conference with my Colonel, and declined a request to accompany the Brigade Commander. He went on his own and his jeep hit a mine. He had to be evacuated wounded and saw no more service. I went to see my friend Scotty Scott-Bowden, who had taken over my old company, 17, after I was wounded. I spotted his sleeping bag cover with my name still on it. In a trice I seized it and put it in my own vehicle, despite his protests! For the rest of the campaign I slept more comfortably, though I fear he may not have done so.

My new company, 246, had established itself in a Dutch Stoettrruppen (SS) hutted camp that lay in the woods just north of the Molenbeck. Life in such a camp showed us just how affected with Nazism Catholic southern Holland had become. This feeling was enhanced by the arrival of a Dutch sergeant from Eindhoven as the company liaison officer with local people. Just before Christmas, my sergeant caught him looting a local house of furniture for transporting back to Eindhoven. He was returned to store and not replaced.

We continued to live in the Venrai area until January as the war ran down for the winter. Clearing mines remained our principal task as we fanned out into the country south of the Maas River. One field was particularly memorable. No fewer than forty-five Sherman tanks lay knocked out cheek by jowl, by German 88 mm and larger calibre fire. The Seventh US Armoured Division had operated near the river before we entered the area. Rudely, we called it the 7th Utterly US Division!

My second-in-command was Chris Edwards, who had been a civil engineer in Pembrokeshire before being called up. He was excellent at his job and quite unflappable. One of my section commanders was Reggie Trench, who continued to serve in the Army for many years after the war. Morale was high throughout the Company which made it easy to command. My excellent driver, Bob Darlow, was a tower of strength. I relied upon him totally and remained in touch with him until, to my sorrow, he died in 2004.

One less pleasant memory was of a night reconnaissance covered by 8 Brigade Infantry to a damaged building suspected of being used by German troops operating from the far bank of the Maas River. In eerie silence we penetrated the buildings on foot, expecting mines or booby traps to go off at any moment. To sighs of relief, we found nothing. Our intelligence had been faulty.

For New Year's Eve I was given a 48-hour pass to visit Brussels. After an alcoholic evening, I was sleeping it off in my hotel room when I was awakened by gunfire outside. I dragged myself to the window to see a German fighter at rooftop height striking the street with machine-gun fire. I decided that life was more peaceful in Venrai! In fact, this attack was the prelude to a German counter-offensive to the south of 3rd Division area, but we were not called upon to stem it. Soon we were under orders to move to the Reichswald Forest area, not far from the Rhine River where an offensive by the British Second Army was underway, to establish positions for crossing that river.

In January 1945 we moved forward to Goch and prepared to pass through the Guards Armoured Division to clear the forest. Once launched into the attack, we came under heavy German artillery fire as we laboured to open vehicle routes through forest tracks after clearing them of mines that had been thickly put down by the retreating Germans. I came forward on foot to see how my leading elements were getting on. I was surprised to see one of my lance sergeants walking fast towards the rear. I stopped him and found that he was clearly shell-shocked from near misses. I sat him down on a log and we talked about his problems. When he was calmer, I gave him the choice of returning with me to his section, or being arrested as a deserter from the front line. We moved forward together and to my delight he never looked back thereafter, eventually winning a Military Medal.

Third Division made steady progress and was able to occupy the designated length of the west bank of the River Rhine. My brigade sector was close to Rees. Our task was to cut through the very high and steep flood banks close to the water's edge so that the assaulting infantry could enter the water in amphibians and cross to the east bank. We used large numbers of shaped charges to blow gaps in the bank. Our bulldozers were there to clear up the breaches in the flood bank, ready for amphibious tracked vehicles to cross and plunge down into the river.

The great day came in March 1945 and as night was falling the charges were ignited. I was on one of our gaps, crouched in a slit trench. The noise was appalling, but the shaped charges did what was predicted and bulldozers came forward quickly to clear the remaining loose earth. They were followed by the amphibians carrying 51st Highland Division infantry. They plunged down the steep and stone-faced banks and disappeared into the darkness. German artillery fire came crashing down on the river bank as the first wave set a course for their landing sites, about 1,000 yards away. Soon I was told that returning amphibians could not climb out of the river to collect the second wave of the assault, because their tracks were unable to get a grip on the stone facing. So it was necessary to lay more explosive charges to rupture the stone, followed by more bulldozing of approach ramps. All this was under sustained German artillery fire that caused a number of sappers to become casualties. We persevered and a regular passage of amphibians was achieved in and out of the river and through the flood bank gaps for reloading. This went on all night and by the early hours we were all exhausted but triumphant, as the crossing had clearly succeeded.

Bridges were constructed over the next few days, and the 3rd Division crossed the river and headed north-east as a follow-up division. The next objective was the large town of Enschede, just inside the Dutch border with Germany. The Germans abandoned it without a fight. As we entered the town, we were surprised to hear the crack of rifle and pistol fire. This turned out to be Dutch reprisals against their own collaborators – not a pretty or edifying sight but no doubt the local folk had had much provocation. For the night we took over some houses in a prosperous suburb. There were many Dutch people still in other houses nearby. In the event we had to invite them in to celebrate their liberation – by drinking our liquor.

North-east of Enschede we crossed into Germany. The Dortmund Ems Canal near Lingen was strongly held by the Germans. A divisional assault across the waterway was ordered. My task was to man assault boats for 8 Brigade infantry and to build folding-boat ferries for loaded re-supply three-ton trucks. Scotty, with 17 Field Company, was to build a Bailey pontoon bridge to take tanks, on a site not far from mine. As so often from the Venrai days onwards, the opposition included German parachutists, a tough bunch. As the assault waves took to the water, down came the Germany artillery fire. 246 Field Company took a few casualties but Scotty and 17 were much affected. Scotty himself was wounded, fortunately not seriously, and removed on a stretcher, but within a week or so he was back with us.

3rd Division continued to advance north-east towards Bremen. A series of minor actions occurred as we moved onward. In one of these we overran a German pioneer detachment under a sergeant-major. He refused to tell us where and how many mines he had already laid. I pulled out my pistol, the only time in the campaign that I did so. Under threat of being shot, he was prevailed upon to tell us what he had been up to. On another night we found ourselves billeted in the Steinhagen Distillery. I regret that we requisitioned a number of their excellent gin products.

One evening we received orders to build a Bailey bridge about sixty feet long over a bridge that the Germans had destroyed. We provided our own infantry cover on the far bank and got down to construction. Around midnight we heard a powerful tank engine coming towards our bridge site. We knew that the Germans still had some Tiger tanks, and this was clearly one of them. Fortunately, it stopped a little way from our bridge site and its crew settled down for a rest. Never was a Bailey bridge built in such silence! As we were dismantling the launching nose on the enemy bank, we heard the tank start up and move away from us. Never before had sappers completed a Bailey bridge build in greater spirits!

The Division reached Delmenhorst from where we could see the skyline of Bremen across the flooded fields south of the city. The

Germans had opened the sluice gates on the River Weser to flood all the low-lying country as the main defence for their big centre. 3rd Division were ordered to assault Bremen across these floods in the same amphibious tracked vehicles with which the Rhine had been crossed.

This time, entry to the water was no problem. There was one main road causeway across the floods into the city itself. I was ordered to clear this causeway while the rest of the Division assaulted eastward across the flood plain. The Germans had destroyed a bridge close to Delmenhorst at the start of the causeway. In a matter of days we built, under cover, what was called a skid Bailey bridge, because we lashed on metal skids under its trusses. These skids allowed an engineer tank to push the Bailey bridge down the road to the bridge site. All we had then to do was to dismantle the launching nose and deck it down, placing ramps at either end. Speed was essential, as German artillery had registered on the water gap.

The day before the assault we heard that a massed bombing raid by Bomber Command was to take place as part of the process of softening up the German defences. A BBC correspondent would be coming to record the attack from one of our infantry observation posts overlooking the floods. That afternoon he appeared, introducing himself as Richard Dimbleby. As the witching hour approached, but we could see or hear nothing, he lifted his microphone and started his commentary:

> '*The sky is black with aircraft – now they are over Bremen – down go the bombs – Bremen has vanished under smoke and debris*'.

We still heard or saw nothing. He put his microphone away and patted his tape. We asked what he would do with it.

'Send it home for broadcasting,' he replied.

We remonstrated.

'No worry,' he replied, 'nobody at home will know that the mission was aborted.' My trust in BBC commentators was extinguished from that moment.

As the light faded, we started our causeway operation with support from a troop of armoured engineers. The bridge was pushed out from cover and the tank manoeuvred it across the obstacle. My section of sappers started to dismantle the launching nose. Down came the German artillery as expected, fortunately not hitting the bridge, but shells burst on the road and in the water. Several sappers were wounded but, despite this, the whole operation was completed in a matter of minutes. The engineer tank crossed and we all took cover from falling shells. By then it was dark and I sent the next section forward to a large metal barrier erected right across the causeway. They found mines in the road and the verges that they lifted without mishap. Another engineer tank came up and knocked down the metal barrier with explosives fired from its gun. Our own bulldozer cleared the debris. Slowly, we moved forward, mine-clearing as we went.

I heard that electric leads had been found leading to large charges, and decided to cut these leads myself. Nothing happened, thank God. Excavation round the charge showed it to be a naval magnetic mine, and a crane was ordered forward to extract it. We found several more during the course of the night. We came to a German anti-aircraft gun position. Fifteen Germans surrendered and were escorted back to our start point by sappers.

As daylight came we reached the built-up area of Bremen. In the road was a large excavation with four 250-pound aircraft bombs in the bottom that had never been set off. These were neutralised. Our own infantry had already reached this point, after a successful amphibious assault. I saw one of their carriers blow up on what I took to be a naval magnetic mine. The whole vehicle flew several hundred feet into the air with the force of the explosion. So ended our last battle of the war. Subsequently, I heard that I had been awarded an immediate Military Cross for the operation. On my recommendation two other Military Medals were given to my Company, in recognition of their bravery in this difficult operation.

Next day I went down into the dock area of Bremen where guards had had to be placed on the wine vats after one or two escaped Russian prisoners of war had drowned in the contents! Soon after that we heard that the Germans had surrendered and that the war in Europe was over, to the immense relief of our troops, not least those who had served throughout the war.

From the personal angle, I had heard that Betty was pregnant with our second child, conceived after I had recovered from being wounded. Janet Lesley, as we christened her after her birth on 2 June 1945, was due, and so I was aching to get home in time for this birth. The end of the war gave me reason to hope and indeed I was granted home leave very soon.

Meanwhile, the end of hostilities did not mean the end of mine warfare. Only two days after peace was announced I was asked to send a party to deal with a large stack of Regel Mines that had been found by an infantry patrol. One of my most reliable corporals went forward with two sappers to cope with this unwelcome find. They started checking these unpleasant anti-tank mines. There was a huge explosion, as unfortunately one or more mines were fitted with anti-handling devices.

Nothing was left of all three men – a sobering start to life in peacetime and a terrible task to write to the next of kin.

We found ourselves billeted in a charming village some twenty miles north of Osnabrück. Strict orders had been issued that we were not to fraternise with German civilians. The officers' mess was established in a substantial German officer's house abandoned in full running order by his wife and family. VE Day celebrations lasted until well into the early hours. I somehow became possessed of a loaded Very light pistol that I discharged, to my horror only narrowly missing my second-in-command! This concluded a memorable party.

After some weeks of relaxation, orders were received to move to another delightful village near 3 Division Headquarters in Bielefeld. Non-fraternisation was still very much the order of the day, so although we occupied a substantial hotel and a number of German houses, we had little direct contact with the locals, other than officially with the Burgomaster and his staff. Light training was restarted, particularly for new intake to replace casualties.

My father arrived to stay with me for a week or two. He had returned from India, still as a lieutenant colonel, and was bound for a new interrogation centre near Munich set up by the Americans. Together, we ranged the countryside, driven by Sapper Darlow for much of the time. Amongst other places, we visited the Mohne Dam to see the results of skip bombing by the RAF. Downstream towards the Ruhr industrial area the damage by rushing waters was awful. We also visited Cassel, where the bomb damage was also devastating.

On another occasion, Scotty and I travelled up to Headquarters 43rd Division north of Hanover at the invitation of our old CRE, Tiger Urquhart, who had been posted there as Chief of Staff during the winter. We had lunch in 'A' Mess but found ourselves ignored by his divisional commander, a notoriously rude man. We congratulated ourselves on how lucky we were to be in 3rd Division under Major General 'Bolo' Whistler, our own revered commander. It will be appreciated that our mental horizons were much restricted by the nature of service in a strictly military environment. This was reinforced by rumours that Third Division was earmarked to land on the main island of Japan in the spring of 1946, should the Far East War last that long. Consequently, we were overjoyed when news came in of the nuclear bursts over Hiroshima and Nagasaki that led to the rapid ending of the war against Japan.

Scotty and myself were delighted when we received news that both of us were to attend the first post-war course at the Staff College at Camberley, starting in August 1945. We handed over our Companies and arrived on leave at home to seek accommodation, in my case for a family of wife and two children. Our only regret was leaving Tiger Urquart's successor as CRE, Lieutenant Colonel Tom Evill. He had been a most understanding and personally congenial commander of the Divisional Engineers. My Brigade Commander, a Guardsman, had been equally delightful since he succeeded Brigadier 'Copper' Cass and I had got to know him well. No doubt both had had a hand in my selection for the Staff College.

There I was one of the youngest on the course – at rising twenty-six years of age at Christmas. But that is the story for another chapter.

CHAPTER 3

Post-war period (1945–1950)

THE STAFF COLLEGE AT CAMBERLEY opened a new era of enlightenment for me. Hitherto, my horizons had been confined to the Corps of Royal Engineers, my job as a serving sapper officer, the brigade and division in which I was serving and, above all, the idea of winning the war against Nazi Germany. My wife and family, my parents and friends completed my circle of vision that did not as yet include the wider horizons of country and global happenings. In the next five years I was to gain practical experience of wider interests that have stood me in good stead ever since.

First priority on return to England was to find somewhere to live for the family for the duration of the six-month course. Tony and Diana Younger agreed to share a house only a few hundred yards from the entrance gates to the extensive Staff College grounds. This we rented and rapidly established the two families. Tony was one term senior to me at the Shop and had won a DSO commanding an Armoured Engineer Squadron that had supported a Canadian Division on the next beach to the west of 3rd Division Sword Beach.

Betty and the two girls had had a tiresome time after the birth of Janet in my grandmother's house in Farnham. The house was left empty after my grandmother died in the spring of 1945. Ownership was vested in my mother and her sister, Evelyn, but the latter seemed to be in charge of disposal. She was awkward to deal with and she and my wife soon fell out. Betty was given notice to clear out soon after Janet was born. My mother came to the rescue, as always, and my family moved down to Charlton while I was still in Germany. Renting the house in West End Grove was a welcome break, the first time that Betty and I had had a home of our own since Ripon days.

On the first day of the course, I found myself allocated to 'A' Division based in Camberley itself; Scotty was at Minley. The student body was mostly older and more war-experienced that I was. John Mogg, later a four-star general of high repute, was in my Division. He had commanded a battalion for some time and was well decorated for his success, so that syndicate discussions were at a pretty high level. Much of our tactical study centred on situations similar to those so many of us had already experienced in practice. Staff duties centred on how to function as a second-grade staff officer at brigade or divisional level. Much guidance was given by directing staff on how to function as Brigade Major, the coveted staff job that we all looked forward to holding after the course.

One of the best features was the succession of lectures from eminent people, mostly Commanders such as Montgomery, Alexander, Tedder and Slim. These addresses opened our minds to much wider events than those that had dominated our thinking while prosecuting the war. Personally, I had not altogether been surprised at the defeat of Churchill in the first post-war election. Some of us thought even then that Alanbrooke and the Chiefs of Staff had been the major influence on UK strategy and relations with the American military. Most of the students had had direct experience of overall American command, particularly Eisenhower. Many had encountered American troops and aircraft in action. So personal knowledge seasoned our approach to Alliance political-military relations. The final address to the course in January 1946 was given by Manny Shinwell, a card if ever there was one as Secretary of State for the Army.

A great family event took place that winter – the christening of Janet. Scotty and Valerie Benyon-Tinker, a cousin of Betty's, were godparents. As the time approached for the christening to start, there was no sign of Scotty. Someone else had to stand in as proxy during the service. He eventually appeared during the reception afterwards, looking shaken, and said that he had had a road accident just outside Minley. Betty did not fully forgive him for a long time thereafter! Another family occasion was Betty's sister, Bridget, getting married at Brompton Oratory to a young American officer with a legal background. They went off to live in the United States, to the satisfaction of Bridget's mother, but less so on the part of her father and my wife. Their history went on to include divorce and re-marriage.

My posting order, delivered in a sealed envelope, was to become Brigade Major of 1 Indian Infantry Brigade now serving in Java in the Dutch East Indies (subsequently to become Indonesia) as part of 23 Indian Division. Twenty-six of the student body had been posted to the Far East; Scotty and Tony were going to Indian Army staff posts in Burma. On the last day of the course I was summoned to see the Commandant who told me that I had been graded 'B'. Half a dozen or so 'A's and 'B's were awarded to students who had done well: the remainder was simply recorded as passing the course. I gathered that 'A's or 'B's looked well on our records in the hands of the Military Secretary

HQ 1 Indian Infantry Brigade in Java, 1946

whose staff would decide our destinies in future years. As one of the youngest and least war-experienced students on the course, I felt flattered.

I suppose it must have been caused by relief at the end of the war, but I have few memories of this six-month interlude in my life. I can remember little about the mass of my fellow students, or of those who taught us. Memories of three years on the teaching staff myself in the next decade are sharper in my mind, as we shall see as this account progresses. Suffice it to say that twenty-six of us found ourselves on a troopship bound for Bombay.

On arrival we were decanted into Kalyan Transit Camp, there to wait till a ship could be found to take us on to Singapore. We languished for nearly two weeks, while visits to the Gateway of India and other such sites passed the time away. Suddenly we heard that a P & O ship was sailing for Singapore and that we were to go aboard forthwith. The ship was full of Japanese internees in India and those wounded Japanese soldiers who had been taken prisoner instead of dying for their Emperor, as their military traditions demanded. Other than an armed escort of Indian soldiers, the twenty-six of us were the only passengers. After we had sailed, we found out quickly that almost all announcements over the ship's radio were to be conducted in Japanese; and I can still hear the opening cry of 'Nipponjin, Nipponjin . . .' echoing in my ears. I resumed playing bridge with a regular foursome including Hugh Oldman, an infantry officer whom I encountered later in Oman.

We approached the Rhio Islands, about fifteen miles south of Singapore, where our cargo of Japanese were destined to be put ashore to join their compatriots: all those Japanese who had surrendered throughout South East Asia on orders from their Emperor. Our ship's Japanese were terrified of what might happen to them ashore at the hands of their fellows who had followed Japanese etiquette and not surrendered until the Emperor's order.

A fellow sapper called John Gillington had been appointed British camp commandant ashore to look after 80,000 Japanese. He invited me ashore to see the sights, and we drove round the island in his jeep. We came to Field Marshal Terauchi, Japanese Commander in Chief, South East Asia, sitting on the balcony of his large hut, built by Japanese labour from local timber. We passed the headquarters of the Japanese Imperial Guards' Division and their Ninth Parachute Division that had been lured to the northern tip of Sumatra by the Allied deception plan for our landing in Malaysia – codenamed Operation Zipper. I returned aboard impressed by the self-discipline of this mass of Japanese soldiery.

We landed in Singapore soon afterwards, and I rapidly found myself on a British-manned Landing Craft Tank (LCT) heading for Batavia in Java. As we were sailing down the coast of Sumatra we encountered the tail of a hurricane, and for the first time in my life I saw numerous water spouts arching up into thick black clouds from the surface of the sea, which the skipper had to manoeuvre hard to avoid.

Batavia docks were full of trading dhows and junks. I was met by an officer from Headquarters 23rd Indian Division who told me that 1 Indian Infantry Brigade was up country at Tjandjoer beyond the Poentjak Pass on the road to Bandung. I could only get there by joining a twice-weekly supply column, well guarded by soldiers and with fighter cover overhead for the mountain section of the road.

Next daybreak found me in the cab of a three-ton truck driven by an Indian soldier heading south towards Buitenzorg and Sukarno's palace. We passed round this ornate building and headed up into the mountains with the bulk of a large volcano looming above us. At the Poentjak Pass we found 1 Seaforth, the one British Battalion in 1 Indian Infantry Brigade, encamped astride the road. The Pass was about 5,000 feet and significantly cooler than the lowlands round Batavia – now Jakarta. We then descended through paddy fields of rice in all stages of growth, from initial planting to harvesting. This I subsequently found out was because no fewer than three crops a year could be grown in this benign climate, with regular rainfall.

At lunchtime we arrived at Brigade Headquarters on the outskirts of Tjandjoer in the same compound as 1 Pattialas, the personal regiment of the Maharaja of Pattiala and as such an independent force, not strictly part of the Indian Army. I was met by the DAQMG of the Brigade, a Sikh officer, dressed as such, but as British as they make them. He took me to the officers' mess for lunch, where the first person I met was a tall Japanese from Hokkaido, the northern-most island of Japan, who spoke good English and ran our mess. He told me that he was a Japanese civilian who had never been inducted into the Japanese Army. On the outbreak of war in 1941, he had been the principal barman in an American bar in Tokyo. He received a message from Field Marshal Terauchi, who had just been appointed to command the invasion forces in South East Asia, to join his headquarters as major-domo of his household. He complied and did his job, still as a civilian, until the surrender in 1945. As a civilian he could not surrender like the rest of the Japanese Army. His case came to the notice of Brigadier 'Pooh' Wingrove, who was at that time Chief of Staff of Allied Forces HQ, Netherlands, East Indies, and AFNEI for short. He had just been appointed to command 1 Indian Infantry Brigade, so he said he would take the Japanese along with him to run his mess. And there he was, all six foot two inches of him, in central Java.

He was not the only Japanese I met in going round the headquarters compound. Most of the Indian soldiers, including the defence platoon, were from 1/16 Punjabis; but they were supplemented by a Japanese signals telephone line section and a light aid detachment helping to look after our vehicles. An Indian signaller would be shot at by the Indonesians if he went to repair frequently-cut telephone lines; a Japanese signaller would not and Japanese fitters were better trained than their Indian equivalents.

My brigadier was a dapper Gurkha officer to whom I took immediately. 'Pooh' was a man of many parts who had acquired in Batavia a Chinese girlfriend of vast riches, sporting a huge Cadillac. Our divisional commander was not so congenial; he had set up house with a Dutch girl whose parents were also in tow. My GSO III was a Seaforth officer whose company I much enjoyed. He had been guard commander in Batavia docks looking after Dutch property, including cars and household goods that had been impounded by the Japanese invaders when they herded Dutch citizens into prison camps soon after they arrived in 1942. He had many stories about senior Indian Army officers and even politicians from Singapore who came to select items for their own use, though the rightful owners were still incarcerated in camps that the Indian Army had still to liberate.

The history of the British occupation of the Dutch East Indies in 1945 was a tangled one. The original plan was for the Americans from Pacific Command to liberate this huge area, some of which they already occupied. Shortly before the Japanese surrender, Mountbatten was notified that troops under his command were to occupy the territory from Bali to Sumatra; but unfortunately no up-to-date intelligence seems to have been passed over to the British together with the change in plan. 23rd Indian Division landed on Java, and Brigadier Mallaby took his brigade to the Soerabaya area. Their orders were to release Dutch civilians from Japanese prison camps wherever they could find them. The brigade therefore dispersed into small parties, searching for these camps in a supposedly friendly environment. In practice, however, the environment was far from friendly. The Indonesians had replaced the Japanese guards on their surrender, and had no intention of releasing any Dutch civilians. Forty-eight hours after the landing, fighting broke out, as the Indonesians whipped out pangas, used to cut rice, and started chopping up Indian soldiers, including Brigadier Mallaby himself. His brigade suffered 450 killed before the situation was brought under control. Further west in Java, where the bulk of the Division landed, similar resistance was soon encountered, not least in the mountains around Bandung where a large Japanese garrison had surrendered and troops had gone in to disarm them. This was why 1 Indian Infantry Brigade was strung out protecting the supply route from Buitenzorg across the mountains to Bandung. When I arrived in February 1946 fighting was desultory with occasional cutting of telephone lines and shooting at Indian troops covering twice-weekly convoys. Stories were still rife of Indian infantry going in to attack Indonesian positions around Bandung, supported by Japanese artillery that had been re-issued their guns as 23rd Division had left most of theirs in Malaya, on the assumption that the occupation of Java would not meet with opposition. I found this confused situation most educational after experiences in Western Europe.

Life in Tjandjoer had its moments. One of these occurred about six weeks after I took over. One morning my Brigadier and I were electrified to hear 1 Pattiala mortars firing repeatedly from just down the road. I was told to ring their commanding officer. 'What gives?' I said. The nonchalant reply came that one of his patrols had been fired on as a Bandung convoy went through so he had ordered twenty rounds a mortar to be fired into the general area to remind the Indonesians not to mess with his battalion.

Unknown to us all, some news correspondents were travelling with the convoy to gain experience on what was happening up-country in Java. On return by air, they reported to HQ AFNEI in Batavia what they had seen and also filed their reports back to London. A most serious view was taken by the Labour Government of what had occurred. A Court of Inquiry was rapidly set up, 1 Pattialas were returned to their Maharaja in India forthwith, and 4/8 Gurkhas were posted in to replace them. We already had 3/5 Gurkhas under Peter Saunders' command, so in all we had one British and two Gurkha battalions in the brigade.

Life was never dull as the brigade continued to patrol its area to keep Indonesians away from the road. Around us peasants continued to till their rice fields, quite oblivious to what went on around them. I used to go up to the Seaforth at Poentjak Pass at regular intervals. On guest nights, Scottish dancing was de rigueur. The sight of the Brigade Major dancing with the commanding officer, a burly Australian, caused some hilarity. With the Gurkhas I attended many functions, including the festival of Deshera. At Brigade Headquarters we lived well, looked after by our Japanese major-domo.

In course of planning patrols to protect the road, it was decided to climb Mount Gunong, the 10,000-foot-high volcano alongside it. A complete company of Gurkhas with their commanding officer and myself set off soon after first light one day to do so. The group route lay through the remains of a Dutch botanical station that had been totally vandalised by the Indonesians. Beyond it the route led to a steep and rough track up the mountainside. The party reached the summit in mid-morning under a rare clear sky. Below us lay the crater, still active, with sulphur blowholes and boiling mud pools. Many Gurkhas refused to descend the few hundred feet into the bottom of the crater because their religion forbade them to interfere with the spirits of the mountain. The British officers present had no such scruples and pressed on to the crater floor. The sulphur blowholes were the greatest hazard; to get caught in a gas cloud wafted across one's path was unpleasing, to say the least. On the way back the route took us part of the way down an old tourist track, where there were hot springs encased in stonework beside the path. Ravenous for lunch, we stopped to heat our bully-beef tins in the boiling water. The homeward path down the mountainside was much simpler than climbing up had proved to be.

New orders arrived in late summer that Dutch troops were coming from Holland to relieve us and that we were to concentrate within the perimeter of Batavia. I was privately horrified to hear that amongst the relieving Dutch troops were Stoettruppen. I earnestly hoped that they were not of the same Nazi background as those whose camp my Field Company had occupied outside Venrai in the winter of 1944: but of this I was to be rudely disabused.

Dutch convoys started arriving carrying Dutch troops. Their Brigade HQ appeared and I was left behind to see them in, while my team drove back to Batavia. That evening I started to hear rifle fire on the perimeter of our camp, something that had never occurred during previous months. I asked my relief what was going on. He replied that a local peasant tilling his field had got too close to the wire, so a Dutch sentry had shot him.

This event shows how bad relations were between Dutch and Indonesians. The Dutch had regarded full-blooded Indonesians as beneath contempt. Even if only one eighth Dutch, an Indonesian gained better treatment and education. Advancement for the mass of the population was another matter. No wonder that some years later the Indonesians rose and expelled the Dutch from control of their myriad islands. No wonder also that 23rd Division had found Indonesian guards on prisoner of war camps set up by the Japanese in the same state as during the war: for they contained Dutch personnel. The British mission to release and repatriate all these people down to one-eighth Dutch blood had cost over two thousand casualties to the largely Indian Army forces by the time we left in December 1946.

Back in Batavia, HQ 1 Indian Infantry Brigade found itself manning the eastern perimeter of the controlled area south of the airfield with headquarters in Polonia, a large and luxurious club. Here we spent our last couple of months in Java before the Division returned to India, largely in cadre-form, as most British officers were leaving now that Indian independence was approaching. British service officers such as myself were at the mercy of the Military Secretary in Singapore. Brigadier Wingrove went on long leave to the UK and was succeeded by another Indian Army officer for the interim.

On the perimeter, skirmishes continued. On one occasion a Gurkha soldier was found by his mates dead with his throat cut. The Gurkhas were incensed but there was not much that could be done about it. The worst incident that we suffered concerned the Seaforth and Dutch Stoettruppen. In the last phase of our withdrawal, 1 Seaforth were in the process of relief by the Dutch unit who had that day taken over responsibility for guarding a railway bridge over the road leading to their barracks. A Seaforth truck bringing Jocks back from the delights of Batavia passed under this bridge. The Dutch sentry challenged the vehicle, which continued on its way. Fire was opened on the unarmed Jocks and several were killed or wounded. The truck continued into the barrack compound and without more ado many soldiers proceeded to the armoury and started issuing rifles and ammunition. Fortunately the commanding officer was told what was happening and went to remonstrate with his men. He succeeded by a great feat of leadership in getting arms returned without use.

That night and all the next day there was a frenzy of activity at staff and command levels. Orders were received to railroad the Seaforths out of Java, which was done within forty-eight hours by sending them to the Singapore garrison. Another furore broke out as the Dutch took over the Seaforth barracks in Batavia. My Brigadier and I were summoned to inspect the barracks with our Dutch counterparts. We found that the Jocks had plastered over every barrack room wall the words: '*The Dutch are Boche without guts*'. Our faces were a study as we toured the barracks.

However, life was not without its compensations. Amongst the Japanese in Batavia there were a number of piratical-looking sailors. They manned a few launches in Batavia port that could be used by parties wishing at weekends to go out to a group of uninhabited islands offshore for swimming. I took advantage of this facility and on one occasion took off on a Sunday with a group from 1 Brigade. Despite my utmost efforts to shield myself from the burning sun, I got seriously sunburned; this was so bad that my shoulders came up in water blisters that evening. My colleagues told me that to relieve the pain they were going to fill me up with whisky until I passed out! This they duly did and I was unconscious until late the following day. On coming to I found my sunburn was much less painful, but my hangover was more tiresome.

A Japanese battalion was allotted for work throughout the Brigade area, and pitched its tented camp in the grounds of the Polonia Club. Every Saturday, as Brigade Major, I used to inspect the lines of those serving in the Headquarters, including the Light Aid Detachment fitters and the Defence Platoon. To this I had to add the Japanese Battalion. So I found myself being received by the Japanese major in command and would be conducted round their immaculate camp, in some ways cleaner even than the Indian Army Lines. This was a further example of how good Japanese discipline had remained long after their surrender.

As December 1946 approached, the pace quickened for the British evacuation and hand-over of Batavia to the incoming Dutch, and I flew back to Singapore to stay with 1 Seaforth. An interview with the Military Secretary at Tanglin yielded the surprising information that I was posted to Kuala Lumpur as DAQMG (Quartering).

I arrived in Kuala Lumpur by the night train from Singapore and was taken to Headquarters Malaya Command, where I met my new Colonel who covered all 'Q' or supply matters under a Brigadier AQ whose function was to control both personnel and supply. Both welcomed me cordially and I was given a room in the hutted officers' mess. I was then introduced to the Chief Engineer, his deputy Harold Lendrum – a Colonel – and the staff of the latter, who controlled building and maintenance throughout Malaya. I was to be the staff link with those sappers who did the actual work of building new camps and maintaining existing ones. This was a field quite new to me, though of course as a user I had had contact with engineer works services for some years. Now I should be responsible as a supplier, with the buck stopping at my desk.

The first thing I had to do was to learn just what my job entailed and how best to set about it. I travelled around Malaya widely from Ipoh and Penang at one end down to Johore Bahru at the other, to see how those serving under Malaya Command were living and working. This I found both educational and daunting. Nearly eighteen months after the Japanese surrender, a great deal still had to be done to make the garrison comfortable – despite dwindling money received from the UK.

At this time, rationing was still in full swing back in England, not least because American money had been cut off shortly after the end of the war and was now flowing into the rehabilitation of our late enemies in Germany and Japan. I was lucky in that I got around Malaya in a jeep driven by an excellent Malayan and I stayed with units and headquarters where food and drink were in good supply.

On arrival in Kuala Lumpur I had rapidly applied for my family to join me, as quarters for married families in requisitioned houses were available. In the early summer of 1947 I heard that Betty and the two girls were to arrive in Singapore by troopship from the UK. At the time appointed I was on the quayside eagerly waiting to greet them, together with a great many others. Family after family came rushing down the gangplank to greet their loved ones. The flow reduced to a trickle, then stopped; and there was still no sign of my family. I spoke to those on duty, and was led into the ship's sick bay where Betty was waiting. Poor soul, she had been incarcerated there for several days as one of the girls had measles. She said that the family would be able to travel to Kuala Lumpur next day, provided that movement was by road. I therefore returned, post haste, to the Seaforth Highlanders, where I saw 'Chu' MacLagan, who had temporarily taken over command. He was so kind as to lend us his staff car and driver for the run next day, and a second vehicle for the luggage. We proceeded at fast speed on the good road from Singapore over the causeway into Johore and then on the long distance to Kuala Lumpur. There I had already recruited an excellent Malayan amah to look after the children and an equally good Chinese cook and his wife and child to look after the house, which was on the approach road into Headquarters Malaya Command.

On arrival we were all exhausted but were made most welcome and in a few days were fully restored to health. Amah seemed well able to keep under control a boisterous near four-year-old and Janet, who was just past two. Lo had been trained before the war in a European household and knew about European-style dishes. Betty and both girls were steadily inducted into Far East cooking, and Lo's curry and Gulam Malacca, a coconut dish, became well-known to Sunday lunch guests.

Almost all engineer works were put out to local contractors, mainly Chinese. In the period before Li Peng's jungle insurrection broke out in the summer of 1948, Malaya was very much at peace, racial relations were reasonable, and work on new camps, from Khota Bahru in the north to Malacca in the south, proceeded apace. My particular function was to prepare cases in draft form for my superiors to sign for dispatch to Whitehall, for approval and allocation of funds. I devised a ledger in book form that set out every project that the Command required, together with columns for progress in getting approval, financial allocation, and progress of the work through to completion. This ledger proved popular with the staff and with the Royal Engineer Works Services at all levels and was taken into wide usage in consequence.

Betty and I were able to take advantage of my way of life in a variety of ways. On occasion she came with me on tour to such places as Ipoh and Penang, while the children remained behind with Amah. On occasion big Chinese contractors staged parties in local restaurants. I developed a passion for all forms of Chinese food and on occasion outate even the Chinese themselves. Such conduct was applauded by our Chinese hosts, though my state of indigestion afterwards left me wondering if the game was worth the candle.

We also made a wide circle of friends. In the next quarters to ours lived Peter Hunt and his wife Anne. He was AAG in the personnel staff at Headquarters and later rose to be a four-star general and Chief of the General Staff. We got to know the family of the Chief Secretary to the Government of Malaya. They lived in a gorgeous house called Carcosa, an old-style colonial building with superb gardens. Outside officialdom we also got to know a splendid couple called Green. He had escaped to Ceylon from Singapore after its surrender. He had then joined the Indian Army and fought with great distinction in Burma, being awarded a DSO and an MC. On the Japanese surrender he was soon released from military service and had returned to Malaya to resume running a large estate out in Selangor State. Curiously enough, his relations with the British element of the Malayan Civil Service were poor. They seemed to regard anyone who had not been in Japanese prison camps, notably Changi, with them as beyond the pale. This did not worry him much.

On one occasion he invited us to go out fishing for crocodile in the Selangor River by night. You had to shine a torch from the bow of a large canoe up river, hoping to light up the eyes of a crocodile swimming on the surface. If successful, the shot was fired, and the paddlers brought the canoe over the spot. The crocodile catcher then leant over the side to encircle the dead crocodile with his arm and flip it aboard. I managed to get one small one, and had it made up into a handbag for Betty. I was more than glad to have an intact arm, as scooping too large a wounded crocodile might not have had so successful a result!

The family had a holiday in Penang some months after they arrived, when we all spent a blissful week in the delightful surroundings of an hotel by the sea. I remember only one discordant note; this occurred one morning when I looked over the sea wall to be confronted by several sea snakes about three or four feet long. This inhibited sea bathing from then on! On another occasion, the motorboat taking us to a barracks at the southern end of Penang Island, grounded on a shelving beach in several feet of water, and we set out to wade ashore. After a few paces I was horrified to see a large area of sea bottom move off in front of my toes. I had disturbed a large stingray sleeping in the shallows! I swear my feet did not touch the ground again as I ran, panic stricken, to the shore.

By 1948 my most agreeable two-year tour as a staff officer was due to end. In early February, a signal arrived in Malaya Command. My next posting was to the Ministry of Defence in London, as a GSO2 in the Joint Planning Staff, and I should report immediately. I therefore had to plan my own return by flying boat while putting the family onto a troopship to come back by sea in slow time. We handed over our married quarters and said goodbye to Lo, the cook, and to his family, and to Amah, who had done us so well in looking after the children.

My flight home was in a converted Sunderland, which managed to fly at about 150 miles an hour. Our mammoth journey involved night stopovers at Calcutta, Bahrain and Athens, as well as other stops to refuel. On the last day we flew across the Mediterranean and Western Europe to Southampton Water. Next morning I reported to the Military Secretary's Office in London.

'How nice to see you,' they said. 'Do tell us how much leave you are entitled to, as there is no hurry to join the Staff.'

I thought rapidly and replied, 'Three weeks.'

'Fine,' they said. I thought about the family grinding home by sea without me to look after them, and ground my teeth!

My parents had moved from Sixty-Six Charlton to Trentishoe near Hunter's Inn in North Devon in 1947. My father had been retired in 1947 as a Colonel, Local Brigadier. So I arranged to spend most of the unexpected leave with them, after staying with Betty's parents who had a flat near the Albert Hall. Her father was then an Air Commodore in the Air Ministry on returning from serving in the Allied Command in Italy in charge of air movements.

I fixed on a rented house in Kew Gardens for the family to settle down in while I commuted daily by underground to the Ministry of Defence. Only a few days before I had to report for duty, the family arrived in Southampton. Betty's parents came with me to greet their daughter, whose first words were:

'How's the new job?'

Imagine my confusion when I had to confess I was still on leave. Betty did not forgive me for a long time thereafter, as she had had a miserable and uncomfortable voyage with no Amah to do the chores for two small girls. However, the house in Kew proved to be reasonable: and very acceptable after the rigours of troopship life. Relations also improved as Robin David, my son, was conceived that summer and arrived on 13 April 1949.

In March 1948 I started my new job in Birdcage Walk. Joint Planning Staff officers were on the first floor. I reported to the Assistant Secretary, 'Splinters' Smallwood, then a squadron leader, later a four-star Air-Chief-Marshal and lifelong friend until he died a few years ago. He introduced me to my team of a sailor, John McClure, and a wing commander, Johnny Iremonger, to the team above us at Colonel level, and finally to the Director, a fire-eating sailor.

The Ministry of Defence in those days was very much an embryo organisation grafted onto the three services that still maintained their independent status. Planning was one of the main central functions, run in parallel with similar staffs in each individual service. Planning had two main arms, strategic and operational on the one hand and administrative support on the other. As an Army man, I depended for advice on the Military Operations Directorate of the War Office, and in particular MO1. Colonel MO1 was initially Colonel Martin Charteris, who later became Private Secretary to the Queen for many years. He was soon relieved by Dick Lloyd, who had been GSO1 of 59th Division in Northern Ireland back in 1943/44. This was a very happy relationship that lasted after our respective retirements, when we both settled in Lymington, where I see his widow to this day.

By this stage I had broadened my experience very considerably, not least by service in the Far East after Europe. The Joint Planning Staff extended this purview worldwide. The major document that my Section had to update annually was called 'The Concept for War in 1957'. In the nuclear age, it was necessary to take into full account to what end the nuclear capacity of Russia and America might be devoted; but I do not remember any direct contacts with our opposite numbers in Washington. Reliance had to be placed on the products of the Joint Intelligence Committee in the Cabinet Office for Russian capabilities. Direct personal consultations do not figure in my memory of those days, only the written word and much discussion in the War Office to guide my pen.

Ideas came mainly from the Chiefs of Staff Secretariat after meetings of the Chiefs of Staff. The important place to meet at lunch-time was the Defence Staff mess in the underground War Cabinet Offices at Storey's Gate. In those days the offices were maintained as they had been in war time. The great treat for guests was to see the bedroom that Churchill used occasionally and to bounce up and down on his bed! The mess was run by a Marine Corporal who was first rate. In due course he moved the mess to the Cabinet Office where it became the Cabinet Office and Defence Staff Mess. It provided an excellent meeting place for many of those serving in the Ministry of Defence.

Gossip was rampant, as was discussion of more serious and relevant issues. Here I met many of those serving in various parts of the Joint Planning Staff, including colleagues from the Army such as 'Monkey' Blacker, later a four-star officer, and Douglas Darling, a well-decorated officer from the Rifle Brigade. Brian Burnett from the RAF, a well-known tennis player and member of the team above mine, was also to be seen regularly. I still see him occasionally through mutual friends. He is a retired four-star airman.

On every mind were the main issues of the day. Stalin's Russia and its threat to the newly-formed NATO were discussed ad nauseam. America's decision to re-arm Germany in face of the threat from Communist Russia was hotly argued, not least against the background of continuing rationing and hardship in the UK. Middle East aspects leading to the establishment of the Baghdad Pact as protection from Russian attack figured in our plans. By contrast, the Far East, other than the Chinese-led insurrection in Malaya that broke out about the time I left that country, did not take up much planning time. One of my friends in Kuala Lumpur had been the MI6 representative. I do not think that he had much inkling of Chin Peng's rebellion. If he did, nothing was indicated to his friends.

In Kew Gardens the family enjoyed life. Kew Gardens themselves were only ten minutes' walk from the house, so the family used to walk regularly in the diverse landscapes open to the public. On one occasion a tall, elderly lady walking furiously with a stick bore down on us. Behind her several ancient gentlemen toiled to keep up. The penny suddenly dropped: this was Queen Mary and her flagging entourage going past us.

Several old friends of mine were working in London. Miles Lovell, who had passed out from the Shop a year before me as top student, was serving as a major in the War Office. He had a beautiful girlfriend whom we also got to know at Kew, and he became godfather to my son Robin. Betty gave birth to Robin at home; an excellent nurse and midwife had moved into our spare room to tend mother and third child. Later in the summer Robin's christening took place in our local church, with the party afterwards in our own house.

Holidays were a problem for an impecunious temporary major, and my parents' new home provided the answer. Trentishoe was a delightful house some three miles by road from Parracombe in North Devon. It suited my father, who had never really recovered from the shock of the enemy shell that had penetrated his tank and bounced off his chest as it rattled around inside the turret, and craved for privacy. My mother was full of enterprise and energy, as usual, and she insisted that we spend our holidays at Trentishoe. The girls loved being there, as they could roam the attractive countryside and local stream leading to Hunter's Inn. Betty and I managed one skiing holiday to Austria on a cheap Army-sponsored scheme. I was delighted to get back onto skis again after four holidays in the Alps before the war. My parents also passed over to me their old Ford car after they had bought a new one in Barnstaple, their nearest large town. The family therefore had mobility, though I still felt too poor to buy my own.

In the winter of 1949 another hazard appeared on our horizon. Betty was declared pregnant once again. We debated endlessly what was to be done. Could we accept another child? Was Betty able to manage another birth so soon after Robin's arrival? Should we be able to look after four children thereafter? We felt that we could consult no one, not even our parents. After much agonising, we agreed to go for an abortion. This was not simple, not least because of the number of charlatans practising. In the end we were recommended to an abortionist who operated in his house in Richmond. A date was fixed and I drove Betty to the house. She vanished inside, leaving me sitting in the car. After what seemed an age she reappeared looking distinctly shaky. I took her home and kept her in bed for a day or two as I had taken short leave. She recovered, thank God. We never told a soul and the topic has never come up until I started to write this book. Now I think that our children should know.

1950 approached and with it my next posting order. I was due for regimental duty once again and I was told by the Corps of Royal Engineers that I was to take over a newly reformed 16 Field Squadron in 35 Engineer Regiment in the Canal Zone of Egypt in the spring. To my delight Jack Gatford, a fellow sapper from the same batch at the Shop as myself, was to succeed me in the Joint Planning Staff. He had been taken prisoner in the desert early on in that prolonged campaign, escaped from the Italians, and been recaptured by the Germans. Our paths had not crossed since 1939, but from then on he and his wife Sheila, sister of another sapper in No 42 Batch at the Shop, remained firm friends for life.

After a suitable hand-over, I went on leave. I then caught a troopship bound for Port Said, leaving the family in the house in Kew until I could get quarters in the Canal Zone and call them forward. Before I sailed for

Egypt, Miles Lovell proposed to his girlfriend and was turned down flat. This festered in his mind, which was already disturbed by his sudden conversion from the Anglican faith to Roman Catholicism, her faith. He resigned his commission and took himself off to a Roman Catholic Jesuit training establishment somewhere in the West Country. On qualifying he was posted to South America, and sadly we lost touch with him for evermore.

CHAPTER 4

To Egypt and Berlin (1950–1955)

EGYPT IN 1950 WAS STILL the great base for British operations in the Middle East, ranging from Libya at one end to Iran in the other, and southward to the Horn of Africa. The British establishment was still of considerable size: Tel El Kabir camp had a circumference of seventeen miles. Politically, however, Egypt was in flux. The regime under King Farouk was in its last stages, and the movement led by Nasser was steadily increasing in strength. None of this showed on our disembarkation at Port Said, where the hawkers came alongside the ship in their traditional craft and offered us everything under the sun; but change was in the air nonetheless.

I was met by David Edwards, second-in-command of 35 Engineer Regiment, and driven to El Ballah, on the banks of the Suez Canal some fifteen miles north of Ismailia, which contained both Headquarters British Troops in Egypt and that of the Suez Canal Company. On arrival I met Lt. Col. Tom Foulkes, who commanded the Regiment, and Basil Rawlins, commanding 42 Field Squadron. All of these remained close friends over many years, together with their wives who were already established in Ismailia.

35 Regiment had already built up from one independent to two field squadrons and a Field Park Squadron. It was established in a largely tented camp close to the Egyptian village of El Ballah. The regiment formed part of a brigade with the most unusual components of a gunner regiment (1RHA), an armoured car regiment (16/5 Royal Lancers) and a single infantry battalion (1R Lincolns). These were the only operational units at that time in the Canal Zone, the remainder being large numbers of RASC, Ordnance and REME units manning the base installation. GHQ Middle East was in Fayid on the shore of the Great Bitter Lake and north of Suez Town. Its bailiwick covered Libya to the west, Iraq and Jordan to the east and the Sudan and Kenya to the south.

As an unaccompanied officer, I lived in the officers' mess and rapidly got to know the officers and soldiers of 16 Field Squadron. My second-in-command was Captain Jim Wade, a shy but efficient officer. My squadron sergeant-major, Calam, was an absolute gem, in that he exerted discipline of a high order while being universally respected by all ranks.

The squadron was partly regular and partly conscript, the latter reaching up to corporal in their final few months of service. Because a number were university graduates, initiative and common sense were very good: although we lacked the full complement of high-grade tradesmen that were the hallmarks of sapper units before the war. This was the third squadron that I had commanded so it was easy to fall into the routine of training that a newly reformed squadron needed.

Exercises began in the desert south of the Suez to Cairo road. On the first occasion that squadron headquarters took the field, breakfast time came and the cook seemed to be in a distracted state of mind. The sergeant-major and I bore down on him and demanded eggs. The cook had a frying-pan full of boiling fat on his gas-fired stove. As we watched, he put eggs with shells still unbroken into the hot fat. Calam's language had to be heard to be believed! It transpired that the wretched cook had never been in the field before. This was what training was all about; soon we had a functioning headquarters in desert terrain. I started using a sun compass mounted on the bonnet of my jeep: it proved to be remarkably accurate. Mine warfare was of fundamental importance. Field Troops, therefore, had much practice in laying concrete replica mines and creating breaches using prodders to test every inch of the ground. Water was a vital commodity in the desert, so building water points, using collapsible tanks on towers, became second nature to all ranks. Demolitions, using live explosives, were much enjoyed by all. As a fully mechanised squadron, we covered many desert miles in trucks driven by our own drivers and maintained by our own fitters.

Later in the summer, Betty and the children arrived by air in the Canal Zone. They had had a bone-shaking and noisy journey in a converted York bomber. I took them to the flat that I had hired in Ismailia on the wrong side of the railroad tracks. The family was met by the cook that I had employed, a Nubian named Mohammed, and an Arab nurse. Both proved acceptable to Betty and all three children, now aged seven, five and one. The flat worked out reasonably, though hot by day despite a number of fans. I commuted daily to El Ballah except when I was absent on exercises. By this time I had acquired a second-hand Ford car for family use in Alexandria. I had got this back to the Canal Zone when I had a succession of punctures near Zagazig! Assistance illustrates the remarkably tolerant attitude of the Egyptian populace towards the British in the year of grace 1950.

For relaxation, I joined the Yacht Club in Ismailia, where a number of dinghies were available for racing. This I did with gusto, though my experience to date was small. Not long after I started racing, news came that the new chief engineer for British troops in Egypt was an experienced sailor and would arrive on a Saturday afternoon to race. He arrived, looking immaculate in a magnificent yachting hat, and was conducted to his boat. This was only fourteen feet long, and he was a burly six-footer. He stepped on the bow: it immediately turned over and the chief engineer was deposited in the water! All that could be seen was the yachting cap floating on the surface, and a lot of air bubbles surrounding it. The committee fished him out and took him to his car, and never again was he seen at the Yacht Club.

On another occasion in winter, racing was in progress out on Lake Timsah when a khamsin or sandstorm blew up without warning, and many dinghies overturned. I was lucky in staying upright by stripping off my sails in time. I took in tow a number of overturned dinghies to await the arrival of the safety boat. Suddenly my crew gasped and drew my attention astern. A few hundred yards behind my back loomed the bows of a large tanker navigating the Canal. It had been dinned into us that ships in transit could not pull up easily, and that we therefore had to keep clear of such vessels. I warned all those in the water with their overturned dinghies that we were going to have to swim for it and that I would give the signal. By some miracle, the tanker captain had spotted us and in the wider waters of the lake was able to stop his ship before he ran us down. The safety boat arrived and dragged us all to safety in low visibility and a howling sand-filled wind. We took some reviving.

Betty and I became good friends with John and Jay Constant and their children. He was staff officer to the chief engineer, and later went to command the Arab Legion engineers in Jordan. He was succeeded by John Cowtan, who had recently married Rose. She had been one of the girls in SIME, the pseudonym for MI6 operations in the Middle East. Scotty, who had married Jos back in the UK, was also posted to Egypt. We saw a lot of these couples, both then and for the rest of our lives, and with so many friends social life was fairly hectic. One friend, however, was sadly not to survive. Audrey Hingston, a most beautiful and talented person, died of bilharzia as a result of contact with the Sweet Water Canal from the Nile.

At duty, a number of brigade exercises took place in Sinai, where British troops could range very widely: down as far as St Catherine's Monastery, and up to the line of the railway from Kantara to Palestine. In the early spring, after a drop of rain, the desert came to life with bulbs of every description, mile after mile of gorgeous blooms that it seemed sacrilegious to drive through. South of Suez on the Sinai shore there were hot springs of volcanic origin. I recall setting up hot showers using this natural hot water and putting much of the brigade units through them – not least ourselves!

On another exercise we had constructed a large water point in a wadi bed in the mountainous area of the Sinai Peninsula. At night, a thunderstorm broke out amongst the mountain-tops, and a wall of water came down as a flash flood. The sappers managed to scramble up the sides of the wadi to escape the flood waters, but two locally-employed Seychellois were drowned. These were the only fatalities on such exercises that I can recall. On another occasion, Colonel Tom Foulkes visited us after dusk, and I had to give out somewhat complicated orders for recovery of equipment and withdrawal to the Canal Zone. I can still picture in my mind's eye the scene that night. It epitomises some of the finest exercises in marvellously scenic country.

As spring 1951 turned to summer, it became too hot for meaningful exercises. This was the period for basic military and sapper training in and around the camp. To my surprise, I received warning that I was to be the sapper member of a training team under a major-general to go to Iraq in October to supervise and run the first large-scale exercise to be mounted by the newly constituted Iraqi Army.

For the summer months Betty and I were lucky enough to be able to rent a Canal pilot's house in the French quarter of Ismailia, complete with garden and fruit trees. Here the children could run around outside as they pleased, only the wearing of sun hats being compulsory. In the garden were mango trees and a lime tree that contributed to our diet. Betty enjoyed this house enormously. As October approached and my mission to Iraq came closer, I had to find somewhere else to live. We found a first-rate flat in the older part of Ismailia, with a garage. No sooner were we established than I was off by air to Habbaniyah airfield, still an RAF base, and home to the Air Force-run Iraqi levies that still functioned in the largely Kurdish areas of the north of the country.

On arrival at Habbaniyah, I was delighted to find that the Station Commander was a group captain who had been in the planning team above mine in the Ministry of Defence. This was a most useful contact, as subsequent events would prove. After several days in and around Baghdad, the training team flew up to Mosul and then on by road to the Rowanduz Pass area close to the border with Persia. I managed to fit in a day visit to the Iraqi Staff College where I found two Iraqis, who had been in my term at Woolwich before the war, both teaching at this establishment. One of them, short and fat, became a minister in the Revolutionary Government after the slaughter of the Iraqi King in 1958.

The road up to Rowanduz was spectacular. In the gorge itself the carriageway was cut into a slot in the cliff wall with the river thundering twenty or thirty feet below. The British team co-located with Iraqi umpires in a tented camp near a bridge over the river on the Persian side of the gorge. The exercise consisted of an attack by an Iraqi mechanised brigade from yet closer to the Persian border, upon an infantry division dug-in on the mountain-tops on each side of the gorge itself. The scenery was magnificent, as was the amount of walking involved. Each day I found myself going up a couple of thousand feet to visit troops guarding one side of the gorge. Then it was necessary to descend the same distance, cross the bridge and repeat the operation on the other side of the gorge. Leg muscles bulged in a big way as a result!

Whilst I was away in Iraq Colonel Nasser led an uprising against the King of Egypt – a development of which I only learned when I received a message to say that my family were safe and well. Safe from what? I asked in puzzlement, and was informed that there was big trouble in Egypt, including the Canal Zone. The Station Commander at Habbaniyah told me that all flights to and from the Canal Zone were suspended. There was nothing I could do but wait; and I used the time to stay with an American friend in Baghdad and to buy a beautiful Kazakh carpet in the souk. My RAF connection allowed me to get it aboard an aircraft, and several days later I returned to Ismailia in triumph, to find that Colonel Foulkes had kindly stationed a lance corporal to guard the family. This excellent man had already opened up with his sten gun to save an RAF officer passing below in the street from attack by a gang of thugs. Betty and the children were anxious, as can be imagined, although the situation in the town was stabilising under a British presence on the streets.

A posting order had reached the regiment while I was away in Iraq. I was to report for duty as staff officer to the Major-General Administration in GHQ Middle East at Fayid. On top of this, news came through that families were to be evacuated to the United Kingdom if they could not be fitted into safe quarters in Egypt. Betty and I were much relieved to hear that we could move to Fayid. I handed over 16 Field Squadron to Hugh Cunningham, later Deputy Chief of Defence Staff and a Lieutenant General, and we set up house in the four large rooms and compound allocated to us. In the place of honour in our living room lay the Kazakh carpet! I still have both the carpet and the memories of Iraq that go with it. In my mind's eye I can see the wonderful cave with the foaming torrent that formed one of the sources of the Zab River; range on range of mountains, the furthest capped by snow and well inside Iran;

and Kurdish families migrating on horseback through to Turkey and even Syria, for in those days the Kurds moved through their mountains unfettered by frontiers.

My new master was Major-General Charles Humphreys, late Northumberland Fusiliers. He had the reputation of being fierce and of not suffering fools gladly. Fortunately he and I hit it off well from the start and we remained friends for life. I gave the address at his funeral in Camberley many years later. He was one of the few people I have met who possessed a photographic memory, and his knowledge of poetry was prodigious. Sometimes at the end of a long and arduous day he would say to me, 'David, I will now recite.' Out of his prodigious memory would come verse after verse of poetry apposite to the subjects that had been dealt with that day. Both Betty and I got on equally well with his wife Doris, who was most kind to the family. To our sorrow the couple had no children.

Equally notable was the Commander-in-Chief, General Sir Brian Robertson. His mind was crystal clear. To read his signals to London was an education in itself. The recipients could have been in no doubt as to his views on diverse subjects, however unpalatable these often were to those in high places in Whitehall. On retirement a few years later he became the Overlord of Transport so, politically, his merits had been fully perceived. His wife was formidable but kindly. I well remember an occasion when Betty and I were bidden to dine at the Robertsons' residence. After dinner they always invited their guests to take part in party games. One of these was to form up in two teams and to transfer a matchbox case down the line from nose to nose. The sight of Betty trying and failing to transfer a matchbox to the nose of General Robertson sticks in my memory!

Occasionally the General used to address the assembled multitude of the headquarters staff. We were warned that he would speak for twenty minutes. Invariably he spoke without notes for this time, plus or minus a few seconds. His Military Assistant told me that the speech had been rehearsed several times in the fastness of his own office.

The Military Assistants' Union was a strong one. The Military Assistant to General Robertson was a cavalryman, his opposite number, looking after the Chief of Staff, a gunner. We used to exchange ideas frequently. Relations with the senior staff were also important. My master presided over two brigadiers who dealt respectively with personnel and supply matters. They were supported by heads of services at major-general level, all of whom I came to know well. With such keen minds at its head, the large staff was a distinctly harmonious one.

The diversity of problems was immense. Egypt was in turmoil: as shown by the evacuation of so many families that could not be housed inside camps because of hostility, particularly from the Buluk, or black-clad Egyptian gendarmerie, who were based in the towns of the Canal Zone. This hostility was quelled by a military operation against police stations and compounds to force the surrender of all armed police, during which there were casualties on both sides. Given Whitehall's determination to hold on to the base, no other solution offered itself.

Kenya and Libya presented different problems that the Major-General Administration, my master, had to look into on the ground. We flew RAF to both countries. In Kenya, Whitehall had decided to put a lot of public money into the groundnuts' scheme at Mackinnon Road. A large area of forest had been cleared by bulldozers, the soil ploughed and groundnuts planted. The project had to be abandoned, largely because the expected rainfall failed to materialise. In Libya there was still a substantial British garrison in both Cyrenaica and Tripolitania, though some had gone to fight the war in Korea, including Tony Younger. The local commander in Benghazi organised a shoot in a valley up in the upper reaches of the Green Mountains. We were loaned guns and had a remarkable day discharging our muskets at the local partridge and pigeons. I had not as yet taken up shotgun shooting and my bag was commensurately small.

Back at Fayid there was a shortage of fresh food. Much negotiation took place to buy eggs, fruit and vegetables from Beirut in the Lebanon, and landing-craft (tank) were used to bring the produce back. Another source of supply was Cyprus. Whitehall was already thinking ahead to a replacement for the base in Egypt, and new construction had been authorised for Episkopi. The MGA and his opposite number, a senior RAF colleague, flew to Cyprus to attend the initial siting board for a joint headquarters, later to be the new GHQ Middle East and the associated RAF HQ. In attendance, I managed to slip into the market in Nicosia and secure a large wicker basket full of vegetables and fruit. These were ecstatically received by the family in the compound at Fayid! My mother in Devon had been told of our predicament, and despatched a sample of her own cheese by post. Unfortunately, this took time to arrive and did so in an advanced stage of decomposition.

Soon we were off on our travels again, this time to Amman in Jordan for an appointment with Glubb Pasha, Commander of the Arab Legion, and a truly remarkable man. Glubb occupied the old Turkish Governor's Office from the days of the First World War. The MGA and I were conducted into the glassed-in waiting room and offered seats in the midst of a number of Jordanis, some of whom had hooded birds of prey on their gloved wrists: a scene almost biblical in its context. Glubb still commanded enormous respect from Arab tribesmen all over Jordan, who exercised their ancient right of access to their tribal chiefs. It was a matter of great sorrow when King Abdullah was assassinated and the new King Hussein, not long out of Sandhurst, dismissed Glubb Pasha.

Inside GHQ Middle East life was never monotonous. Problems arose constantly for staff consideration and recommendations to the Commander-in-Chief. There were, of course, distractions, such as the annual tattoo in Ismailia, a great spectacle as the massed bands from Colonial territories took the stage. In the office that winter I blotted my copybook. One night in the early hours, my telephone rang. Sleepily, I answered it. The Duty Officer at GHQ was ringing me to say that Queen Mary had just died. I replied that there was nothing that I could do about it, and put the phone down. Next morning, I realised the extent of my error when I reached the office. 'Why wasn't I told?' stormed my General. I had no answer. Fortunately the Duty Officer had carried out the necessary actions, but it took some time for me to live down my mistake.

Christmas in the Canal Zone came and went, with a few flakes of snow in our suddenly frigid compound. Celia and Janet attended an Army school nearby. The Army Education Corps provided good, dedicated teachers, so both received adequate grounding for future schools to build upon. In the autumn of 1952 all five of us took a holiday in Cyprus. We booked in to a small family hotel in Kyrenia that proved to suit us well. Two bicycles were hired and the heavily-laden convoy took off daily for the sandy beaches west of the town, or further westward towards Morphou. Local people of Greek or Turkish extraction lived in complete amity at that time, and the shadow of Archbishop Makarios had yet to fall on this peaceful land. Despite the climb up to St Hilarion, we managed to explore the crusader castle inland from Kyrenia. People from both communities kindly invited us into their houses for cool drinks on seeing us toiling past on our bicycles. Holidays in Cyprus sold extremely well to every member of the family.

My three years in Egypt were drawing to an end. My fate lay in the hands of the Corps of Royal Engineers, and in the early spring a posting order arrived. I was to take over as Officer Commanding Royal Engineer Troops in Berlin. I was due for leave at home before taking up this job, so we packed up our possessions into boxes provided by the Army for despatch by ship. Reduced to hand luggage only, we rejoiced in a great round of farewell parties before flying back to UK in more comfort than the family had endured in 1950. We were met by Betty's parents and taken to their excellent quarters at Bicester alongside my father-in-law's headquarters of 42 Group RAF Maintenance Command.

The main task back in the UK was to choose schools for Celia, who would be ten in September 1953, and Janet, who would be eight in May. Both had been enrolled since soon after birth to go to the Royal School at Bath. Betty and I went to the school to interview the headmistress. She seemed, however, to think that she was interviewing us, and we did not take to her at all. We asked to look round the school, and an under matron was eventually found. On the way she filled us up with stories of what really went on at the school. We liked little of what we heard and decided then and there that the Royal School was not for our daughters. Time was short before departure to Berlin, and in a fever of activity we decided that we liked St Michael's School at Limpsfield in Sussex, which had originally been a mixed school. Celia would go there in September, and Janet when finances permitted. This decision stemmed in part from interviewing an impressive headmistress, not knowing that a year later she would retire. However, the die was cast and both girls eventually stayed on to take A level exams, despite none of us having much time for the new headmistress.

The family also stayed with my parents at Trentishoe in North Devon. By this time my parents had built a leat across their fields to an electrical turbine run by water power, thereby making their own electricity. More land had been acquired to run a herd of cattle and a nearby cottage acquired to house paid help. But all too soon my own family had to move once again to Berlin – this time by air to the British airfield at Gatow.

The quarter allotted to us was in Kantstrasse, near the 1936 Olympic stadium. This house was substantial, with a useful bit of garden and a built-in garage, and the family took to it at once. An excellent East German woman was engaged as cook, and in addition Betty employed Frau Gläser, an Englishwoman who had married a German between the wars, as tutor for the two girls. I had a car and German driver. After four large hutted rooms in Fayid, living conditions were ideal.

The city was split into four sectors: British, French, American and Russian. There was an international headquarters or Kommandantura, but it had ceased to be effective after the Russians blockaded the city. This led to the air bridge operation that had provided sustenance for the three western sectors as a whole until such time as the Russians admitted defeat. Only a matter of weeks before I arrived, Russian tanks had driven over East German citizens demonstrating against Russian occupation in

Topping-out Ceremony, British HQ Berlin, 1953

the eastern sector of the City. Tension was still at a high level for some months after our arrival, despite road and rail communications having been restored with western Germany. In East Berlin and East Germany the police, or VOPOs, lorded it over the local populace, supported by some twenty divisions of the Russian Army.

RE Troops Berlin was a tailor-made unit for support of the British garrison. It consisted of a DCRE Works, complete with a number of garrison engineers and clerks of works, senior warrant officers who controlled nearly 500 German engineers for maintenance work and planning new construction. In addition, there was an independent field troop of combat engineers to support the Berlin Brigade of three battalions, and there were troops to look after plant and stores. Money was available in large quantities because all our expenses came from occupation costs that were met by the West German government in Bonn and not by the British taxpayer. Headquarters was in the Olympic Stadium complex commanded by a major general. The Berlin Brigade and its commander led a separate existence in the British Sector. The largest works task that occupied most of my tour in Berlin was the rebuilding of the headquarters blocks close to the Olympic Stadium.

My DCRE in charge of works was older than I was and held a short service commission. He and I established a harmonious relationship. He was kind enough to teach me a lot about Works Services, a subject that I had not hitherto encountered at first hand. I had become a substantive major at last in 1952, after completing the necessary thirteen years. This step helped my authority in my new unit.

We shared a barracks at Spandau on the western outskirts of Berlin with the tank squadron supporting the Berlin Brigade. Next door was Spandau Prison where Hitler's Deputy, Rudolph Hess, and others convicted of war crimes at Nuremberg were incarcerated. The prison garrison, an infantry company, was rotated every month between the four occupying powers, so that once every four months there was a Russian guard company on the other side of a wire fence separating the two barracks. On one occasion this company marched out of the prison gate onto the road below the windows of our barrack rooms, singing as they went. The British soldiers emptied the odd bucket of water over them, and the Russians lodged a formal complaint at the Kommandantura. The tank commander and I had some fast talking to do. The Russians seemed not to bear malice, and on several occasions I met their prison staff at lunch in the prison.

Several joint exercises with the French and American garrisons were staged, in which our combat engineers always participated, once building tank ferries to cross the river and lakes running through Berlin from the British to the American sector. Berlin rejoiced in substantial lakes, particularly the Wannsee. The British Yacht Club had taken possession of the German fleet of Stars that had been built for the 1936 Olympic Games. The helmsman and crew of two had to cling on to the side of a fully-heeled yacht with one hand on the extended tiller and I enjoyed helming these boats enormously. Sailing in Berlin is an abiding memory of great yachting occasions.

Berlin Brigade commanded three infantry battalions. One of these was 1 Royal Lincolns that I had seen much of in the Canal Zone. Betty was great friends with several wives, particularly Margaret Goulson, whose husband later commanded a brigade in Nigeria and was tragically killed in a road accident on his last few days in that country. Our brigade commander had an idiosyncrasy; he could never remember names, even of those whom he dealt with day by day. At parties in his house, what I termed a stately gavotte took place; to introduce a member of his immediate circle to a guest he first withdrew a few paces to allow your name to be whispered in his ear, then moved forward to make the introduction.

Another specialist team in the British sector was BRIXMIS – British Mission to the Soviet Zone of Occupation. This team, headed by a brigadier, engaged in a game of cops and robbers with Russian troops stationed in Eastern Germany to observe and report on their state of training. Large-scale exercises were particular targets. On one occasion a BRIXMIS team managed to conceal themselves on the Elbe riverbank and recorded much of a major river crossing exercise by the Russian Army using the latest Soviet bridging equipment. But their mission was distinctly dangerous. With fluctuations in East/West tension, the Russians occasionally allowed shots to be fired at British, American and French teams operating in their zone of occupation. The East German police were not permitted to arrest them, but went to great lengths to obstruct their movement. One pay-off for me was that BRIXMIS could visit the Meissen showrooms near Dresden. Through friends in the Mission, I bought several Meissen pieces of porcelain. An exchange rate of five to one in favour of the West mark helped the purchase price vastly.

That winter Betty and I decided to take the children skiing in Austria. To get there, we travelled with a special permit through the Russian zone of occupation in East Germany – a process that we managed with no great difficulty. For our return journey, however, I was ordered to take the longer route. BRIXMIS had objected, I gathered, to our travelling through 'their' territory.

Works Services took up much of my time, not least because I was keen to learn the ropes. Unusual tasks came our way. One of these was to prepare the Olympic Stadium for the annual British Berlin tattoo. This attracted large numbers of Germans, as well as many British, French and American soldiers with their families. Even some Russians came from their representation within Berlin itself. Stands had to be erected, together with accommodation for performers and sets for some of the acts. The performances were always to a capacity crowd; in one's minds eye lurked memories of Hitler reviewing jack-booted troops and SS units in the same location not so long ago. British military massed bands were extremely popular with all spectators.

The DCRE's chief clerk was a German professor, only too glad to find employment. The office staff were largely German, although my chief clerk on the British side was an excellent British citizen, who had married a German woman and settled in Berlin. Mr Bocock spoke good German and was a tower of strength. Occasionally things went wrong, such as when the German habit of informing on their fellow men and women came to the fore; and I could not but reflect on the role of the Gestapo in Nazi society.

We often went out to German pubs and restaurants. Local people were uniformly friendly, and I formed a very high opinion of the Berliners, who seemed to be determined to remain an independent island in the midst of a communist-dominated East Germany. On occasion it was possible to attend opera performances in the Russian sector of the city. These were first-rate, though, as all officers had to go in uniform, we tended to stand out like sore thumbs in the midst of a largely communist audience. East and West vied with one another to produce the brightest and latest productions on stage. The main opera house in West Berlin was much in demand, as were the theatres in the Kurfürstendam, the main cultural centre of the city. There was a splendid British Club in the British sector, where in winter the tennis courts were flooded and used for skating; and the family all acquired skis or toboggans.

In the days before the Berlin Wall was built to prevent East Germans escaping into West Berlin, movement in uniform using official cars was easy. The family went to see the Russian Army war memorial in Treptow, and the room where the German surrender document had been signed. Beyond the Brandenburger Gate lay the appalling street of flats built by the Russians, called Stalin Alley, to ape Moscow, though on every side behind them war-damaged buildings remained untouched. The Russian sector of Berlin left a nasty taste in the mouth.

The biggest challenge for me lay in occasional visits by the Chief Engineer from HQ British Army of the Rhine and from his deputy in charge of works services, Harold Lendrum, my old friend from days in Malaya Command, now promoted to brigadier. They were my immediate seniors within the Corps of Royal Engineers. My annual reports, initiated locally, passed through their hands and were above average.

In my first year in Berlin, I was summoned to the Olympic Stadium headquarters to receive a top-secret briefing. I was to help with a joint CIA/MI6 project. The Americans had worked out that the main telephone cable from the Russian headquarters at Potsdam back to Moscow and beyond ran only a few hundred yards from their boundary with the Soviet Zone of Occupation. They planned to dig a tunnel to intercept this cable. The British part of the project was to build a chamber at the end of the tunnel, to allow for the interception of messages. I was required to house Major Merrill and his team, and certain pieces of the chamber were to be made in my engineer workshops. When 'take' from the cable started to be received, I was to arrange storage before dispatch by air to the UK. Security, I was told, was vital.

Some months later the Russians found that there was some sort of 'short' in their telephone cable. They started to dig trial pits along the length of road beside which our underground chamber lay, and one corner of our chamber was uncovered by mischance. Other reports suggest that the British traitor George Blake had blown the gaffe. In any case, the whole operation had to be aborted. Security on the British and American side remained absolute for a great number of years, and only after the Cold War ended did some fragmentary accounts appear of this great intelligence triumph.

While all this was going on, life remained amusing and fruitful in Berlin. On occasion we were invited to the Russian headquarters in Potsdam for a reception under the auspices of BRIXMIS. We visited the famous palace at Potsdam that had been built by Frederick the Great, removing our shoes and donning felt slippers, as its floors were built of beautiful wood. Celia came out for the holidays from school in England. Janet went to the Army school in West Berlin for our second year in the city in the autumn of 1954, and Robin started in nursery school. Sadly, all nice things come to an end. I received a posting order in the spring of 1955 to take up an appointment as a member of the directing staff at the Staff College at Camberley. This post was graded as a local lieutenant colonel, although still paid as a major. With great regret the family said its goodbyes to Berlin and, after a break for leave at home, I reported for duty in Camberley.

CHAPTER 5

Camberley and Aden (1955–1960)

T HE STAFF COLLEGE AT CAMBERLEY, recently removed to the Defence Academy at Shrivenham, was a bulwark of the Army establishment that had long existed to train staff officers. The Directing Staff mostly lived in comfortable wooden huts within the extensive grounds. These were contiguous with those of the Royal Military Academy at Sandhurst, which had combined after the war with its similar academy at Woolwich, through which I had passed out as a sapper in 1939. When I arrived in the early summer of 1955 some of these wooden huts were being rebuilt. My family therefore had to occupy new student-type married quarters at the north end of King's Ride on the edge of Barossa heathland.

Several other teachers, including Matt Abraham, a cavalry officer next door, were already established there. Between our houses ran a gully that flooded soon after we moved in. I complained and was taken to see the Commandant as the final arbiter. This was a fellow sapper, General 'Splosh' Jones, whom I had never met before. He turned down my request for an early move to the grounds of the Staff College. He furthermore indicated his displeasure and I formed the impression that he had not asked for me to be posted to his staff. The animosity he displayed continued for the rest of my service, as this account will show. However, we did move to a new house in Everest Road, off the top end of King's Ride, when this was finished.

Life as a member of the Directing Staff was arduous. Most of the students were only three or four years younger than I was. Though I was disguised as a Lieutenant Colonel, in fact my pay as a major was the same as theirs. I found myself allocated to 'B' Division at Camberley under a charming gunner Colonel. 'A' Division was also in the main building; 'C' Division lived and worked at Minley about three miles away. They came to the main building for central lectures and discussions, which took place often. In the late summer the whole establishment migrated to Normandy, where battlefield tours were run, partly built around 3rd Division and 6th Airborne Division operations on and after D-Day, 6 June 1944. On the strength of my personal experiences, I joined the team putting over the capture of the Orne Bridges, particularly Pegasus Bridge, by the gliders carrying infantry. Other portrayals were given by wartime 6th Airborne participants invited as guest artists. On the first occasion that I could, I went into the Café Gondrée to thank Monsieur and Madame for their kindness when I had lain on a stretcher in their parlour. Both became firm friends. Monsieur Gondrée told me that for so long as he lived he would ensure that the modest plaque on the Canal Bank that marked the site of our first ferries, followed by a bridge, would remain intact. He was as good as his word, despite burgeoning 6th Airborne publicity exhibits. The year after he died the plaque vanished.

Work for syndicates of about ten needed preparation. For discussions and tactical problems proposed party line solutions were issued. These had to be digested beforehand, even though on occasion discussion yielded a different answer. The art of the game by my reckoning lay in judging the best answer and declaring it as such, if necessary alongside the official solution. A number of written answers, including essays, were demanded of each student. These had to be corrected using the official notes provided by the Staff. Many hours, on occasion over the weekend, were needed to annotate each paper with meaningful comments. Tactical exercises without troops (TEWTS) required much reading up and study before conducting discussions on the ground.

On top of all this an exercise was allotted to each syndicate Directing Staff (DS) to update or rewrite as the faculty had decided the previous year. I was given a crossing of the River Thames at Goring in a nuclear environment to prepare from scratch. This required much reconnaissance on site, as well as a study of how best to graft a nuclear environment onto well-known drills for river crossing. Back in 1941 I had even crossed this stretch of river on a 4th Division exercise. I was required to present this TEWT in the spring of 1956 to the Directing Staff headed by the Commandant before the students came out from Camberley to discuss the various questions set them as the theoretical river crossing proceeded. All three Divisions of the course would be participating, plus a full turnout of DS and the hierarchy above them to listen in to student solutions.

I laboured long and hard to prepare the setting, the narrative and the questions for discussion. On the day appointed the whole of the Directing Staff assembled. As the originator, I asked permission of the Commandant to proceed. Instead of doing so he turned to the assembled company and said, 'Before we hear from Willison, I want to be sure that we need this exercise at all. What are your views?' A stunned silence followed. One or two voices spoke up in favour of an exercise of this sort being needed. Then silence reigned once more. 'Oh, very well then, let us hear what Willison has to say.' Not too abashed, despite this arrogant attempt to bully me, I got on with the job. The day was in fact successful. A new exercise had been accepted by all those present. Eventually, General 'Splosh' Jones stamped off without a word to me. I may say that this animosity was not uncommon between him and his staff. On another occasion a clever gunner DS was presenting a new nuclear attack exercise on Salisbury Plain. He was torn to shreds by the Commandant, in our view gratuitously, and had to recast parts of his solution to the problems he had himself set before the students came out on the ground for his TEWT. Other events of bullying DS occurred before General Jones was posted and General Nigel Poet, whom I had met on D-Day across the River Orne, took his place. As can be imagined, his arrival was a breath of fresh air. Needless to say, none of this percolated through to the student body. General Jones was popular and well regarded by each year during his stewardship. But he was to plague me again when I commanded 38 Corps Engineer Regiment at Ripon as this narrative will explain, and again thereafter.

Family life became progressively strained as the years 1955, 56, 57 and the first part of 1958 unfolded. I felt myself under strain while General Jones was Commandant. Under his successor, strain was less but there was still a mountain of work, not least corrections, to do. Celia was at boarding school while Janet went to a local school in Camberley for the first year and then as a day-girl to a private school in Wokingham. With no allowances for children's schooling this meant very little money to spend on the rest of the family. Holidays entailed motoring down to Trentishoe where my mother coped magnificently with the whole family. She herself showed signs of strain, though continuing to minister to Christian Scientists in North Devon. In 1957 she announced that she was going to the Mother Church of her sect in Boston. She came on a short visit to stay with the family before taking ship from Southampton. She looked most unwell. Looking into her eyes one could see that she was constantly in pain. True to her faith, she refused to see a doctor and insisted on catching her ship.

A week later my telephone rang late at night. It was my father, who told me that he had heard from officials in the Mother Church that my mother had died of cancer on the steps of the church. She was to be cremated in Boston. He did not feel up to flying over, and asked if I had the time to go. I had a great deal on my plate and to my shame and regret I decided not to go either. So my mother was cremated on foreign shores with no family member present. She had done so much for me, for Betty and for the children, in addition to looking after my father. He had become a Magistrate in Barnstaple, had bought himself a 1927 Rolls-Royce and despite nagging pain from his chest wound, he continued as

My mother and father, 1952

best he could the life of a country gentleman. My mother, at heart a country woman from Ireland, kept bees, made her own honey and butter from milking a small herd of cows below the house. She gardened with great skill, growing fruit and vegetables as well as shrubs and flowers. The children adored her and our holidays at Trentishoe. Her passing left a large hole in all our lives. It was not till the Millennium year that I visited Boston.

Betty insisted on keeping a cat. This creature produced large litters of indeterminate parentage far too often for comfort. I got detailed off to drown them and bury the corpses out on Barossa Heath. This job I really detested. I am afraid I took this bad temper out on Robin, who was six when the family arrived in Camberley. He was at a difficult age and got smacked all too regularly. Bad temper from a general sense of strain rebounded on Betty and on the girls when they were on holiday. In many ways, Camberley was not a happy period for the family.

One saving grace was sailing. After experiences in Egypt and Berlin, I was determined to remain in the game. So, early in our life at Camberley, I decided to invest in a GP14 of my own, plus a boat trailer to tow behind the car. I joined the Frensham Pond Sailing Club and raced there most weeks throughout the season. Norman Speller, a fellow DS, often crewed for me; Toby Caulfield occasionally did so, as did Betty. In the holidays the girls came out with me on occasion. By this time I had gained a lot of experience as a racing helmsman. I was fiercely competitive, as my crew can no doubt attest. One year at Frensham the Sailing Club attracted the South of England championship for GP14s. As the last race approached I was in the lead overall. To my sorrow I did not do so well in this last race and was placed second overall. Of course, I blamed a fickle wind; in fact I had failed to read wind changes in time. Such is racing on the water. On other occasions in summer the family trailed the boat down to the coast and sailed in Channel waters. What an asset this GP14, that I christened *Zephyr*, turned out to be.

Life as a DS, though hard work, had its compensations. Each year a number of students passed through one's hands as syndicates changed over. Writing reports on them at the end of each changeover was challenging. Many were excellent; one of my students later became Chief of the General Staff and Field Marshal on retirement. Some were not so good and how to grade them fairly was not easy. There were foreign students mixed in amongst British Army types, with the odd sailor and airman thrown in. Air Force students included one who finally succeeded me as Director General of Intelligence as a four-star airman many years later. Amongst foreign students was Ariel Sharon, the current Prime Minister of Israel, who came to Camberley from commanding a parachute battalion with distinction at the Battle of the Mitla Pass across the Suez Canal from Suez town.

Each year joint exercises were run with the Royal Air Force Staff College at Bracknell. For several days those lucky enough to go found themselves working at Bracknell to attend joint Army/RAF exercises in the lecture hall and classrooms. In 1956, I happened to be at Bracknell at the time of the ill-fated operation to take back the Suez Canal from Egypt. This was after the expulsion of the Suez Canal contractors who ran the base installations after withdrawal of British troops from the Canal Zone. (Incidentally, these contractors had as general manager my old boss at GHQ Middle East, Charles Humphreys, who had retired and taken this job.)

In the central lecture hall at Bracknell the RAF Commandant made a brief announcement about the cessation of hostilities in the Canal Zone as a result of pressure from America upon the Eden Government in London. Up jumped a Canadian Officer who made a fierce attack on British policy in Egypt. This did not go down at all well, although the wretched man was only expressing views that were common amongst Canadian students. Americans present did not say a word, many of us thought wisely. The extent of liberal feeling amongst Canadians at that time surprised us all.

Living at the Staff College meant that many of the staff and students had good contacts with both the forces committed to the landing of Suez and to the Ministry of Defence in London. In the preparatory period before some of those participating sailed from Portsmouth to the Mediterranean, word had got around that the original plan had been to land at Alexandria. Landing ships had been loaded to support the plan. Combined operations with all three Services were part of the teaching curriculum each year at Camberley. There was therefore a proprietary interest in learning the extent to which operations against Egypt were being mounted in accordance with the teaching that was given annually.

As the force was assembling in the Eastern Mediterranean, word came of dissension at the top level in Whitehall. Rumours started that the landing had been switched from Alexandria to Port Said. There was much gossip about American pressure not to land at all, as no assistance from across the Atlantic was to be expected. When the landing took place at Port Said, followed by a dash down the Canal towards Suez at the southern end of the Canal, this was of little surprise to the audience at Bracknell. We already knew that the ships were loaded for a different concept. Equally, we were aware of adverse American pressure. So the sudden cessation of operations on the ground surprised no one: nor did the subsequent fall of Anthony Eden from power. War against Egypt had been an object lesson on how not to plan and conduct operations.

I fear that many present that day failed to appreciate just how dire would be the effects in later years of this botched affair. In political terms it marked a watershed between independent military action by Britain in defence of what were still regarded as legitimate purely British interests, as opposed to such action only in conjunction with allies, and in particular America. NATO would assume a more global significance in the decades ahead. Macmillan's famous 1960 address about the 'winds of change' represented a belated recognition of this fundamental shift in British thinking.

The course went annually to Portsmouth where the dockyard was shown to us, including going on board HMS *Victory*. We then went to sea in a variety of HM ships. Guns were discharged at targets south-west of the Isle of Wight on at least one occasion. Fortunately, splicing the main brace was still practised in those days, and I acquired a taste for naval rum.

Towards the end of each year an increasing number of guest speakers addressed the multitude, culminating in a talk by the current Chief of the General Staff on how he saw the Army developing. Field Marshal

Appletree Cottage, Charlton, Andover, 1964

Montgomery, who lived west of Farnham at Bentley in his latter days, also spoke his mind. Guest nights took place in the mess at Camberley, to which outside guests were invited to talk to us after dinner in the main ante-room. On one occasion Randolph Churchill, son of Winston, was the guest speaker. He arrived one hour later than invited and was clearly under the weather on arrival. After dinner he was asked to sit on the fender in front of the open fire to give us his thoughts. After being lowered onto the fender by helpers, he promptly fell forward onto the floor and had to be carried up to bed. No one took his place on that occasion to offer words of wisdom.

Came my last winter at Camberley and the list of brevet lieutenant colonels was announced. My name was among them, together with Jim Wilson, a fellow teacher in 'A' Division, and several others elsewhere in the faculty. General Poet had done us proud. A brevet entitled one to advancement in seniority back to the date of award on eventual substantive promotion to lieutenant colonel. In fact I gained almost three years seniority on this account. This was a useful bonus but brought in no additional money. This is what I really needed most, not least to meet ever-increasing school costs. My mother's will had left me only Appletree Cottage at Charlton, which she had bought originally in 1945 for her Aunt May. The latter died soon after and the cottage was let until it passed to me. After meeting landlord's costs, letting did not yield much at that time. For some years before she died, my mother had helped out with school fees by a thrice-yearly payment into my own account. When she died this assistance ceased. On balance, the family was slightly worse off in consequence.

One great asset of belonging to the Directing Staff at the Staff College was the high calibre of teachers and their wives, and the very social existence that we led. Betty made many friends whom we continued to meet for many years to come. We saw a lot of our small colony of neighbours, Matt and Iona Abraham and the Parsons. (He was a Marine.) Jim Wilson introduced me to his father in London, a sapper major-general long since retired. In due course Tommy Cochrane joined the staff, as did Jack Gatford. Both were from my batch from the RMA Woolwich before the war, and both had been taken prisoner in the desert war. At the level above us were some delightful characters and their wives, notably the Graemes. The Spellers were good friends, as was Toby Caulfield. Our family, therefore, felt well integrated into a community of like-minded people.

Army pay at that time was at a very low ebb. The wife of a senior sapper officer in London led a movement of Army wives in raising the public profile of Army families. She was received in the House of Commons by ministers and by the press en masse. Betty attended a number of her public meetings in London that went down well with the newspapers. Helped by this furore, pay was at last increased in due course and school allowances, with one paid holiday overseas for schoolchildren per year, were introduced. The tide had at last turned on a very penurious period at Camberley.

In the spring of 1958 my next posting order arrived from AG7, the sapper posting branch in London. I was to go to Maralinga in South Australia to be the military assistant to one of the scientists conducting nuclear trials there. I would still be a major. I made inquiries and learned that the scientist concerned was a decade younger than I was. Prospects therefore seemed bleak and I went to see the Commandant on the strength of already being a brevet half-colonel on his recommendation. He was horrified at my news and promised to look into the matter. A week or two later I received a revised posting order from the Military Secretary. This sent me to Aden as AQMG (operations and plans) to HQ British Forces, Arabian Peninsula. I was to be promoted to Temporary Lieutenant Colonel in this post, a considerable increase in pay. I expressed my gratitude to General Nigel Poet and set to with Betty to make family plans.

We decided to send Janet to St Michael's, Uckfield, to join Celia. Robin would go to a preparatory school at Rottingdean, near Brighton. These ideas would stretch our resources to the limit; promotion to half colonel at increased rates would just make this possible. I went to the local Army hospital to be inoculated for Aden. A few days later I felt very poorly and had to be admitted to the Cambridge Hospital in Aldershot. There I languished for a week or so, suffering in my view from the results of the many jabs that I had received, though this was never admitted by the doctors. I recovered and caught a Britannia flight to Aden, leaving Betty to get out of the quarters in due course and move the children to their new schools. Quarters were difficult in Aden, and she was unlikely to be allowed to join me before the autumn. Fortunately, her parents had retired to a house up on Crawley Ridge above Camberley. She therefore had a local base from which to achieve all these tasks.

Looking back on the years at Camberley, I am not conscious of any big new ideas entering my mind. Most of the time attention was directed to learning more about the nuclear environment in which ground force action might take place. The Russian threat, coming from Eastern Europe, was the predominant issue during the Cold War. Russian activities to stir the pot worldwide were widely discussed. The latest news from the Congo, from Cuba and from any other centre of communist activity, including arms provision, was eagerly seized upon. Nevertheless, the pattern of events seemed reasonably constant.

This confrontation was rudely altered by the murder of the King of Iraq by a revolutionary government in Baghdad. British interests in the Persian Gulf and South Arabia were seen in Whitehall to be at enhanced risk. Hitherto this theatre of British control had been an RAF fiefdom based on Aden. Soon after the Kassem regime was shackled on to Iraq, a British Army build-up was ordained. An initial Army staff element under a brigadier was added to the RAF command. I was selected to become one of this new Army staff increment to HQ British Forces Arabian Peninsula in Aden.

Because of uncertain relations with many Arab states following the revolution in Iraq, the main supply and reinforcements air route had been switched to West and Central Africa from direct flights over the Mediterranean. This meant a long flight with refuelling stops at Gibraltar, Kano and Bangui in the Central African Republic, before crossing the southern Sahara to Aden.

Considerably shaken by this experience, I was met by my new Colonel AQ and taken to a hotel at Steamer Point where senior officers without families were accommodated. After a long sleep in air-conditioning I set off for the Headquarters offices in prefabricated huts not far beyond the point overlooking Aden harbour entrance. Here I met the other members of the administrative staff, plus our opposite numbers in the RAF. These included Brian McNamara, the Group Captain Administration; he and his wife Aline settled after retirement in Lymington, where Betty and I bought a house some time after they did.

HQ BFAP controlled British Forces in a wide area from the borders of the Rhodesian Federation through Kenya and British Somaliland to Masirah Island off Muscat and Oman, where there was an RAF airfield, and finally to Bahrain and Kuwait. In Bahrain the senior British representative was the Political Representative Persian Gulf (PRPG). In the next two years I was to visit every part of the Command, from the Federation of Rhodesia at one end to Kuwait at the other.

Tension in the Gulf was still high because of the revolutionary government established in Baghdad. In Muscat and Oman a tribal rebellion against the Sultan was already in being, centred on the Jebel Akhdar area. In Aden itself there was incipient trouble from a left-wing trades union movement that was preaching anti-British sentiments. In Kenya the effects of Mau Mau were still in minor key. Tanganyika was quiet, as was the Rhodesian Federation. I received detailed briefings on all these subjects. I also met the brigadier deputy commander and the head man himself, a four-star RAF officer.

In the late spring, Aden was really stoking up its climate. From late April to early October the south-west monsoon blew, and the temperature rose to 100° Fahrenheit, with humidity not much less than the hundred mark. Come evening the wind usually dropped away and under the full moon the roof terrace was especially inviting. Kindred spirits were the heads of the services that lived in the hotel, particularly Wally Meekin of the Ordnance Corps and the chief of electrical and mechanical engineers. Wally had a great stock of classical music recordings. These we used to listen to under the stars that shone so brightly only ten degrees north of the equator. So many years later, I can still visualise the beauty of those moments. Beethoven's Fifth Symphony invariably recalls such nights.

My job was to evolve policy for the three commanders of the services, including the Royal Army Service Corps. Living together as we did, this was made easy. I started getting around. The RAF had Beverleys in service in Aden. These ran a regular service through to Bahrain. The Beverley was as high as a house and almost as slow: 135 knots was cruising speed. It had to be refuelled with distressing frequency. This took place at Masirah and Sharjah on the way to Bahrain.

At Sharjah, I dropped off to meet the Trucial Oman Scouts who were based, under command of a British brigadier named Carter, in that sheikhdom. In Bahrain I met PRPG and the senior naval captain who commanded British ships stationed in the Gulf. On the way back I called in at Muscat to see the Sultan of Muscat's Armed Forces based on Beit el Falaj, not far from the ancient walled city of Muscat itself. I found Hugh Oldman, with whom I used to play bridge on the way out to Singapore in 1946, installed as a contract officer military adviser to the old Sultan – who spent most of his time on the south coast of the Sultanate many hundreds of miles away across the desert. Hugh Oldman was the real commander of the local Armed Forces, not least as budget holder for them.

Returning to Aden, I soon set off for Nairobi to meet 24 Infantry Brigade, the resident British garrison in that country. Their DAQMG was Hugh Beach, a fellow sapper who rose to be a full general and my successor in 1982 as Chief Royal Engineer. Having suitably explored the area, I settled back in Aden to prepare for the next important tasks that came my way. These were the arrival of my wife Betty in October – and the start of the sailing season! To these were added an overriding task of operations in Muscat to defeat rebels in the Jebel Akhdar area. My part in this fascinating assignment was to go round with Tony Deane Drummond, Commander of the SAS Regiment, to make the original plan and to arrange to receive and support the soldiers in their assault on the 10,000 foot-high Green Mountain.

As soon as the summer holidays were over and all the children installed in their boarding schools, Betty flew out to Aden to join me. I hired a flat on the Maala Straight, a new road connecting Steamer Point with the RAF airfield at Khormaksar. Only one air conditioner was allotted to me and this I installed in our bedroom. There were two other bedrooms and a large living-room, not too much to take three children out from England for the Christmas holidays. Nearby was the local Trades Union building at which frenzied meetings were staged at intervals, accompanied by equally frenzied and tiresome Arabic broadcasts. I managed to hire an excellent Yemeni cook who did wonders with both western dishes and south Arabian curries. Ahmed was immensely loyal, and we both swore by him. One huge joke was when I gave him a substantial Christmas present. I asked him what he would do with the money. 'Buy a refrigerator,' he replied. I asked if there was the electricity to run it. 'No,' he replied. He wanted an old one to keep his clothes from being eaten by moths.

Betty settled in quickly; but it did not take long for me to see that she was unhappy. Eventually she broke down late one night and told me that she had had an affair during the previous summer with the French member of the teaching staff at Camberley and that she was still in touch with him. I agonised long and hard over this, as can be imagined. We discussed it at great length and decided to stay together. She took a local secretarial job with a British member of the administration in Crater, the old capital of Aden, and seemed to perk up in consequence. The following summer I developed dengue fever, a wretched disease that put me into hospital for several weeks until my daily rise and fall of temperature subsided. I found out later that she started an affair with her boss while I was in hospital. Troubles do not come singly, but in the end we surmounted them.

As soon as the south-west monsoon subsided in September, the sailing season in Aden started. The Aden Yacht Club had originally been started by the civilian community. After the build-up of all three services, the membership contained more and more sailors from the Army and RAF. To obtain grants from Ministry of Defence welfare funds in order to buy new boats from England and have them shipped out, membership included all ranks from both services. GP14s were the most popular and newest class, together with some older twelve-footers and Snipes. As the north-east monsoon grew in strength, humidity lifted and the wind came up every morning through to the following April, reaching Force 4 or 5 for most of the day, till dropping away by late afternoon. Such conditions offered ideal racing conditions for GP14s that could plane downwind for much of the day. I entered into racing with great gusto and hardly missed a weekend race throughout the season, except when on tour elsewhere. After the rather tame racing on Frensham Pond, courses in the Bay were a real challenge, as we sailed the waves of the Indian Ocean; and my helming skills improved in consequence. I won a number of cups, donated by earlier members of the Aden Yacht Club, in the two winter seasons that I enjoyed in Aden, my most skilled opponent being a corporal from the RAF Station at Khormaksar airfield. My opposite number as AQ Quartering imported a brand new racing catamaran from England in my second season. Together we unpacked it from many crates and assembled it ready for launching. After a suitable ceremony to christen the new boat, we set off to sea. Sailing catamarans is different from dinghies in some respects, particularly when going about. We rapidly mastered the art and took her out onto the really big seas of the Indian Ocean offshore. At times we were sailing close to 20 knots, surfing down the big seas. I can still recall the excitement of doing this;

planing on GP14s was nowhere near the same, though trickier because of instability.

Back at work, the main preoccupation was mounting the operation to take the Jebel Akhdar in Oman. I flew to Muscat to meet Tony Deane Drummond – who had been a DS at Minley during my time at Camberley – and Frank Kitson, the representative from the Army Military Operations Directorate in London. He had been one of our students at the Staff College and rose to be a full general subsequently. From Beit el Falaj we drove round to Nizwa on the inland side of the Great Mountain; then we had a look from the Batinah Coast side to the east. Tony decided to mount his attack up the steps that had been built many centuries ago up the eastern face of the Jebel Akhdar for use by men and donkeys landing on the coast and making their way to villages near the summit. We decided to fly up to look at these villages that were heavily defended by dissident tribesmen. We were disconcerted by shoals of tracer bullets coming up at our aircraft from several heavy machine guns defending villages around the summit. Our skilled pilot took evasive action, and we returned to Muscat appreciating that the SAS had a difficult objective to capture.

My task was to buy two hundred donkeys accustomed to carry loads up to 10,000 feet, get saddles and gear made, on which to fit SAS weapons, ammunition and food, and assemble them in time for the regiment to fly out from England and mount the attack. I also had to provide base camp facilities near Muscat for the regimental group before they set off on their assault. I returned to Aden to plan my side of things, together with the Heads of Services. My Commander Royal Army Service Corps was a most experienced officer. He advised buying the donkeys in the high country on the borders of British Somalia and Ethiopia, driving them down to the port of Berbera, embarking them on a converted Landing Ship Tent (LST) that could be sent down from Cyprus and finally landing them at Muscat after a substantial sea voyage. All of this was done in a matter of some weeks.

I flew to Muscat to see the donkeys arrive. At that time there were no suitable port facilities in Muscat harbour to offload an LST. The improvised solution was to lay a large carpet of rope on the tank deck, drive about a dozen donkeys onto it, lift the four corners by crane till a mass of heads and legs of donkeys protruded, hoist them over the side and onto the quay and release the four corners of the rope carpet to allow the animals to walk away. Out of two hundred donkeys bought on the borders of Ethiopia, 199 landed safely in Muscat, only one breaking a leg on disembarkation that required it to be destroyed. Local donkey herdsmen took charge and drove them to their lines where they were fed and watered. Their equipment had been made in the bazaars of Crater in Aden to the order of Wally Meekin and flown into Muscat. These were duly fitted and just about fulfilled their task of supporting the SAS assault.

The Regimental Group flew in a day or two later from England and were accommodated in the camp that had been built for them by the Sultan of Muscat's Armed Forces, and the assault was duly mounted. After a rearguard action, the dissident tribesmen poured down the western face of the mountain and escaped from Omani territory. I flew up to the caves that they had occupied near the summit. Outside, the desert was littered with bomb cases. Shackletons had bombed here on a number of occasions. Even aircraft from a passing Fleet Carrier had attacked these caves. But inside there were acres of space that no bomb could penetrate. No wonder that dissident tribesman had held out against the Sultan for so long. The villages and orchards around the summit appeared to be largely intact. The only sour note was struck by the final report on the operation. This recorded the SAS view that they had to carry the donkeys on the final stages of the assault. I took this with a grain of salt. I gathered that in later years, progeny of these donkeys were in general use throughout the Jebel Akhdar area. The following summer I figured in the Queen's Birthday Honours in having been awarded an OBE. Tony Deane Drummond received a DSO.

All three children arrived by air from England to spend the Christmas holidays. Friends made on the flight meant that each had a built-in community in Aden to enjoy. Swimming had to be behind shark-proof netting. Nothing deterred them from enjoying such facilities to the full, and there were parties galore. Betty and I were constantly driving them somewhere and collecting them in due course. By this time one free visit per child per year was authorised, as was an education allowance to help with school fees at home. The weather at Christmas was perfect, up to 85°F by day but cool by night with no humidity. I think the children had a ball, not least in the swimming pool, suitably netted. At Easter we arranged for Betty's parents to look after them at times when they were not staying with friends. For the summer holidays Betty flew back to the UK to act as a base for them at Camberley.

That summer the planners in Aden were ordered to go to Kuwait to arrange with the Kuwaiti authorities how best to receive a force from the UK, should the Iraqis threaten to invade. The team flew via Bahrain to Kuwait, where we were welcomed by the Kuwaiti military authorities. Kuwait City at that time was an extraordinary city. Oil revenues were

With Betty, Janet and Robin at the OBE Presentation at Buckingham Palace, 1961

pouring in to the treasury. The Emir of Kuwait had decided to enrich the Bedouin Arabs of his state by progressively building them substantial houses around the old city and then buying up their land, giving them cars and money to set themselves up in their new houses. The walls of the old city had been breached in many directions and arterial roads built out into the desert. Connecting these roads were concentric rings of new houses, built on either side of feeder roads. On the outskirts were a number of camels, donkeys and goats. We gathered that as the Bedouin came into town they abandoned their animals, got into their new cars and were driven to their new houses.

We were taken to see the Deputy Ruler who was also Minister of Defence, a typical Bedouin aristocrat with long beard and flowing robes. The next item on our programme was to drive out into the desert, northward towards the Iraqi border. The temperature by midday was around 127°F, so whether to wind the windows down and be burned by the hot wind or wind up the windows and stew was a real conundrum. There was a low ridge not far from the border, and this was the obvious line for a defensive position. Finally, we went down to the oil port of Mena-al-Ahmadi and the extensive oil fields inland, run by the Kuwaiti Oil Company. Here I had extensive discussions, as only the Oil Company could provide a maintenance area for a British Force.

On arrival at the port we walked out onto the jetty that bifurcated left and right some many hundreds of yards offshore to provide deep water berths for a number of tankers. The evening before, a blue whale had come in slowly through the piles supporting the jetty into the large triangle formed by bifurcation. It had then panicked and started swimming furiously round and round. The faster it went, the more solid an obstacle was presented by these piles. Next day it was still swimming round and round, surfacing at intervals to sound off. To see a 100-foot whale so close was a remarkable spectacle.

Having produced a draft plan agreed by both sides, we flew back to Aden. In 1961 this plan had to be activated with success. By then I was in Ripon, Yorkshire. In the summer of 1959 I flew up to Nairobi to attend 24 Infantry Brigade exercises in the Tanah River Valley area of north-east Kenya. This was great fun, not least because of the mass of African wildlife along the river itself. Yet another expedition that Betty and I undertook was to British Somaliland, as it then was. Maurice MacWilliam, who had been a DS at Camberley with me, was in command of the Somaliland Scouts. We took advantage of a visit by General 'Frankie' Festing, by now Chief of the General Staff, to take a lift in the back of his aircraft to fly to Hargeisa for a fortnight's leave. Drawn up on the tarmac was an immaculate guard of honour of Somalis, every man over six-foot, with headgear towering up a further foot. The CGS was dressed as usual in a far from immaculate shirt and shorts, and looked remarkably ill-dressed by comparison. Maurice saluted and accompanied the great man around on his inspection before putting him into a staff car. As he dismissed the guard, its Commander came up to him and asked a simple question. When was the CGS going to arrive?

Next day Maurice and his wife Norah, Betty and I set off for Ethiopia. For many hours we drove across featureless desert country in high temperatures, until at last some low hills appeared. Amongst these were the Somali and Ethiopian frontier posts. Formalities were minimal. We drove for many hours more, as the track steadily ascended into greener country. As evening approached we saw the outskirts of Harar where both families were to stay with an Indian Military Mission to the Ethiopian Army. The evening with our Indian hosts was most convivial, only spoiled by our refusal to go on a lion hunt with them next day, on the grounds that we had booked seats from Diredawa on the Djibouti to Addis Ababa railway the following morning.

The road from Harar to Diredawa had been built by the Italians just before the Second World War, and was an excellent one. At Diredawa Station Betty, Norah and I awaited the arrival of the train. Maurice departed in the Land-Rover to drive on the roughish track beside the railway, all the way up to Addis Ababa – cheaper than using the railway flat. After a wearisome but not unpleasant journey, soon overtaking Maurice, we reached the main railway station in Addis, an ornate building constructed by Italians. We were met by the British Defence Attaché and taken to his spacious house. At over 7,000 feet the climate was a delight after the heat of Hargeisa.

That evening our host had arranged a cocktail party for the international community in the capital of Ethiopia. We three kept glancing at our watches as Maurice had hoped to arrive by 8 o'clock. The last guest departed; still no Land-Rover. We had a late supper and started yawning after a long day. Eventually, as midnight approached, Maurice arrived, filthy and dishevelled. His story was pathetic. Parts of the track had been washed away in flash floods. He had had several punctures that he had needed to mend himself. He was quite exhausted and needed the next day to recuperate.

We then set out on road journeys to the north towards Dessie and the Rift Valley of the Blue Nile, and to the west of Addis. To the north we had lunch with a delightful British couple to whom Maurice had an introduction. The husband had been a special adviser to the Emperor, Haile Selassie, during and after the war and on retirement had built his house with a view over the upper valley of the Blue Nile.

Back in Addis we attended a number of parties at night. At one of these we were slightly surprised to be introduced to a half-grown lion cub that lived on our host's veranda. The time came to catch the train back to Diredawa. This ran overnight, and this time Maurice and I decided to put the Land-Rover on a railway flat! As pilfering was endemic, I had to get into the vehicle and travel the whole way sitting aboard. Fortunately nothing untoward occurred. Early next morning we disembarked at Diredawa. We found a café to have breakfast. I asked to wash and shave, putting my jacket down on a chair behind me. After shaving I put it on again and checked the pockets. The wallet had been pinched. The proprietor pleaded innocence. We called in the local police, but I never saw my wallet again. Somewhat deflated we retraced our steps to Harar where the Indian Mission were as hospitable as ever. Next day we drove back to Hargeisa and finally flew RAF to Aden. Betty, of course, was an indulgence passenger.

Later, in the winter of 1959, the planners, Army and RAF in Aden, were ordered by Whitehall to fly down to Salisbury in Southern Rhodesia. We were instructed to carry out preliminary staff talks with the Federation of Rhodesia Army and Air Force should it prove necessary at any time to carry out joint operations. On arrival we were received most hospitably and got down to business. General Anderson, a large South African of British extraction, commanded their Army. That evening he invited us to a lion shoot out in the bush, some many miles out of Salisbury. We were given rifles and ammunition and invited to sweep through a large area of long grass. This was six-foot in height. I could not see a thing, though our host was well over six-foot and was obviously having a high old time. Relief was uppermost in my mind as the long drive, mainly by sound rather than sight, drew to a close. The team duly reported results of the staff talks to London.

A second holiday in British Somaliland with the MacWilliams also took place. This time they took us to a fascinating cedar-forested area, right in the horn of Africa away to the east of Hargeisa. An advance party in a three-ton truck moved and repitched our tented camp each day. Meanwhile we were free to explore the forest tract. A shoot for wild pig was arranged using Service rifles. To hit a running pig from a moving Land-Rover took a bit of doing, I found. I managed to get only one; Maurice did better. One was kept and the others given to local tribesmen.

Back in Aden there was much to do in building up local forces. In the Aden Protectorate there were the Aden Protectorate Levies under a British brigadier. In the Hadhramaut Valley to the east was another local force that I visited up-country from Mukalla. The valley itself was remarkable, with several cities containing multi-storied blocks. The Hadhramis had traded since time immemorial with both Zanzibar and what was now Indonesia. Money had poured back into the rich families, who had raised these buildings.

In the summer of 1959, Brigadier Mike Hutton was replaced by Major General Bobby Bray as Deputy Commander under the RAF Commander-in-Chief. I enjoyed serving under him and continued to keep in touch with both himself and his charming wife till he rose to be a full general and Deputy Supreme Commander in SHAPE. He was a keen sailor and became Commodore of the Aden Yacht Club. In the winter of 1959/60 I became Vice-Commodore and continued to enjoy success on the water. Further grants of sports funds became available and a successful bid was made for a number of Flying 15s to be sent out to Aden in the summer of 1960.

I did one more trip to Kenya on duty, and Betty flew over RAF indulgence for a short holiday thereafter. David Edwards' successor as 2i/c 35 Engineer Regiment in Egypt was born and bred in Kenya and had retired there. We stayed with him and his beautiful and much younger wife at Kipkabus across the Rift valley. Another night was spent with his sister, who lived with her husband and children near Limuru, not far from Kenyatta's home village. This was a delightful farm, half coffee and half arable, that had been developed by her parents.

Nearer home, the Aden planners took a trip to Kamaran Island. An RAF aircraft flew us along the coast, west to the Straits of Bab el Mandeb, where we circled over the old coaling station, now disused in the era of oil-fired engines, and then up the Red Sea to Kamaran off the Yemeni Coast. Kamaran was still administered from Aden and had one British civil servant still in charge. He met us and drove us around his bailiwick that had been the quarantine station for Muslim pilgrims from Africa and Asia to Mecca until recently. Now the large settlement for these pilgrims was silent and deserted, as the Saudis had transferred quarantine arrangements to Jeddah.

Over lunch he regaled us with stories of how recently he had seen Russian ships carrying tanks, delivering them to the port of Hodeida to the southward. After lunch in his echoing house, the ageing master of all he surveyed said that we must take a present back to Aden. He strode into his hall and opened wide an enormous refrigerator. Inside stood a number of kingfish on their tails, all of five foot in length. He took one of these out and presented it to us. On return to Aden we dashed with the huge fish to the Officers Mess at Steamer Point. The mess caterer was somewhat bemused at this handsome gift. He promised to serve it up for lunch on succeeding days, and did.

In the spring of 1963 my next posting order arrived. This was to command a Territorial Army Engineer Regiment in Lancashire. As I had received confidential reports at outstanding level in Aden and was already a brevet as well as a temporary Lieutenant Colonel, I raised the matter with General Bobby Bray. He promised to look into it with London. A few weeks later came in a new posting – to command 38 Corps Engineer Regiment at Ripon.

I heard subsequently that my old master, Tom Foulkes from 35 Regiment days in Egypt, who was now Engineer-in-Chief, had personally looked into the matter. He found that his postings branch AG7 had brought in a new rule that reports before 1950 were to be ignored. My only sapper report subsequently had been from Berlin, when I had only been graded above average in a Works Services appointment. As Engineer-in-Chief he kindly changed my next job to one far more congenial. Betty and I packed up our flat in the Maala Straight and flew back home for leave and then to establish a new home in the Commanding Officer's quarter in Ripon.

With hindsight, it is possible to see that 1958 to 1960 was the beginning of the end of the British Empire in the Middle East and Africa. In the sixties, withdrawal was very much the order of the day. Yet peace had been maintained in these colonial territories, and though of a low standard, Arab and African living conditions were acceptable. Aden was fortunate in having an outstanding Governor, Sir William Luce. He had previously served as PRPG in Bahrain, after starting life in the Sudan Civil Service. It is hard to believe that even in the twenty-first century inhabitants throughout this large area are better off. For many, the reverse remains the case, not least in Somalia.

Scenically, South Arabia, the Persian Gulf and East Africa were superb. Even in Aden, superb country lay inland. On the Yemeni border the mountains rose up to 7,000 feet. The old trade route from Oman ran along these mountains, and here and there remains of cities could still be seen. At Mukheiras, the RAF Commander-in-Chief had a bungalow, and in the summer months it was blissful to fly up and enjoy the cool air by night, as Betty and I did on several occasions. To sum up my time in Aden, despite the climate, it was generally rewarding.

CHAPTER 6

Command in Ripon (1960–1963)

AFTER A BUSY LEAVE spent visiting the children, Betty's parents at Camberley and my father in Devon, we hurried up to Ripon to take over the commanding officer's quarter from my predecessors, the Clutterbucks. He and I had been DS at Camberley together, although he left after my first year, as he was senior in service to me. The quarter was in the midst of a new patch of officers' houses with majors' quarters around it. Nearby were substantial numbers of other ranks' married quarters, many of which were fairly new. About half a mile away was the barracks that was still in the same huts that I had known when posted here as Bridging Assistant Instructor in 1942. It was only in my last few months in command that funds were made available to start building a new barracks in brick, adjacent to the old huts.

Command of a regiment is always regarded in the Army as the apex of a Service career. I took over in October 1960 in high hopes that this would prove to be the case. 38 Corps Engineer Regiment, as it was then designated, was one of two regiments in the Engineer Group within the Strategic Reserve held in the UK. The Group Commander for 36 and 38 Regiments was a Canadian colonel, ex-Kingston, whose service had subsequently all been in the British Army. The Regiment had a headquarters, two Field Squadrons at that time, 12 and 48, plus 15 Corps Field Park Squadron, a bit larger than a similar unit supporting a divisional engineer regiment. Within Yorkshire, 38 Regiment came under the local Area Commander, a major-general, and HQ Northern Command in York with a Brigadier Chief Engineer who was another Canadian, Jim Carr.

Ripon also provided temporary accommodation and training facilities for Territorial Engineer Regiments in the North of England and Scotland. Bishopton Park alongside the River Ure provided 800 acres of War Department land. In addition there was an extensive 'wet' bridging site at Bishops Monkton about three miles down the river from Ripon towards Boroughbridge. 'Wet' refers to everything needed to cross a river; adequate stocks of equipment were stored there. Close to the barracks lay the bridging sites and training land inherited from the wartime School of Military Engineering in which I had taught bridging

Commanding 38 Corps Engineer Regiment at Ripon, 1962

to classes back in 1942/43. For larger exercises we could go to the Otterburn Ranges in Northumberland, where my predecessor had been until just before he handed over to me. Most of the facilities needed for training an Engineer Regiment and a large Field Park Squadron were therefore to hand.

The first few months were spent in getting to know everyone, no mean task in a regiment of 650 people with a considerable percentage of families. When I took over, nearly 50 per cent were still conscripts, the remainder being regular soldiers. These were the days of running down conscripts to zero and forming an all-regular Army. By the time of handover in 1963 the regiment was all-regular. This turned out to be a mixed blessing in the short term, because initiative was not so strong amongst junior NCOs and soldiers. Longer term, as NCO training became better and the percentage of tradesmen increased, as most soldiers became both combat engineers and, for example, chippies or bricklayers, the Regular Army became yet more efficient.

Much time had to be spent on looking into the administration of the regiment. This needed buffing up in time for the annual administrative inspection carried out by the Area Commander and his staff. 15 Corps Field Park Plant Troop proved to be in a shocking state. Its plant spares account was impossible to square. Some straight talking with the Military Plant Foreman concerned eventually yielded results. Later he told me that he received a tip-off to dig in a certain area of his compound. He arranged this and to his great surprise, and mine subsequently, he excavated a number of cases of plant spares. With their help, the plant account at last made sense.

In the early spring there was torrential rain day after day. York became flooded because of the River Ouse breaking its banks. 38 Regiment were ordered to build a relief bridge across the river in case the main bridge should collapse. Much reconnaissance and planning yielded a design to construct a multi-span Bailey bridge with two piers, three spans in all. Within hours work started to build both piers while equipment started arriving at the site in trucks. When the piers were ready with rollers on top of them, bridge construction started with the assembly of a long launching nose followed by the three-span bridge. Using bulldozers to push the whole structure, the launching nose reached the far bank pier rollers. More and more bays were added to the back end until the whole bridge reached its final position over the flood waters. Jacking down went well; decking and ramps each end were added and the new bridge was ready for use. For much of the time I watched the whole process that took over twelve hours to complete, as did my wife for part of the time, together with an anxious Chief Engineer Northern Command. My wife came too because I thought that she wished to show solidarity with me after recovering from aberrations in Aden. This was a great relief to my mind.

Ripon proved to be a most special place. Willisons had come from the North Riding in past generations. Assimilation into the community was rapid as a result. The regimental doctor was a local GP because doctors in the Services were in short supply. Douglas Ridout, his wife Carol and their children were also keen dinghy sailors and came regularly to our bridging site on the River Ure at Bishops Monkton. The Ridouts settled in Milford-on-Sea on retirement. This was close to our retirement home in Lymington, so contact was resumed.

The Mayor of Ripon, Miles Coverdale, also became a great friend, as did his wife. Relations between the Regiment and the Town Council were close, not least because the Corps of Royal Engineers had been granted the Freedom of the City back in 1949. Fifty years later I was invited back to Ripon by the present commanding officer to celebrate the 50th Anniversary of this event. Together with all living previous COs and their wives, it was a pleasure to attend the mayoral parlour, witness a parade in the market square and then proceed to the Cathedral for a memorial service.

Back in 1960 relations with the Dean and Chapter of the Cathedral were already close. Betty and I got to know local Members of Parliament who lived around Ripon, notably James Ramsden, who represented Harrogate and later became Secretary of State for the Army. We also

Inspecting the Guard of Honour with the Mayor before the Cathedral Service, Ripon Square, 1977

knew Bourne Arton, the member for Darlington. Nearby were several large RAF airfields. Their commanders and their wives added to our circle of friends. Ripon was a microcosm of English country society at that time. It proved to be an antidote to life in Aden in a big way for both of us.

Another abiding interest was works services in aid of the civil power. At that time, local authorities could apply to Whitehall for military engineer assistance for jobs that would be of benefit to their communities, subject to meeting strict provisos as regards trades union acquiescence and so on. One of these was to build a road north of Mallaig on the West Coast of Scotland to connect up a number of crofts that could only be reached by boat. In the summer of 1961 I arranged for a party from the regiment to undertake this work. I myself visited Mallaig and formed a taste for Mallaig kippers that has lasted until this day. The authorities at Tobermory in Mull applied for the demolition of a derelict mansion that had become a menace to children because of falling masonry. This was done by a troop from Ripon. The work involved much drilling of walls and loading of charges. On the day appointed I was present to see the building subside totally as the charges were fired. I stayed the night with an old Seaforth's friend who had retired to Tobermory; he and I had last met in Java.

Yet another tricky task was given the Regiment by the Corporation of Plymouth. They wanted to develop Drake's Island in Plymouth Sound into a recreational park after the site had been de-requisitioned by the Navy. The task was to destroy a number of Second World War anti-aircraft gun emplacements that had been built on top of some of the defences dating back to Elizabethan times. Part of the remit to the Regiment was that there should be no damage to these earlier defences. I sent a troop down to Plymouth to prepare the charges and went myself to inspect them before they were fired. This was done to the approbation of all and sundry.

The most important task of all was sited in the island of St Kilda. The population of St Kilda had been evacuated before the Second World War. After the war the rocket range based on Benbecula in the Outer Hebrides was established. In due course the range was offered to a number of American rocket regiments stationed in NATO countries. A fall of shot radar was needed on St Kilda to record where rockets had pitched into the ocean. 38 Regiment were given the task of building suitable accommodation for the radar crew and preparing a small jetty to offload stores. Hitherto these had had to be landed over open beaches as and when wind and wave conditions allowed. A clerk of works was seconded to the regiment to supervise construction. His team came from selected tradesmen sappers. In the summer of 1961 the project got up steam. On several occasions I took the steamer service from Oban to Benbecula; there I was met by a jeep from the range headquarters. On one occasion an American rocket regiment from Italy were in residence for a week to fire their Corporal missiles. I was invited to see their first firing. In the command bunker we looked onto the missile standing on its tail ready for firing. The count went down to zero – fire. Nothing happened, apart from an escape of steam at the base of the rocket. The Commanding Officer turned to me and said:

'Gee, you'll have to come again tomorrow.' I replied that by then I should be on St Kilda after getting out there by landing-craft.

'Well then, we'll fire into the sea near you so that you can see the fall of shot.' With some trepidation I acquiesced in this idea. Next day I got out to St Kilda and spent the day with my team. At the time appointed we all looked to seaward to see the splash. Nothing happened. I returned to Benbecula and asked the Americans what had happened.

'Gee,' they said, 'We had another failure. We'll try again tomorrow.' They did but I heard subsequently that they failed consistently for the whole week. I also heard that this was the poorest result ever recorded. Perhaps something in the Italian air disagreed with rocket propulsion?

St Kilda was a major bird sanctuary. I walked over much of the island to see the remarkable structures left by the inhabitants of previous generations. These were of stone; they were designed to dry out seabirds with good top cover and sides and air holes to allow entry by the wind. There were also a unique brand of sheep, called 'Soay' if I remember rightly; a type of fieldmouse was indigenous to the island. Visits to St Kilda were a delight. I was sorry when the job was finished.

In early November 1961, Betty and I planned to visit London for a weekend. We were to stay with the Royal Engineers Territorial Army Parachute Regiment. On the Friday afternoon we drove down the A1 and then into west London where the regiment was located. We found our friends the Cowtons' quarters and were received with a welcome glass of whisky.

'By the way,' said my host, 'Bill Woods, the Colonel E on the staff of the Engineer-in-Chief War Office, rang just now and said he must speak to you urgently.'

'Tell that to the Marines,' I replied, not believing a word from a well-known practical joker. My host kept on at me over a second glass of whisky and eventually I agreed to do so if he would make the call. He did so and sure enough it was Bill Woods on the line. He had much to say. Had I heard, he began, the radio news about hurricane Hattie having struck British Honduras near Belize? I had not, so he gave me a rough estimate of the resulting damage. He told me that one squadron from 38 Regiment had been ordered to fly out early the following day from the RAF transport base airfield at Lyneham. 12 Field Squadron advance party were moving in the early hours from Ripon to the airfield. The Engineer-in-Chief wished me to go too, to report back on what resources would be needed to restore the situation. My second-in-command had been instructed to break into my house and pack up suitable clothes and kit for me to use on arrival in Jamaica, which was our initial destination. (Fortunately, he had the key to my house.) I was to proceed to Lyneham under my own steam in the early hours, to join 12 Field Squadron advance party in flying to Jamaica.

After an admirable dinner party I got ready to drive to Lyneham. The telephone rang again after midnight to say that the flight was delayed until the afternoon of 4 November. After a short night's rest, Betty and I drove to the airfield. An RAF Britannia was due to leave that evening. Only five seats could be allotted to sappers. John Notley had already handed in both his and my kit from Ripon, so I had to fly to Jamaica in my thick London-style suit. The Military Plant foreman, squadron sergeant-major and a stores sergeant completed the party. En route we discussed amongst other things the hazards of membership of the Strategic Reserve in the UK.

On arrival in Jamaica I reclaimed my luggage and did a rapid change into tropical uniform. In a hot and humid climate a thick suit was not the ideal form of wear. Headquarters Caribbean Area sent a car for me. I was briefed on all they knew about conditions in Belize. A company of Royal Hampshires was normally stationed at the airport for Belize. The CO and two more companies had already flown in, as had American assistance from the Panama Canal Zone. A frigate stationed in the West Indies had moved to off Belize port. I rejoined John at the airfield. He had three seats on a freight aircraft leaving almost at once; its engines were warming up as we climbed aboard. On arrival at Belize Airport an American fork-lift truck flown in from Panama allowed us to offload the heavy stores brought from the UK. No transport had been provided for sappers, so the Military Plant foreman commandeered an ancient car found abandoned on the airfield. Being a man of infinite resource, he got it to go in clouds of blue smoke. Belize lay eight miles away. Wreckage was everywhere on the airport and roads into town; big trees were down and power lines sagged from their pylons.

The city itself presented an even more distressing sight. Waves up to twelve feet in height had swept through the streets that were only a couple of feet above high water level. Most houses were built on stilts so cars and stores below had been swept into local swamps. The main street had been cleared one way, although several inches of muddy water remained on its surface. Some vehicles were moving about, mostly relief agencies or US Army. Police HQ was reached in the town centre; here the Governor presided over the heads of the Civil Service, Police Chiefs, a US Army Colonel from Panama and HQ of the Royal Hampshires. The latter had control of the city after sorting out looting and imposing curfew. I entered the tower of Babel that the operations room resembled, while John Notley went off with Douglas Manning, the Director of Public Works (PWD), to visit his ruined offices and park that were already a hive of activity. They were able to use what had been salvaged after the tidal waves had receded, leaving inches of black mud over everything. It was decided on the spot to set up a joint task force with the PWD. The leading troop and 12 Squadron HQ would be set up in the badly damaged Belize Club nearby but no transport could be provided because so much had been drowned.

The Port was next on the visits list. A Naval Commander from Jamaica was already installed as Queen's Harbour Master. Local working parties under Royal Hampshires' control had already partially cleared debris from one of the quays. Some flat-topped barges had been salvaged. Meanwhile, I had established contact with all and sundry at Police HQ. With the airfield usable and the Port soon able to receive stores, the first priority was to get 12 Squadron built up quickly and to order vehicles and plant from Jamaica.

That night a series of signals was dispatched to Jamaica and London, reporting how things were and ordering up vehicles and stores. I was allotted an American car to get around. The local American Oil Company offered some discarded marsh buggies, if the sappers could resuscitate them. Next day the squadron 2i/c, some plant operators, and 1 Troop arrived from the UK. Under the Military Plant foreman, four marsh buggies were brought back to life through combination of the remainder. The sappers had some wheels at last! On 8 November the rest of 12 Field Squadron arrived and were ferried into town. We were in business.

While all this was going on, the American Army were a tower of strength; they were running large field cookers to feed the populace and had set up a big clean water point in the city. That same day a second hurricane warning was received. Fortunately this storm turned north into the Gulf of Mexico. Heavy rain deluged Yucatan and flooded down into low lying Belize, causing three feet of water on the only road inland for several weeks thereafter. Some communities up country were isolated for many days by fallen trees and then flooding. US Marine Corps helicopters from the carrier *Antietam* were providing their main source of food.

To the south of Belize City and 100 miles by road lay the town of Stann Creek. The hurricane had cut a path, many miles across, through the rain forest just on the Belize side of the town and up into the mountains of Guatemala. Much of the landscape around Stann Creek had been cleared for orchards of red grapefruit to be planted. These had been stripped of fruit and leaves by the wind. Within weeks, blossom appeared. The scent pervaded the landscape, thereby replacing the stench of rotting vegetation. For thirty miles to the south, coastal communities had suffered grievous damage. 2 Troop had been put into Stann Creek; one section went aboard HMS *Vidal* to bring succour to coastal communities.

Within days of my arrival, the Governor asked me to go and see the First Minister, George Price, about his proposal to build a temporary township for 5,000 homeless people about ten miles inland from Belize. Devolution from direct colonial rule had started several years before, and I gathered that relations were prickly. I found George Price at his house

Hurricane Hattie, British Honduras, 1962, with (centre) George Price, Chief Minister

loading timber into a large tipper, and he at once asked me to help. I did so and, when the truck was full, he invited me to join him in driving out to the site. On the way, the truck fell into the swamp as the road was under water. I organised a passing bulldozer to extricate the vehicle. On arrival, the First Minister and I offloaded the truck at the proposed new site organised by his American advisers. Ever after, George Price was my friend. I kidded myself that I had passed muster as a Brit who was not standoffish. I used to get letters from him regularly – after full independence for the territory.

I had to give technical approval for the work and promised full support from both Royal Engineers and the PWD. Next day I put one of my Clerks of Works on site. 12 Squadron later provided much assistance to Hattieville, as it was called.

George Price co-opted me onto his New Capital Committee, presided over by himself with a mixed group of his ministers and technical people. It was already plain that a new city was needed on higher land inland or at Stann Creek to replace low-lying Belize. Once relief work in the existing city was organised, I was a member of a party that examined alternative sites. In this capacity I visited Stann Creek, where 1 Worcesters, who had followed 12 Squadron from the UK, were dealing with rehabilitation. I also went up-country to delightful Savannah country, close to the border with Guatemala, and to Corozal, close to the Mexican border to the north. I even went across the border to the city of Chetumal for a brief visit.

My group commander, Mike Stevens, and his HQ had been sent from the UK to take control of all three services in the country. He established himself alongside the Governor, and I reported to both on my efforts to support the First Minister. Soon I had to up sticks and return to commanding 38 Regiment at Ripon. I left British Honduras on 28 November after arranging for the withdrawal of 12 Field Squadron during December and seeing the arrival of the stores and plant ordered from Jamaica. After a day in the Blue Mountains of Jamaica spent with Douglas Manning of the Public Works Department on short leave, I flew back to the UK via the US airbase in the Azores, where the RAF aircraft refuelled. The last member of my regiment to return from British Honduras reached Ripon on 24 December.

38 Regiment bailiwick stretched as far as Aden and the independent Field Troop there came under my command. I had to sign confidential reports on the two officers and their NCOs, so it was necessary to visit them and get to know all concerned. This I did in the winter of 1960/61 and early in 1962 and 1963. Jeremy Rougier, later Engineer-in-Chief War Office, as a major-general, was the first troop commander. When he was posted, I sent out Neville White who, on retirement as a brigadier, became general manager of Slough Estates. I remain in contact with both to this day.

To revisit Aden was most agreeable. On one occasion Air Marshal Sir Sam Elworthy, later CDS in the Ministry of Defence and a Marshal of the RAF, invited me to crew him on the newly-arrived flying 15s that I had ordered before leaving Aden. We did not fare too well on the Sunday morning race, as I made a nonsense of hoisting the spinnaker.

With Neville White one day I had coffee in the market place in Crater. An Arab at the next table rose to his feet and embraced me. To my great joy it was my old cook Ahmed! Aden in the winter season remained a delight. The troop did good work in support of the garrison in Aden, until replaced by a squadron for operations in Radfan.

If I have given the impression that I was seldom in Ripon, this is not the case. Commanding a regiment is in itself a full-time occupation. On return from Belize I spent many weeks in mulling over confidential reports on officers and NCOs. My own were also sent me for initialling; it was most satisfactory. In the spring of 1962, orders came in to form a third field squadron – 30 – from scratch. This caused a lot of work for most of 1962. Officers and men arrived in dribbles from the training establishments. During the changeover period from conscripts to regular soldiers, much turbulence resulted. I formed the habit of occasionally assembling the whole regiment in the Camp Cinema and talking to them about the future as I saw it, as well as current problems.

Early in my tour of duty I decided to take advantage of game shooting facilities available to the regiment. These included shooting rights over the extensive tracts of training ground, in which keen volunteers put down and fed pheasants. I went to the Harrogate shooting grounds to acquire a new Aya 12-bore shotgun. This gun was made in Spain and came new at a reasonable price. Clay pigeon shooting was also available to improve swinging with a fast-moving bird at any angle to the firer. Shooting became part of my life in winter for a great number of years thereafter. I never did enough to become really expert; nevertheless, I did manage to shoot a reasonable number of birds each season. Kind friends invited me to their private shoots, not least a retired officer on my camp staff who lived near Ripon. Only in 2003 did I pass on the gun to one of my grandsons.

In the summer of 1962 a new GOC in C Northern Command was appointed. This was General 'Splosh' Jones, a sapper whom I had crossed swords with as Commandant while teaching at the Staff College in Camberley. Such a dignitary seldom, if ever, crossed my path, so I thought no more about the change. Later in the summer my regimental sergeant-major came to see me one day and told me that he suspected that certain wives were running a sexual favours business in their married quarters while husbands were away from Ripon. He had already identified one particular woman as a possible ringleader. We discussed what was to be done and decided that the RSM would keep a sharp eye out for further evidence. Several weeks passed and he raised the subject again with me. This time he had had his suspicions confirmed as to who led the group and who the members were. We decided to tackle this ticklish subject head on. The RSM would get hold of the husbands and take action through them to sterilise the ring of wives. This he did and reported success; we thought no more about it.

Several weeks later I was in my office planning training schedules for the Regiment when my adjutant burst in to say that the GOC in C, followed by several staff cars, had passed through the barrack gate and that his party was just getting out of their cars outside the office. I went out to greet them and found that General Jones was accompanied by Brigadier Jim Carr, Chief Engineer, my Group Commander, Colonel Mike Stevens, and several staff officers. The three senior officers stamped into my office. General Jones said that his headquarters had received a written complaint that there was deep trouble between officers and men in my regiment and that bullying was rife. My adjutant and I were to remain in my office while those accompanying him would fan out to ask questions of all and sundry.

He then got back into his car and departed while the remainder fanned out to do his bidding. By lunch-time they were finished and departed. Before leaving I was informed that nothing untoward had been found. Subsequently I learned that the complainant was a wife in the regiment. It did not need much brainpower to guess who this must have been. The regiment was in a bit of an unsettled state after this visitation but soon settled down. My excellent RSM told me that the wives' ring had gone to ground. I recommended that the relevant husband be posted away as soon as possible. This was done. No word of explanation reached me from General Jones.

In the autumn of 1962 orders came that 48 Field Squadron under Peter Jackson was to proceed to Germany to form part of a regiment in the British Army of the Rhine. By this time, 30 Field Squadron was in operation and I therefore still had two field squadrons and the Field Park under command for the six months that Peter and his men were away. By this stage most conscripts had wasted out on replacement by soldiers on regular engagements, and individual training was therefore very much the order of the day for all ranks. The reporting season on officers and NCOs arrived and I found myself deeply immersed in paperwork. My own report was a severe shock. All senior reporting officers, including the district major-general and the chief engineer, had graded me as outstanding. General Jones as GOC in C had downgraded my report to above average. There was no redress, so I had to put up with it – despite forebodings that this would have repercussions hereafter. It did. I can only put this down to malice of the same order that I had experienced while teaching at Camberley. Nothing had come of the extraordinary visitation after the complaint by a wife in the married quarters at Ripon.

Family life also had its problems. Celia took her A levels in the summer of 1962. In the spring of that year St Michael's School had staged a mock election. My eldest daughter stood as the Communist candidate. She became progressively more left wing in her thinking. Unknown to us at the time, Communist Party Headquarters in London somehow got to hear about the mock election and sent her literature. Not surprisingly she failed to get elected. But her exam results seemed to have been affected; her A level results were poor as a consequence. This was a great shock to her parents, who had always had a high regard for her talents. These were real and led eventually to the award of a Ph.D. in 2002.

But back in 1961 the great conundrum was whether to pay for her entry into university life at a place not likely to develop her talents to the full. We decided against sending her to university, as two younger children were yet to follow in her footsteps. She opted to become an executive officer in the Civil Service, was accepted, and set up house in London with several girlfriends. Within a couple of years she was given a job in the outer office of a minister. Celia then decided to enrol for an external degree at Birkbeck College in London. This entailed work in her own time, over and above a Civil Service job for two years, and full-time study for the last year before taking final exams. One can only commend such determination.

Janet had two years to go before taking A levels at St Michael's. Robin sat the entrance exam for Wellington in 1962 at Rottingdean School. He passed and went to the Blücher, my old dormitory, for the autumn term of that year. Under Graham Stainforth as headmaster, we found that Wellington was still in the doldrums. The Blücher had a bachelor housemaster; Robin did not take to him too well. All three children enjoyed holidays in Ripon, where there were many diversions to amuse them.

One of the joys of commanding at Ripon was the annual weekend in summer, to be attended by the Colonel Commandant or Chief Royal Engineer. In 1962 this was General Sir Frank Simpson, who visited us with his charming wife in that year. He had been a fellow student with my father at the Staff College in 1931 and 1932. The programme included a series of events on the Barrack Square on Saturday afternoon organised by the regiment. Saturday evening centred round an all ranks dance. Sunday morning gave the chance to cultivate relations with both the City of Ripon and the Cathedral. A guard of honour was mounted in the City Square for inspection by the Mayor. City councillors and army representatives then processed to the Cathedral for a church service. The Dean conducted the service and preached the sermon; the commanding officer read a lesson. Led by the Corps of Royal Engineers band that came to Ripon for the weekend, the procession reformed and marched back to the barracks for lunch in the various messes. As Ripon was the centre for a number of Territorial Army regiments in the North of England and Scotland, and also for associated branches of Royal Engineer old comrades, many representatives came to spend the weekend with 38 Regiment to take part in the festivities. By Sunday evening all ranks and their families were exhausted, but triumphant.

In early 1963 I was expecting a posting order once again, as two and a half years was the most that I could expect in command. This duly arrived; to my surprise this was to take over as Colonel of MI4 in the War Office in the early summer. After the downgrading of my report by General Jones, I had appreciated that placing me might be difficult. Just how difficult I learned later from General Dick Lloyd, who was still in the job of Director of Military Intelligence at the time that the selection boards met. My name was passed around staff directors and Dick Lloyd said he would have me, although he himself was on the point of retirement. How lucky I was to have a friend in need. The course of the rest of my Service life was set by his decision.

The winter of 1962/63 was one of the coldest on record. The ground was frozen many inches down and snow had compacted above it. The North Yorkshire Moors had deep snow that gave good ski slopes. For a number of weekends we were able to take advantage of these conditions by taking over skiing parties. Main roads were kept clear and it was still possible to get down to London by car.

Betty and I set about house-hunting in London. James Ramsden came up trumps, as he had much influence with the Duchy of Cornwall Estate in Lambeth. He suggested that we go and visit the estate manager. We did this, and went to see what was on offer. A ground floor apartment with four bedrooms looking out onto a green sward was available. At the back ran a street leading to the Lambeth Walk. I could walk to the War Office across Lambeth Bridge in about twenty-five minutes. Without hesitation we agreed to the let, at a price that was most acceptable. In early summer we moved house from Ripon to London and I prepared to beard the War Office in Whitehall.

CHAPTER 7

London (1963–1966) Colonel MI4

LONDON IN 1963 WAS STILL resonant with the song 'The Lambeth Walk'. This lay some hundreds of yards from our back entrance along Black Prince Street towards the embankment. Every day I walked to the office past the end of this famous road to reach the old War Office building in Whitehall via Lambeth Bridge and Parliament Square. On Saturdays we often did our weekend shopping in Lambeth Walk market. On the other side of our rented ground floor apartment lay an expanse of grass and a quiet road. Rents were still low at that time so life was worth living in an area now much changed – for the worse.

Military Intelligence 4 (MI4) was a scene quite new to me. I wondered what to expect. I was introduced to the director, a gunner who had taken over from my old friend Dick Lloyd who had been instrumental in my selection for the job. I met my fellow colonels in charge of segments of military intelligence such as the Communist Bloc and Far East. John Constant, my old friend from days in Egypt, was Colonel of yet another section. Above all, I met my own staff of two majors, running intelligence analysis for the Middle East and Africa respectively. Each had two staff captains who acted as desk officers for a group of countries. They collated intelligence as it was received and controlled the database of knowledge accumulated down the years. A mass of papers crossed their desks every day, from which new facts were winnowed. The more important facts, and opinions derived from them, were passed upwards through the various staff levels above them. If sufficiently important, copies went to the Foreign Office, Colonial Office and to the Heads of Sections in the Cabinet Office. These reports would be discussed at weekly meetings or at special meetings, as needed, of the Heads of Section. After approval by the Joint Intelligence Committee they would be circulated to Ministers, Chiefs of Staff and so on throughout Whitehall. This basic procedure continued throughout my subsequent career in Whitehall.

Jim Eyre, later Major-General commanding London District, was General Staff Officer Grade Two (GSO 2) in charge of African affairs. Jonathan Hall-Tipping was one of his desk officers; he served under me later in two other more senior capacities and remains a good friend to this day.

My job was to learn a great deal more about Africa, an area that hitherto I had only experienced in Egypt, Libya and East Africa. Simultaneously I needed to cultivate a wide range of people in the War Office and the Foreign Office, not least those serving within the intelligence assessment staff. This was centred on the Cabinet Office that lay across Whitehall from the War Office. I joined the Cabinet and Defence Staff's mess that was still run by the Marine corporal, now retired, who had presided over the mess in the old Ministry of Defence at Storey's Gate back in the late forties. The Middle East was an area that I knew better, but there was still a great deal to learn about the historical background to the recurrent crises in that turbulent part of the world.

One of the prime sources of intelligence throughout the area of my responsibility was the constant flow of Foreign Office telegrams that poured in each day. In each capital city an army attaché was usually to be found as part of the Embassy staff. They all reported direct to me from the Middle East and Africa. At intervals they came in person to London, often on vacating their posts. Briefing new attachés plus debriefing outgoing ones was very much part of my function. A number of soldiers served in overseas stations of Government Communications Headquarters (GCHQ), notably in Cyprus. GCHQ output flowed ceaselessly across our desks to add to the great load of reading that intelligence staff work required. Handling high security papers was a constant headache for my military clerical staff, who were highly experienced at their jobs.

One of the great joys of military intelligence work was the ability to go on tour of most of one's parish. This extended to all officers of my branch. I formed the habit of going out each winter for a tour of about five weeks around much of the Middle East and Africa down to the Cape of Good Hope. British interests at the time lay particularly in Jordan, Iraq and the remainder of the Arab world southward to the Indian Ocean. From the Sudan right down to South Africa were many places of significance for British policy makers. My tours therefore took in the bulk of countries within this wide bailiwick. The first of these tours took place in the autumn of 1963 and was followed by similar tours in 1964 and 1965. It was also necessary to go to Washington to cultivate the American intelligence community. This I did on a number of occasions, combining it with visits to Ottawa.

On tour I always visited embassies in each country. I stayed with army attachés in the main. My first tour took me to the Near East, then down to Aden, Muscat and up the Persian Gulf to Baghdad. I then retraced my steps to Kenya, Zanzibar and Dar es Salaam before going on to Pretoria via Salisbury in what was then the Rhodesian Federation. In turn I visited what were then called the High Commission Territories of Swaziland, Bechuanaland and Basutoland. These were still administered by the Colonial Office in London through our Ambassador in Pretoria. Each had a Resident Commissioner alongside the paramount chief of the territory. In Zanzibar Arab rulers had traditionally held power over the indigenous population, most of whom were close relatives of the people of Tanganyika. The Arabs had come from Muscat and Oman many centuries before. The north-east trade winds had filled their sails for the long voyage down; in the summer the south-west monsoon wafted their passage back home. Arab slave traders had operated from Zanzibar until abolition of the slave trade; despite its abolition, a number of Africans had continued to be dispatched to southern Arabia until much more recent times. On my visit to Zanzibar, I received a very gloomy picture from the Resident Commissioner, who informed me that in his opinion Arab rule was about to come to an end. The stage was set, according to my informant, for Julius Nyerere in Tanzania to take advantage of an uprising that was due to take place in about one month's time.

On my return to London I issued my report to all interested parties, including the Foreign Office and the Colonial Office. The latter had been told by the Resident Commissioner on a number of occasions that Arab rule over Zanzibar was about to end. I reiterated what the Resident Commissioner had told me; but no one reacted. Some weeks later the uprising duly occurred. Nyerere seized control and formally incorporated Zanzibar into Tanzania. British ministers in London were aghast. Why had no one told them that this was about to happen? An internal witch hunt was ordered as to how this had occurred. The Africa section of the Assessments Staff, of which I was a member, had met on a number of occasions to evaluate what had been occurring recently in Zanzibar. Nothing significant had been published in Whitehall. My report forecasting events was the only document that could be found within the intelligence community. This was reported to the Secretary of the Cabinet. Hitherto, the Africa Section of the Assessment Staff had been presided over by the Secretary of the Joint Intelligence Committee in the Cabinet Office – a Foreign Office man. A change was ordained and I was told that in future I was to preside over all meetings of the Africa Section.

This I did for the remainder of my tour of duty. It meant that amongst other things I had to attend each weekly meeting of the Joint Intelligence Committee, when the heads of all the Intelligence Agencies met, to consider current intelligence assessments for submission to Ministers and their heads of departments. This brought me into contact with many influential people and redounded to the credit of Military Intelligence. This work, of course, came on top of membership of the Middle East Assessments Section, and in consequence I found myself reading yet more papers each day. My contacts with the Foreign Office, Colonial Office and the intelligence collecting agencies were equally enhanced.

These events had an interesting sequel. That winter my annual confidential report initiated by the Deputy Director of Military Intelligence, a brigadier, landed on my desk for initialling. No mention of my upgrading within the Assessments Staff in the Cabinet Office appeared, nor was the grading of the report to my liking. I went to see the brigadier. He had never heard of developments over Zanzibar, as his work was largely administrative; I explained the course of events that had occurred. He agreed to consider again the contents of my report. After further consultation, a revised report reached my desk. This was much more to my liking and I initialled it.

In the spring of 1964 rumours began to spread that Major-General Kenneth Strong, who since his retirement had run the Joint Intelligence Bureau (JIB), was making a strong play to amalgamate all three Service intelligence machines with his own organisation. Admiral Lord Louis Mountbatten was due to retire as Chief of Defence Staff that summer. Strong, who had been Eisenhower's chief intelligence officer in wartime days, was known to have the ear of the Chief of Defence Staff. The JIB comprised Logistical Intelligence, Scientific and Technical Intelligence and Economic Intelligence on all communist countries. At the height of the Cold War no doubt it was the latter task that allowed its head to have and request access to the Chief of Defence Staff. Service Directors only had access to their respective Chiefs of Staff. As midsummer approached and the departure of the Admiral of the Fleet, Lord Mountbatten, drew near, no decision had been announced. On his last but one day in office, the order was promulgated for the Defence Intelligence Staff to be formed from the intelligence assets of Navy, Army and Air Force, together with those of the JIB under Strong as Director General of Intelligence. The three Service Directors of Intelligence were to be phased out.

The proposed new organisation was rapidly announced. I ceased to be Colonel MI4 and was metamorphised into Colonel DI4 with sections of naval and air force intelligence added to my original army staff, all of which had dealt with Middle East and African affairs in their own Service departments. We were to come together on the second floor of the new Ministry of Defence building across Whitehall Place from the old War Office. This we did in surprisingly short order. I found myself with a wing commander deputy and a naval lieutenant commander, supported by several desk officers keeping the desk level files on navies and air forces throughout the joint area of responsibility. This amalgamation worked well and so far as I know persists to this day.

Similar reorganisations took place for those studying Europe and the Americas, the Soviet Bloc and the Far East. We all came under a two-star level Director of Services Intelligence, a post to be rotated among the three services. Residual single service interests were looked after by a one-star level officer from each service. At the top level stood the Director General and his deputy, a three-star officer, the Deputy Chief of Defence Staff (Intelligence) – DCDS(I). Little did I know at the time, but I was to fill each one of these posts in subsequent years.

This change increased significantly the strength of central staffs under the Ministry of Defence but it did not derogate from the prime importance of the three single service chiefs. Career planning and advancement still lay in the hands of the Navy, Army and Air Force – not of the central staffs. The Chiefs of Staff Committee collectively still held sway, with each chief of staff having access to the Prime Minister, if needed, to represent the views of his own service. At lower levels, however, we took no cognisance of such affairs of state and concentrated on making the new amalgamated machinery work.

Alongside the Directorate of Service Intelligence were directors for management and support, economic, scientific and technical, including the old individual service technical intelligence branches. This amounted to a formidable staff of around 1,200 at the time of formation of the Defence Intelligence Staff (DIS). One of the deals struck before the deed was done was that my old friend Dick Lloyd, who had retired, was to be re-employed as Secretary of the DIS. He duly replaced a career civil servant but, though achieving much, he clearly did not hit it off with his master, Kenneth Strong. Within a couple of years he was ousted and joined the Foreign Office as head of their disarmament branch.

I visited Washington, where a small DIS liaison staff was maintained to cultivate the American intelligence community. Much of my time was spent in discussions with the Defense Intelligence Agency (DIA). I also called on my opposite numbers in the Central Intelligence Agency (CIA) and NSA, the equivalent of GCHQ at Cheltenham. This was to be first of many such visits. They were to be of particular value in the exchange of ideas and complemented visits to the Middle East and Africa.

In the winter of 1964 I set off once again on my annual extensive tour of my large parish. On this particular visit I concentrated on South Arabia, the Persian Gulf, East Africa, Central Africa, including the

Tour of Congo, 1965

Congo, and South Africa. In Aden, operations in Radfan against dissident tribesmen armed and supplied from the Yemen was in full swing. The mountains in the common border area had always been tiresome. In my days in Aden we had had to run armed convoys up to Dhala in the western part of the Protectorate up-country. These difficulties had multiplied until substantial forces had to be deployed in subduing dissidents in a way that no doubt would have been familiar to my father in Waziristan in the North West Frontier Province of India pre-war.

Next, I proceeded to Kenya where Mau Mau gangs of thugs were just starting to murder isolated white farming families. British troops were already engaged in support of the King's African Rifles and I went to visit both. Farm properties were protected by extensive wire entanglements covered by external lights at night. Farmers carried rifles or pistols. Movement by car was usually by convoy. My friends out at Kipkabus were still all right, as was Deirdre Welsford, who had married a sailor before he retired to farm near Mau Summit.

From Kenya I flew to Kinshasa in the Congo where the military attaché, a charming gunner colonel, met me. Together we paid a call on Mobutu, who had recently taken over control of the country. He lived in what had been the Belgian Governor's palace looking out onto a broad reach of the River Congo. Our talk, I fear, was somewhat stilted: but from my angle fruitful in meeting the man who would be decisive in

Congolese affairs for a great many years to come. The attaché and I then went off by road to Matadi, the port in the pool at the mouth of the great Congo river below a series of rapids, and then on towards the Cabinda enclave, on the Atlantic coast. Oil had recently been struck in the Angolan portion of the Cabinda enclave but at that time production had hardly started. Today Cabinda oil is the mainstay of the Angolan economy. Finally we flew down to Elizabethville in Katanga on the Copper Belt. Here I went down a copper mine. Some 2,000 feet below the surface the air was fetid and water seeped everywhere.

North of Elizabethville was disputed territory between the Congolese government and mercenary-led locals in revolt. To my sorrow I was unable to meet mercenary chiefs because I was on the government side of the line. I parted from my attaché escort and flew on to Lusaka in Zambia and after a brief stopover there, to Pretoria, the part-time capital of South Africa. For the hot season the government migrated to Cape Town after half a year in Pretoria. After talks within the Embassy I paid a brief visit to Johannesburg. On the way out of Pretoria by road I noticed that we were driving beside a railway on an embankment. Suddenly I saw not one but two pedestrian tunnels under the embankment. One was marked *Blankies* and the other *Ne Blankies*. This brought home to me just how absurd apartheid measures could get, in that segregation was mandatory to pass under a railway line. I was glad therefore to take off for Swaziland, where the Resident Commissioner kindly put me up. He told me that he had arranged for me to see King Sobuza of the Swazis next day at his kraal some distance south.

'What time do we leave?' I asked.

'Oh, you go on your own,' was the reply. 'The King asked for you to go alone.'

So next day I sallied forth by car and reached the King's kraal, a modern-looking structure. I was conducted inside and there was the King in his council chamber surrounded by his councillors, including many members of his Dlamini family. The King invited me to sit opposite him and launched into a series of questions about the state of the world in general and Russian machinations in the territories to the north of Swaziland in particular. The King was about sixty years old, and spoke good English. Whether the councillors did I never knew as none took part in the dialogue between the King and myself. He was clearly already well informed. His questions were searching and required rapid thinking on my part, so as not to prejudice sources in my replies. After a couple of hours of discussion over cups of tea, the King indicated that the audience was at an end. I retired gracefully to recount to the Resident

Commissioner all that had transpired. That night I was entertained by several British officers on secondment to the Swazi Police at a local restaurant. The prawns that had been caught off the port of Lourenço Marques in what was then Portuguese East Africa were the largest and juiciest that I can ever recall. They even came in special plates with grooves in for each prawn – truly memorable.

My next port of call was Basutoland, high in the Drakensberg mountains. Much of the population worked in the gold mines of South Africa as indentured unaccompanied labour. As preparation for independence, a Prime Minister, Jonathan Lebua, had been appointed. He had already usurped much of the power of the Paramount Chief and was engaged in dispute with the Colonial Office. When I went to see him, he insisted that I help him compose his latest diatribe back to Whitehall. He struck me as intelligent and forceful and he continued to control his small state for many years after independence was granted. Later I drove out into the high country to the east of Maputo, reaching nearly 10,000 feet in glorious mountain scenery. To the north I reached the South African border in the lowlands before turning back to Maseru. From there I flew back to Pretoria to catch a flight to London. This was a memorable trip and my tour report was commensurately long.

I returned to encounter problems on the home front in Lambeth. The flat on the Duchy of Cornwall Estate proved to be a great success. In the summer of 1964 my younger daughter Janet had taken her A levels at St Michael's, Uckfield. Her results had not been as good as both she and her parents had hoped. Educational standards at the school were not as high as they should have been. Janet's strong suit was mathematics. She decided to capitalise on this rather than to go to a second-rate university. She took a job with some aircraft designers, commuting from Lambeth. But she found the work of little intrinsic interest and decided to go for Chartered Accounting. Interviews were the order of the day on my return from Africa. Eventually Janet chose to become an apprentice with Jacob, Cavanagh and Skeet in the City of London. This worked out splendidly and two years later she passed all her exams with flying colours and became a fully-fledged chartered accountant. Janet continues to pursue this trade and now specialises in tax affairs for individual accounts.

The Intelligence world continued to occupy my mind in a big way. The heads of section in the Cabinet Office were often required to produce special assessments for ministers and chiefs of staff in addition to their weekly product. I got to know Teddy Youde of the Foreign Office well, in his capacity as chairman of the heads of sections. His mind was crystal clear, and it was an education to listen to him presiding over the

Middle East section that I attended. This section was always busy, because of the number of Arab states in which it had to monitor developments. Within my own staff area, I had much to learn about navies and air forces throughout my parish. Naval and air desk officers were most knowledgeable about the many countries that they covered, many of which kept close military relations with the UK. The Defense Intelligence Agency in Washington had a liaison staff in the Ministry of Defence. After my first visit across the Atlantic, I kept in close touch with this liaison element. One of the locally employed folk in this staff was a particularly attractive girl called Virginia Fyler, daughter of a retired major-general. I took her out to lunch – to be told that she had just accepted a job in our equivalent staff in Washington. There she was a tower of strength for many years, until she married a millionaire dentist.

Early in 1965 I started planning my next big tour around the Middle East and Africa. Highlights were to be visits to Iraq, Abyssinia and Bechuanaland from Rhodesia. For my third tour I decided to go to Africa first before tackling the Middle East. Abyssinia was still ruled by the Emperor Haile Selassie, although not for much longer, as he was to be deposed and executed by communist conspirators. My cousin Desmond Vigors was the defence attaché in Addis Ababa. I stayed with him and missed by only a day my relative, Wilfred Thesiger, who had been staying in the same house. He was a legendary figure in Abyssinia, and further enhanced his reputation by crossing the Empty Quarter of Saudi Arabia and then living for a year or so with the Marsh Arabs of the delta formed by the junction of the Tigris and the Euphrates Rivers in Iraq. His mother was a Vigors, well-known to my mother, and I was sorry to miss meeting him. Desmond and I got around widely in Addis Ababa. I remember particularly going round the newly completed headquarters of the Organisation for African Unity, where all the door handles were shaped as a map of the African continent.

Salisbury in Southern Rhodesia was my next port of call. I had called an attaché conference to meet my attachés of all three services in central and South Africa. The defence attaché from Pretoria had come up to Salisbury by road. After a most useful *tour d'horizon* with the assembled attachés, he and I set off in his car for Bulawayo. Here we attended a passing-out parade for young officers being commissioned into the Rhodesian Federal Army. The instructors included seconded Guards NCOs, so the drill was impeccable. It was startlingly similar to a passing-out parade at Sandhurst, as the students were white and their families attended. Next day we drove south-west past the Rhodes Memorial to the Bechuanaland border. Thereafter the road was dirt, not tarmac, but well-maintained and fortunately dry. On reaching the then capital, we spent the night with the Resident Commissioner and saw the local sights. These included the house where Seretse Khama lived with his English wife. Unfortunately they were away, and our host declined to introduce us to any of his Government. I guessed that the last stages to independence were proving somewhat fraught. Already the new capital, Gaborones, was being built and this was to be our next port of call – some 250 miles yet further south. We reached there by lunch-time and were shown round the new set-up that looked promising – as in fact it turned out to be following independence. In the evening light we carried on across the South African border to Mafeking for a second night. After a brief tour of the sights of what had been one of the focal points of the Boer War at the turn of the twentieth century, we took the good but narrow tarmac highway leading to Pretoria. Driving in South Africa had its moments as on the long straight stretches drivers were apt to go to sleep.

Next day I lunched with the South African Director of Intelligence, an hospitable Boer who introduced me to the excellent red wines of South Africa that in more recent times have graced many a table in the UK. I went on to Swaziland and Basutoland as before, including a further meeting with Chief Jonathan Lebua; then to Lusaka in Zambia and Dar es Salaam in Tanzania. In Dar I called on the Minister of Defence to Nyerere, a smooth African who later fell out with his master. He seemed well informed and we had a useful exchange of ideas.

After six weeks it was time to familiarise myself with the Middle East portion of my parish. Visits to Aden, Muscat and Bahrain went smoothly, and I took off from Bahrain to Baghdad to stay with the defence attaché. The plane had to make an unscheduled stop at Basrah, and all passengers were asked to disembark and spend an hour or so in the transit lounge. When approaching the immigration desk I was concerned to see that passports were being removed from all those in the line ahead of me. I thought quickly about whether I should part with mine and decided against doing so as my name was bound to figure on Iraqi intelligence lists. I refused to part with it and was told that I could not enter the building but would have to stand out in the sun under armed guard. This I did for well over an hour till we were all allowed back on the plane.

I was much relieved to be greeted by the defence attaché in Baghdad as he wafted me through immigration and customs. He lived in the embassy compound, in those days a gracious oasis in the desert just west of the River Tigris opposite Baghdad itself. It was fun to get around the city again. The Ambassador was most helpful in setting out his view on the development of the dictatorial regime of Saddam Hussein and the Baath party. A visit to Near East Arab countries followed. Beirut was the ugliest situation with Maronite Christians and Shi'ite Muslims already at each other's throats.

Arrival back in London felt anti-climactic, not least in the writing of a mammoth tour report. In my absence the Defence Intelligence Staff had continued to evolve and life in the Heads of Sections across Whitehall in the Cabinet Office was as busy as ever. In the Ministry of Defence I had much briefing to do, particularly of the army hierarchy. Amongst these was General George Baker, initially Vice-Chief and then Chief of the General Staff. His son was at Wellington in the Blücher Dormitory, the same vintage as my son Robin. The families met on various occasions such as Speech Day that Betty and I always attended while Robin was at school. His daughter, a fine artist, remains a great friend of my second daughter Janet. One of her pictures now adorns my dining room wall.

This contact proved to be of importance in late 1965 as I received my next posting order from the Corps of Royal Engineers. This was to be chief engineer in Aden, where the Radfan operation was still in full spate. Betty and I were horrified, as we had already done one tour of duty there. The job was still at colonel level. I talked it over with General George, and he kindly said that he would look into my case with the Military Secretary. Soon afterwards I heard that I had been given a last minute vacancy on the Imperial Defence College course in Belgrave Square, London. This made no less than three sappers on the course: myself, Mike Lewis and Richard Clutterbuck from whom I had taken over 38 Engineer Regiment in 1960. I was quite delighted and in January 1966 I reported to Belgrave Square for this excellent course, having handed over my job in the Ministry of Defence. It had been great fun and most educative. I had got on well with Charles Earle, a four-star airman who had succeeded Kenneth Strong as Director General in 1965, which was to be fortunate indeed for my future.

Belgrave Square is a delightful area in which to work, and easy to reach. Work was hardly onerous; the morning lecture was obligatory, as was some syndicate work to prepare presentations to the course as a whole. There were many visits, both at home and overseas. Students could write a thesis if they wished; I did so for comment in due course by the senior army instructor, a major-general named Fitzgeorge Balfour, who later became Vice-Chief of the Army Staff and finally UK military representative in Brussels. The Commandant, a four-star general or equivalent, was, for 1966, from the army. There were many foreign students including Americans and Commonwealth – about one-third of the course in all. Their presence gave an excellent leavening to both question periods and course presentations following syndicate discussions. In addition the staff organised a series of events for wives that gave Betty an invaluable chance to meet her opposite numbers, both UK and overseas.

Above all, a course lasting a year, without responsibilities other than family and with plenty of spare time, was a marvellous relaxation for all students. I certainly needed it, not least because of family problems. My father-in-law died that spring and I had to arrange with the Air Ministry for his memorial service in St Clements Dane Church in the Strand – the RAF Church for London. Leslie Bates had retired some years previously as Director General of Equipment in the Air Ministry. He had bought a charming property on Crawley Ridge above Camberley with quite a lot of land. Here he had much enjoyed retired life and my family had made a great deal of use of my in-laws' house in recent years. Poor soul, he had suffered from rheumatic fever in his early years and this was a main cause of his death. The same fate overtook his daughter many years later.

For the first time in our lives Betty and I decided to buy a house. We started looking at various properties and soon latched onto a delightful place in Pilgrims Way, Guildford, that lay in the parish of Shalford in the valley of the River Wey. Number One was at the western end of Pilgrims Way. It had four bedrooms, up to an acre of garden, containing both a hard tennis court and a swimming pool, and a splendid sun room overlooking the patio round the pool. Behind this lay a big vegetable garden and some fruit trees. On the eastern side a very tall hedge covered the next door garden.

As we were negotiating to buy the house, with savings that I had managed to make in recent years plus a mortgage, news hit us that my father had burned his house in North Devon to the ground, and had died in the fire. Since my mother had died back in 1957, my father had been looked after by a couple in the cottage next door to Trentishoe Manor. Unfortunately, they had accepted an invitation to stay a night with friends who lived just over the ridge to the south of Trentishoe and out of sight of my father's house. In the morning they saw smoke from our valley and rushed up the ridge to be greeted by the sight of Trentishoe already largely burned down. They summoned the fire brigade and dashed home, but were unable to do anything until the fire was finally damped down.

They contacted my father's friend and solicitor who lived near Barnstaple. He telephoned us and said that he was arranging the funeral in Parracombe Church. Betty and I, together with all three of our children, dashed down to North Devon. Trentishoe was a deeply distressing sight. The family still had a lot of possessions stored in the attic. All of these were burned, as was my father's furniture and pictures that had come from Ireland from my mother's family. These included family portraits going back several centuries, including a 'hanging' judge who had been forced to convict his own son. My parents had also bought some fine Dutch marquetry furniture; and my father had one of the largest and finest collections of thousands of 'penny black' Victorian postage stamps in albums in the sitting room. All of these were totally destroyed. The cause of the fire was never fully determined. There was a coke-fired Aga cooker in the wall between the kitchen and the dining room. The most likely cause was that my father had left this fully open and that it had become red hot – thus setting fire to the house. He had woken because of smoke but only made it to the landing before he collapsed.

The funeral at Parracombe was a sombre affair, well attended by local people. I caused a stone to be erected to mark his grave at Parracombe churchyard. All the estate came to me. Unfortunately none of the contents of the house proved to be insured. I sold the site of the house for a miserable £5,500. In all, about £48,000 came my way but it did allow me to buy 1 Pilgrims Way outright. We moved in during the early summer.

At home Janet continued to live with us until we moved out to Guildford. Celia was still sharing a flat with friends and Robin was at Wellington, soon to move on to King's College in London. Betty settled in well to life in Guildford. We continued to week-end occasionally in my cottage at Charlton near Andover. This had been let for some years, but I turned it back into a week-end cottage before the year I spent at the Imperial Defence College.

The course continued on with a fascinating variety of speakers. These included scientists, administrators, media men and trade unionists. Various visits took us away from Belgrave Square, the most remarkable of which was a visit to the north-east. We went down a coal mine that had galleries running out under the North Sea. A shipyard was of great interest but we were surprised to find that, although much money had been spent on automating the cutting and assembly of large sections of each ship, once construction started on the slipway, time-honoured methods prevailed, with no sign of speeding-up devices. Needless to say only a few years later I read of the demise of the yard.

Getting the house in Guildford to our liking absorbed much of our energies in the summer months. As summer leave approached before the long overseas tours, we looked forward to a period of relaxation to enjoy the fruits of our labours. With the house I had acquired an immensely tall ladder that was needed to cut the high hedge between our own garden and the neighbour's garden; unfortunately, that belonged to us. On the first day of the summer break I set about cutting the top of the hedge with an electric hedge cutter. To do so meant mounting the free-standing ladder to its top platform. The legs stood on a slight slope down towards our house. Without warning the ladder toppled sideways, leaving me suspended in space clutching the electric hedge cutter. This I managed to leave on the top of the hedge so that it did not bite me. But I failed to adjust my non-existent parachute and hit the ground with an alarming thud.

I found it difficult to move and croaked out a call for help. Betty came running and fortunately did not try to move me but dashed for the phone to ring for an ambulance. The crew were experienced and lifted me with great care onto a stretcher and then parked me in the back of their ambulance. They took me to a private hospital just north of the Hog's Back where a doctor examined me. He announced that I had fractured my spine and would have to remain prone for some time. He was right and I did not emerge for a month – thereby, to my rage and impotent fury, missing the IDC visit to South East Asia, Australia and New Zealand!

I was looked after by a charming nurse whose husband was out of the country on prolonged business. Under the guidance of the physiotherapist we soon started to do remedial exercises for a crushed vertebra in the middle of my spine that had showed clearly on the X-ray. I was told that within six months, if I maintained remedial exercises throughout this period, it would grow again. On release from hospital there was only a short time before the course reassembled after various visits to all parts of the world had been completed. I was able to resume commuting to Seaford House and was not best pleased to be regaled with stories of how excellent had been the experiences of colleagues who had gone on the Far East tour. I was allotted a room on the top floor to do my exercises. Lectures, presentations and exercises continued full blast. As the end of the course approached, dignitaries from the Ministry of Defence and Foreign Office addressed us. These included permanent under-secretaries and Chiefs of Staff. Presentations of overseas tours by participants were excellently performed after much rehearsing – and I was green with envy.

That autumn, posting orders for students reached the students. Mine was to return to the Defence Intelligence Staff, this time on promotion to brigadier, as Brigadier General Staff (Intelligence). As part of the checks and balances set up on formation of the Defence Intelligence Staff in 1964, each service had a one-star post to watch over single service interests and to brief his Chief of Staff. The Director General of Intelligence (DGI), Air Chief Marshal 'Tubby' Earle, had asked for me to return as the senior army man, and in the New Year I was due to return to a staff that I knew well. I looked forward to doing so with keen anticipation.

A bumpy year at the Imperial Defence College drew to a close with final addresses and parties. We said goodbye to new friends, many of whom we should meet again in years to come, both at home and overseas. The course of 1966 would remain a close-knit union for many years to come. I attended a number of reunions.

Chapter 8

London and Germany (1967–1971) BGS (Intelligence)

Life back in the Ministry of Defence, Whitehall, was never dull. I found myself in a new office not far from my old one as Colonel of DI4. My essential task was as a watchdog for the Army. I had to see that the centralised Defence Intelligence machine continued to give the same input of processed intelligence to all relevant parts of the Army machine as they had previously received from the single service Director of Military Intelligence and his staff. I was the focal point for all Army Staff Officers up to Colonel throughout the Defence Intelligence Staff, including their confidential reports that were passed to the Army Military Secretary's department after I had made my comments, as had the Senior Army Officer serving in the Defence Intelligence Staff.

This meant that I had to get to know a large number of Army Officers serving not only in the branches under the Director of Service Intelligence (DSInt), but also those in other Directorates such as the Director of Management and Support (DMSI) and the Director of Scientific and Technical Intelligence (DSTI), on occasion a civilian scientist seconded from Defence Science.

As time went on, Northern Ireland loomed ever larger on the horizon as a large single service requirement. The Army Intelligence Corps came under DMSI, as did soldiers of all ranks in GCHQ stations and others in JARIC, the air photography and other collection specialists. In addition, the Director General of Intelligence, Air Marshal Sir Charles Earle, asked me to become the DIS member of a team headed by Sir Dick White in the Cabinet Office to look into the organisation of intelligence at national level. This took a great deal of time, not least in visiting all collection agencies and hearing witnesses at regular meetings in the Cabinet Office. So my time was well filled with meaningful work, supplemented by visits throughout the world, including America, Canada, Australia, New Zealand, Europe, particularly NATO, the Middle East and the Far East, not least Vietnam.

All this widened my mental horizon yet more, and fitted me for further advancement in the intelligence world. But this was still subject to Army planning and not to central staff control. This led in due course to further problems, as this account will disclose. Fortunately, my duties included briefing the Chief of the General Staff weekly and addressing conferences and audiences of Army commanders and staff world-wide: so I became well known to large segments of the Army in consequence. Of significance were the personality and knowledge of the Senior Army Officer in the DIS. When its turn came to nominate the DSInt, the Army put in Major-General Miles Fitzallan Howard, later Duke of Norfolk, with a view to his selection in due course as DCDS(I) – the deputy to the DGI. Unfortunately, he had little interest in intelligence. Much of his work tended to come my way, in the form of advice on what he should do. This was particularly the case over developments in Northern Ireland that led to me having to run the build-up of intelligence there after the destruction of Burntollet Bridge in the summer of 1968, the start of Army operations.

Miles was eventually turned down as his potential deputy by the DGI, colloquially known as Tubby Earle, and he retired soon after. The DCDS (I) was for some time Vice-Admiral Denning, brother of the former judge and Master of the Rolls, Lord Denning. He was deeply steeped in naval intelligence, having first entered the scene as a young officer in Room 40, the redoubtable naval intelligence centre in the wartime Admiralty. He was a somewhat aloof figure, but I found him easy to deal with insofar as our paths crossed. He was one of three brothers who became well known – the third reaching the rank of Lieutenant General. They were born and bred in Whitchurch, Hampshire, sons of a shop owner in that town. Admiral Denning retired in 1969 and Lieutenant General Sir Dick Fyffe replaced him.

Enough of personalities. I much enjoyed getting to know a wide range of army officers doing intelligence work. These included the Intelligence Corps that came under the Director of Management and Support (DMSI), a rotational post. Some of the Intelligence Corps worked as analysts in the intercept world of GCHQ. One task given me by the Army was to run an inquiry into whether these analysts should remain as part of the Intelligence Corps, or should be transferred to the Corps of Royal Signals, who provided the operators of intercept sets. This led me into numerous visits to the Intelligence Corps Centre at Ashford where the inquiry was held. The Brigadier in command there was initially Bill Vickers of the King's Own Yorkshire Light Infantry, whom I had known as a first grade staff officer in the Kommandantura during my tour in Berlin. After much thought and discussion, I came to the conclusion that analysts should remain members of the Intelligence Corps, as their training was largely concerned with interpreting foreign armies' activities rather than in the Signals aspect of these communications, essentially the business of the operators manning intercept sets. In due course this decision was endorsed by the Army Board and, in consequence, the Intelligence Corps remained large enough to survive intact the manifold cuts in Army manpower that have become such a feature of Army life to this day. The main function of the Corps remained gaining and interpreting intelligence within the Field Army and maintaining security therein.

The DMSI was assisted by a staff officer at lieutenant colonel level from the Intelligence Corps. Ken Meares filled this post at one time, before joining the burgeoning staff in Northern Ireland and finally becoming the brigadier commanding the Intelligence Corps. He remains a good friend of mine to this day, together with his charming wife. Over and above the Intelligence Corps there were many other Army elements in Defence Intelligence. DI3 Army was an Army staff branch in its own right studying the Russian and Eastern Europe communist armies alongside similar bodies from the Royal Navy and the RAF. There were some Royal Engineer Survey officers and men working with JARIC, the experts on air photography amongst other things. Cultivating all these and more within the Scientific and Technical aegis required much legwork.

Intelligence input into purely Army studies gave me access to many audiences. I had to talk to the Army Staff College at intervals. I attended a study period in Singapore presided over by the Commander-in-Chief, Mike Carver, later Chief of the General Staff and Chief of Defence Staff. On this occasion I fear that my views were not too much to his liking, and had their repercussions in later years. Another task was to address a large conference convened by the Quartermaster General, Bill Jackson. Once again, my views were slightly heretical and did not sell too well. On the other hand, addresses to 1 British Corps conferences at Bielefeld in Germany went down reasonably well. There was a direct weekly briefing to the Chief of the General Staff (CGS). In my early days as BGS (Int) this was General Rowley Gibbs, who was interested in what I had to say, although he spent much of his time on tour. He was replaced by my old friend from 1947/48 in Kuala Lumpur, General Peter Hunt. Briefings to him were both hilarious and fun. On his retirement, still as a general rather than a field marshal as was customary, he became Constable of the Tower of London and enjoyed a flat within the Governor's House. On one occasion he attended a function in the City and returned late to the gate leading into the Tower. The sentry demanded his pass. He had left it in his flat, so replied that he was the Constable of the Tower. The sentry looked him up and down (Peter was well over six feet tall) and said firmly that he could not enter. Peter remonstrated, and the sentry agreed to summon the officer of the guard. The latter eventually agreed to summon the Governor himself to identify the prospective entrant to the Tower. The Governor – a retired two-star general – was woken from sleep and in due course arrived grumpily at the gate. Finally, Peter was cleared for entry into the Tower and his own bed! As a Highland Officer, Peter had a great sense of humour and carried this affair off with his customary aplomb.

In his time as CGS he invited me to various regimental functions, as he was also Colonel of his Regiment, the Seaforths. It happened that the regimental secretary was my old friend from days in Kuala Lumpur and Java, Chu MacLagan, who had commanded 1 Seaforths in Singapore. So I was doubly glad to attend the odd reunion of the Seaforths in London, latterly in the Tower itself. Here the Royal Fusiliers had their depot and officers mess, and I was invited to several functions at the site where a notorious spy was incarcerated before the Second World War.

In retrospect, very much of my time as BGS (Int) seems to have been taken up with travelling. In my view, this was right and proper, because intelligence requires a personal feel for places and people if it is to convince audiences in London who have not themselves borne personal witness to events. Intelligence analysis necessarily requires a forecast of things to come, as well as a recital of what has actually happened of late. Best guesses require a wealth of personal knowledge, and a briefer who can describe a scene from having been there is in a much stronger position to establish consumer confidence than one who has stayed at home. The habits that I learned in MI4 regularly stood me in good stead in the Cabinet Office as well as the Ministry of Defence.

True to my instincts, I spread my wings by touring Vietnam, Australia and New Zealand as well as countries between there and the UK. I made contact with a number of people in the Australian intelligence community in Canberra and the New Zealand counterpart in Wellington that stood me in good stead in future years, when, as always, a familiar face is much more welcome than a stranger. Many Australian and New Zealand people had served in most parts of the earth, either as serving officers or as civilians, and were well informed on what went on. I also cultivated their counterparts in London. Amongst many other functions, the DIS had a section devoted to liaison with both Commonwealth and foreign embassies. Through them I could cultivate those resident in London. Intelligence indeed has a wide network of contacts.

My tour of the war in Vietnam in 1968 was particularly noteworthy. I flew into the American-controlled airfield outside Saigon to be met by the defence attaché. The city itself was teeming with people on bicycles and in rickshaws and appeared reasonably prosperous at that time, some three months before the Tet offensive that symbolised communist Vietcong resistance. Next day I called on the American headquarters in the city, and our own embassy headed by the Ambassador Peter Wilkinson, whom I was later to re-encounter as a Deputy-Under Secretary in the Foreign Office in Whitehall. I then made my mark with the South Vietnamese Army headquarters, also in Saigon.

The air attaché piloted his own aircraft over Vietnam. In this we set out next day for Danang in the north, headquarters of the Marine Corps covering that area. After an interview with the Corps Commander, I found that arrangements had been made for me to visit a marine regiment on a lake near the border with Cambodia. Taking off by helicopter from Danang, we flew inland to find the regimental headquarters on a small hill overlooking a lake. Although they had been there some days, I was concerned to see that only one coil of wire surrounded the position and that the entire regimental headquarters, signals and supporting artillery regiment of self-propelled guns were not dug in. I found that the regimental commander had recently taken over after attending a course at the Joint Services Staff College in England. Like all officers, he only did six months in Vietnam before returning to the States, in my view one of the prime reasons that the Americans failed to learn much battle experience while serving in Vietnam. We got talking as we walked round his position. I asked about Vietcong strengths.

'Gee', he said, 'them gooks are cunning. Ma men think that up to a company might be hiding in the water below us breathing through straws to the lake surface.' As can be imagined, I took this with a grain of salt. I asked him about actual contacts. He replied that only the day before his men who were laying the wire fence had laid down their coils of wire and come into the camp for chow time. After eating they went back and lifted up their coils. A local explosion occurred and several marines were killed and wounded. While they had been away the enemy had crept up and booby-trapped the coils.

On balance, I was delighted when my helicopter took off without further incident. We flew to a nearby marine post, where a combined action platoon was stationed. This was a mixed force of marines and South Vietnamese Army soldiers, the latter liaising with the local population. They seemed vulnerable to me, in an isolated position where Vietcong strength could rapidly be assembled against them. We flew back to Danang and then on to Saigon for the night. En route I was looking forward through the windscreen while talking to the pilot, when streaks of light screamed down not far in front of us. 'American fighters above us engaging ground targets with rockets,' said the air attaché. I shuddered slightly.

Next day we set out to visit two Korean divisions occupying Central Vietnam and providing protection for the naval base at Camranh Bay, through which much food and military support entered Vietnam. The Koreans had arranged for me to visit a regimental headquarters and gun area followed by a battalion base. Both were fully dug in with massive overhead protection. On arrival at the battalion base by American-manned helicopter gunship, I noticed that we were substantially beyond the reach of the supporting artillery at regimental level. I asked the battalion commander how he controlled his area. He replied that two thirds of his men were constantly away from base on patrol. Artillery support did not bother him as few contacts ever occurred with the Vietcong. If they did, Korean reserves would be deployed to help him. He insisted that from lessons learned in the Korean War from watching British troops, his men were trained on British and not on American lines. Later, I lunched with the Korean divisional commander. In the presence of his advisory American 'chicken' colonel, I asked what he would do should one of his battalion bases out of artillery range be seriously threatened. Would he call in the American Air Force to assist him? He looked up to heaven before saying:

'Never would I invite the American Air Force to support me.' It was good to see such professional soldiers deployed, an experience repeated that afternoon when visiting the second Korean division.

An old friend of mine from IDC days in London was commanding the Australian Brigade in Vietnam. They were occupying a sector south of Saigon that was much disputed by the Vietcong. Mine warfare was in full swing, with occasional infantry attacks against Australian positions. I flew down to see them and once again was greeted by a thoroughly professional force. It was good to see my old friend in excellent form and enjoying the challenge. On return to Australia he was promoted Deputy Chief of Army Staff in Canberra, as a major-general. I last saw him after we both retired and I had bought a small house on the Sunshine Coast north of Brisbane, while he had settled on the Gold Coast south of that city.

On my final day in Vietnam I flew south-west to see the South Vietnamese Army operating in the river delta area. This was equally interesting in that much of their forces operated in boats. I went some way in one of these and visited Army posts way out in the delta. Fortunately, no untoward events took place: but I was impressed by the little that I saw of the efficiency of the South Vietnamese Army. On my last day in Saigon I again went to their headquarters and had a long talk with the Chief of Staff, of whom I formed a reasonable impression.

I also made good contacts in Saigon with senior officers seconded from the DIA in Washington and with the CIA. My visit to the latter was amusing. Their station chief would not disclose their location to me. Instead, I was told to go to a certain street corner in Saigon and dismiss my vehicle. I was then to walk along a certain road till I came to a bungalow, where I was to go up to the front door and knock. This I did and lo and behold the CIA station chief was inside to greet me. We had a fascinating, though scarcely illuminating, talk over lunch. Sadder but little wiser, I returned to London. So ended my sojourn in Vietnam, a memorable occasion that stood me in good stead when back in London for assessing the after-effects of the Tet offensive.

Getting to know the large number of officers and soldiers working in intelligence was a major task. Within the Defence Intelligence Staff itself there were several hundred. The Intelligence Corps was over a thousand strong and spread throughout the Army. Visits to the Intelligence Corps Centre at Ashford were always fun. Once the Army build-up in Northern Ireland was authorised by the Army Board, Intelligence Corps officers and men were in the vanguard of those sent over from England to underpin the work of the Special Branch, itself expanding fast.

At this point in my narrative it would seem sensible to set out what I remember of the early days of developments in Northern Ireland. In the spring of 1968, the activities of the Civil Rights movement representing the Catholic community became increasingly threatening. At that time the IRA did not figure significantly in exacerbating tension between the Catholic and Protestant elements of the population. For some months beforehand the Joint Intelligence Committee in the Cabinet Office in London had foreseen major trouble brewing. An additional Heads of Section group was therefore formed to assess weekly how the threat from the Civil Rights movement was progressing. I was appointed as the Army senior member on behalf of the Defence Intelligence Staff. Each week we attended the Joint Intelligence Committee meeting presided over by a Foreign Office chairman and comprising the chiefs of MI5, MI6 and GCHQ, plus a senior Home Office official and latterly a representative from the Northern Ireland Office, an offshoot of the Home Office, for consideration of the weekly report to go out to Ministers, senior civil servants, Chiefs of Staff in the Ministry of Defence and so on.

For many weeks before the Burntollet Bridge incident that led to Government authorisation for the Army to deploy in support of the

Royal Ulster Constabulary, I had constantly asked for permission to send an officer to liaise with the Special Branch. This was consistently refused, after a regular statement by MI5 that the Special Branch was totally on top of the problem and that everything that needed to be said was in the draft in front of the meeting. In the aftermath of Burntollet Bridge, at which blood had been spilled, I was given permission at last to send an officer to Belfast. I selected an Intelligence Corps major, briefed him myself and sent him on his way. Some days later he returned and rushed into my office with the cry: 'You sent me to liaise with the Special Branch – there is hardly any to be found.' After calming him down I found that there was much substance in his view. Special Branch was indeed very thin on the ground. In their headquarters little effort was available to file reports efficiently. At lower levels there were single officers deployed whose main task was to extract information from the B Special (police reserve) units, exclusively Protestant recruited, and located throughout the Province. These, of course, were IRA orientated rather than building up information about civil rights activists. The end product was that distressingly little intelligence had been collated on those activists that were causing the trouble. I applied at once for permission to be granted by the JIC for Army Intelligence Corps officers and men to be sent over to Northern Ireland to aid the build-up of intelligence by Special Branch and to underpin collation and administration. I went myself to Northern Ireland to talk to the Army Headquarters there with the object of gaining their support for this build-up and to ask for support for this increment. Both ends of the equation agreed and Intelligence Corps build-up started soon thereafter, in line with deployment of Regular Army Units in support of the Royal Ulster Constabulary. At the same time, a number of intelligence staff officers were sent to HQ Northern Ireland Command.

This was the first stage in a very substantial increase of community-wide assets. MI5 appointed a Chief of Intelligence for Northern Ireland and sent several other operatives over. GCHQ entered the field, largely with soldiers and airmen initially. Army intelligence provided a deputy chief. This expansion grew and grew as the IRA belatedly entered the field from 1969 onwards. By 1970 the system was really beginning to pay off, as our weekly JIC reports indicated. Intelligence Corps training for officers and men posted to Northern Ireland was progressively built up at the Centre at Ashford. I found myself going over to Lisburn, Army HQ in the Province, pretty often as events unfolded.

I have already mentioned that Sir Dick White, having already been chief of MI6 and M15 and with a background of outstanding service stretching back to Second World War days, had been appointed in 1969 as the first Coordinator of Intelligence in the Cabinet Office. He was charged with examining the national intelligence structure with a view to recommending improvements. The Foreign Office representative was Christopher Ewart Biggs, who had been in the Blücher Dormitory with me at Wellington, although several years younger than me.

With representatives from the three collecting agencies, we met regularly for some months in the autumn of 1969 to interview witnesses and consider our report. This recommended that the Heads of Sections that had survived from wartime days should be reorganised into the Assessments Staff under a formal Foreign Office chief. The composition of each team within the Assessments Staff to study all available intelligence material, together with unclassified publications, was formalised. Teams for the Middle East, Africa, the Far East, Northern Ireland, and so on remained unchanged. Arrangements for exchanging information with Canada/UK/US countries, plus Australia and New Zealand, were confirmed. In all of this work, Christopher and I worked closely together and out of hours our wives met one another. It was a great shock to Betty and me when, in 1975, Christopher was murdered by the IRA in Dublin, where he had been appointed Ambassador.

Outside Whitehall, my interests proliferated. I had taken up shooting at Ripon. On posting to London I joined the Royal School of Military Engineers shoot at Chatham. As the Navy ran down their shore establishments in the area, the shoot inherited the naval ammunition depot area on the north side of the River Medway and later on the area beyond the dockyard on the south bank. Both areas were productive, so shoot members enjoyed many a day of reasonable bags during the shooting season. It was good to meet many old friends in the Corps of Royal Engineers and to make several new ones. On one occasion the shoot was operating in an area close to the naval dockyard that was still active. I swung at a low-flying bird and spent pellets pattered down onto roofs nearby. An infuriated dockyard matey appeared, red-faced with rage, shouting that he had been hit on the arm by a pellet. A naval member of the shoot was invited to pacify him, as he did not appear to be injured. As the guilty man, I was not popular that day! My membership of this shoot continued for three years until I was posted to Germany, where I joined the Rheindalen Shoot.

Skiing in winter had continued to be an abiding interest once school fees had run down to a less burdensome level. Betty and I went to Austria for several holidays, under arrangements made by the Army Skiing Association. Later we also went to Switzerland several times. We particularly loved Zermatt, where we could manage most pistes if we took our time in doing so. Racing was not our cup of tea.

Gardening was in my blood, coming as I did from forebears who were keen gardeners. With about an acre of garden, the house in Guildford provided much scope. I had always been a keen vegetable gardener. There was a large vegetable patch behind the swimming pool patio and this I brought to a high standard of production for much of the year. My back had largely rebuilt itself after the fall from a ladder in the late summer of 1966, so I did the whole thing myself while Betty concentrated on the flowers. The bane of my life was badgers that had built regular runs through my garden and that of our neighbours. One particular run included a considerable excavation under my back fence. I blocked this with a large and heavy block of concrete. Next day this block had been moved to one side. Later on, Betty and I were woken up by loud crashes and bangs in the night. We got up at once and rushed downstairs thinking that burglars were breaking in. Nothing was found, so we returned to bed. Next day, my neighbour told me that he had found our mutual fence splintered that morning. Badgers had used their powerful fore paws to smash a hole through the fence. I did not try to block the badgers again, although they forbore to thank me.

Swimming was another activity that I had been keen on since Wellington. Bought with the house in Pilgrims Way was a twenty-five-foot pool with a diving springboard opposite the deep end – a delight when the sun shone and the winds were kept at bay by a splendid patio room on the north side. Robin ran several parties at the height of summer in this room and the adjacent pool. Celia and Janet were already working in London, so they benefited less from the amenities of the house in Guildford.

In 1967, Celia announced her engagement to Deane Clark, an architect who worked in London. We had met him on a number of occasions. His parents lived in Southsea, where his father had built up a business of managing a number of houses let to people working in Portsmouth. Soon we were busily engaged in planning the wedding, an expensive business even in those days, and in which Betty bore the brunt of the organisation. Fortunately, dinner dances were then not de rigueur, so we could lay on the marriage in our local Shalford church, followed by a reception at the parish hall on the village green. Guest lists were organised even before we had taken the vital decisions on the total number to be accepted (well over 100), the share each family required, the number to be asked by the bride and bridegroom, and finally the number of local friends to be included. NAAFI were invited to lay on champagne, wedding cake, other refreshments and staff. The wedding dress provided a certain amount of fuss, as did the choice of bridesmaids and the many other arrangements including transport. The great day at last was reached, the marriage service went beautifully, the reception seemed to be enjoyed by all, speeches were mercifully short and the bridal couple departed with due ceremony, tin cans rattling in their wake. Bride and father even reached the church on time.

Within the month Janet announced her engagement, and in the spring of 1968 we were faced with a repeat performance. This time Andrew Baines was the lucky man. He was a serving sapper officer and he had known Janet for many years. His father was also a sapper from a vintage about eighteen months senior to me. Peter Baines was a highly intelligent officer who qualified as a barrister before retiring to a house on the hill west of Rochester. The wedding was a repeat performance of Celia's, and once again the weather was kind, and we were finally able to relax. Only the cost was a problem for some time thereafter, but even that faded away quite quickly.

I used to walk daily to Guildford station, a discipline that helped keep me fit. A second walk, from Waterloo, over the Thames via Charing Cross Railway Bridge to the Ministry of Defence in Whitehall Place, completed my daily sojourn. The train journey was usually amusing in that those in the compartment became known personally as month succeeded month. Twice-yearly visits to Washington broke up the monotony of commuting. There I was looked after by the Defence Intelligence Staff liaison team. They were co-located with the DIA, and in addition the range of other intelligence agencies serving the American administration, notably the CIA, National Security Administration (NSA) that covered the same field as GCHQ, the Air Photography Service that did the same as our JARIC, plus Army, Navy and Air Force Intelligence Agencies that had survived the establishment of the Defence Intelligence Agency (DIA) in a typically American way. The assessments staff for production of national intelligence assessments consisted of a number of retired officers and civilians from all these agencies and produced documents that were models of distillation and deliberation. We in London read every product and set great store by them. Some years later this excellent body was abolished by President Carter, advised by a particularly tiresome Admiral whom he had appointed as Director of the CIA. Ever after, I suspect to this day, each agency presented its own assessment of any situation to the President who picked whichever he and his advisers wished, no doubt to suit their policies. One fears that even in the case of Iraq this pernicious system still prevailed, though this is pure surmise on my part.

Commissioning of Jeremy Nittle into the US Navy at Philadelphia Naval Base, 1969

One diversion from visits to Washington was to take part in the commissioning ceremony for Betty's nephew Jeremy at the US Navy Base in Philadelphia. I flew down from Washington while Betty flew direct from London. Her sister Bridget had asked me to participate as the nearest male relative; her husband had divorced and there was no contact with Bridget and Jeremy, her only son. In the morning I attended the graduation ceremony in Philadelphia University main hall at which Jeremy received his degree, together with a large number of other graduates. After lunch we moved to the Naval Base. Betty was due to arrive at this time at the nearby airfield. She did so and joined me in the hall, where Jeremy was to be commissioned into the US Navy, minutes before the ceremony started. The presiding Admiral administered the oath to the President of the United States to Jeremy and his colleagues, none of whom had been given their degrees at the University that morning. Dressed as a British brigadier in full uniform, I then joined them and pinned the insignia of a sublieutenant in the United States Navy onto Jeremy. The nearest male relatives, mostly fathers, did the same for the remainder. On conclusion of the ceremony we adjourned to the naval base officers mess for suitable refreshments. Throughout, many curious glances were directed my way at my uniform, as can be imagined. It was indeed rare for a brigadier from Britain to take part in such a ceremony.

I have set out these details at some length because, as I moved up the British chain of command of the Defence Intelligence Staff (DIS), so I visited the American Intelligence Community more widely. As BGS (Int) and a single serviceman, I only took in the DIA, Army Intelligence, and courtesy calls on the American collection agencies. I went on to visit Ottawa where again my talks were with their Army element. Both visits were well worthwhile, not least in forging contacts that stood me in good stead in subsequent years. Visits on an easterly course as far as Australia and New Zealand, via the British headquarters in Singapore, were equally useful.

As BGS (Int), I was the Army's man with divided loyalty to the Chief of General Staff and to the Director General of Intelligence. My colleagues as Commodore (Int) serving Naval interests and Air Commodore doing the same for the Air Force were in certain respects more single service in their outlook than I was. Nevertheless, I was not aware of any movement to revert to single service directorates. The merits of a tri-service approach soon proved themselves conclusively, as various international crises required analysis from the military viewpoint in its widest sense. This viewpoint went down equally well with politicians. All of these were served by the Assessments Staff product through the Joint Intelligence Committee to ministers collectively.

Yet the vital provision of serving officers to man an inter-service and civil servant organisation still lay completely within each single service. This paradox remained throughout my time in Defence Intelligence. I was reminded of this when in the autumn of 1969 I was warned that my chance of selection for major-general lay in late 1970. My tenure of duty as BGS (Int) was due to end early in 1970, so I had to wait one more year in some other brigadier appointment. My name was hawked around by the Military Secretary's department. General Sir Desmond Fitzpatrick, whom I had served as Vice-Chief of the General Staff and who had recently gone as Commander-in-Chief to the British Army of the Rhine, said that he would welcome me as his Brigadier General Staff Intelligence & Security at Rheindahlen in Germany. This job also carried with it responsibility as Assistant Chief of Staff Intelligence of Northern Army Group under a German general as Chief of Staff. My case was put before the relevant Board of selection and confirmed. I was due to take over the job in late January 1970.

Meanwhile, I continued with my multifarious duties in London. Northern Ireland remained a major headache, as the IRA progressively ousted the civil rights activists as the opposition to stable government in the Province. A new Chief of General Staff was appointed in late 1969,

General Mike Carver. I well remember my first briefing for him. No doubt with some memory of our previous encounter in Singapore, he scarcely allowed me to get a word in edgeways but harangued me for about twenty minutes on his view of what went on around the world. I retired hurt and next week returned to the charge. Once again my views were not asked for and I was treated to a dissertation of his opinions. On the third occasion I decided that nothing but confrontation would do. Before he could launch into his usual diatribe, I cut in.

'General, I am here to brief you on behalf of the Defence Intelligence Staff. Please allow me the chance to do so.' He looked thunderstruck but allowed me to proceed. I had taken advice from those who knew him – that he only respected those that stood up for themselves. This judgment was correct and ever after he listened to me rather than the other way about. We became reasonably affable with one another, a situation that had its rewards when he became Chief of Defence Staff.

Northern Ireland continued to provide a series of crises as Army deployment in support of the Royal Ulster Constabulary increased in the face of more and more violence instigated by the IRA. Nevertheless, sources of intelligence improved steadily as the Intelligence Corps build-up progressed in support of a Special Branch that itself grew and grew. We still applied interrogation in the same way as had been used against suspects in colonial territories. This included the use of white light in cells to keep suspects from sleeping before interrogation. IRA suspects that had been arrested rapidly told us most of what they knew. In consequence, the Army Commanders and the Northern Irish Government were well briefed on the state of the opposition to stability. The opinion amongst hawks was that during 1969/1970 enough was known to snuff out insurrection, if political authority to take the necessary measures were forthcoming. Unfortunately, Home Office civil servants predominated in the build-up of the Northern Ireland Office. So the necessary decisions were not made by the Government in Whitehall and the opportunity to act decisively was missed.

In due course the IRA protested about Army interrogation methods. This protest was fanned by the media and led to a Commission of Investigation being set up by Whitehall under Lord Scarman. Colonial style methods were banned as a result and, in consequence, intelligence flow from arrests ran down rapidly, leading to less accurate assessments in London and Belfast.

Northern Ireland was peripheral to the main thrust of DIS work, which remained locked on to the Cold War with Russia. Estimates of Russian activity in Eastern Europe and Russia itself, plus influence of anti-western activity in many states throughout the world, remained the bread and butter activity of many of the Defence Intelligence Staff and of the Assessment Staff in the Cabinet Office.

I visited army attachés in many countries on regular tours in the years 1967–1969. Talking to ambassadors, friendly intelligence services and prominent personalities in the country concerned was rewarding.

One visit to the embassy in Lebanon I landed in Beirut, then drove on the switchback route to Damascus in Syria. Here the tanks were on the streets; tension was high as Hafez Assad consolidated his position as an Alawite minority leader of a mixed Islamic community. My contacts were largely confined to the Embassy quarter. We then drove southward, crossed over into Jordan, and spent an hour or two at the remarkable Roman ruins at Jerash. Here I walked down the main street, in which it is still possible to see ruts cut by Roman chariot wheels, to the Roman amphitheatre. We finished at Amman: a trip that is indelibly imprinted on my mind.

In my third year as BGS (Int), I visited Jerusalem once again and stayed with the army attaché. Ari Sharon had by then become the commander of the Northern Front, facing Syria and Lebanon. He insisted that I join him on a short tour along the Israeli salient reaching up to the source of the River Dan. At that time the Syrians had control of the Golan Heights. Their tanks were dug in right on the border so that their guns could fire across the low country occupied by the Israelis. Ari insisted that we should drive along the border perimeter track. As we did so, every Syrian tank turret revolved to follow our path. This was an eerie sensation, but grist to Ari's mill. Despite adverse publicity over operations in Lebanon in 1982, I am not surprised that this brave man became Prime Minister of his country.

On 6 June 1969, 3 Division Association, to which I had belonged since its formation soon after the end of the Second World War, decided to wind itself up by staging a big function over in Normandy. This would wipe out their residual funds. Accommodation had been arranged with French families in Luc sur Mer, close to where I had myself landed in 1944. The day dawned fair and bright. The initial ceremony took place in the War Graves Cemetery adjacent to where Division HQ had set up in 1944. Many hundreds of 3 Division officers and men were buried there. Commemorative stones are beautifully maintained as always, everywhere, by the War Graves Commission. A Church of England service was held in the cemetery, while French schoolchildren carrying flowers took station by each of several hundred gravestones. These included stones for my second-in-command and a subaltern killed by a German aircraft dropping bombs on the beaches on $D + 1$-Day.

For the rest of the day individuals from the Association were free to visit their own particular sites, all meeting again with some hundreds of local French families that evening at a reception paid for by the Association. A meal and much calvados went down the hatch with general approbation. So ended annual visits by 3 Division Association to the Normandy beaches. This body was much missed in latter years, notably the 40th, 50th and, in 2004, the 60th anniversary of the landing.

My three years as BGS (Int) were coming to an end. Betty and I began to plan for a year in Germany. After much discussion, we decided to let our house in Guildford at 1 Pilgrims Way through a local estate agent. A new tenant was soon found, a nice American and his wife who only needed a house like ours for one year. The deal was struck. We planned to move to Germany in late January 1970 leaving a lot of furniture and effects in store as the Americans wanted a largely unfurnished house. This caused certain problems, but with only one remaining child – Robin – having started at university in London, money became a lot easier for the first time in our lives.

The move over to Rheindahlen, some twenty miles north-west of Düsseldorf, went smoothly. I reported to Headquarters Rhine Army – BAOR – which was co-located with Headquarters Northern Army Group in a specially constructed barracks including many married quarters that had been built and supervised by the Royal Engineers works services in the years after the Second World War. I had two staffs to control: one of purely British officers with full access to all sources of intelligence for national purposes; the other of British, German, Dutch and Belgian officers with access slightly limited to intelligence sources that were not of the highest sophistication. This distinction was made, of course, to maintain security on those sources that were for Canada/UK/USA eyes only. This separation pertained in all NATO headquarters from the Supreme Command then in Fontainebleau outside Paris downwards. It could only be changed in the event of hostilities occurring. It seemed to be accepted by all nationalities without dissent: but it did lead to certain problems in handling both staffs side by side, though separate in their offices in different parts of the same building.

Betty and I could and did put up our children. Janet's husband Andrew had been posted to Iserlohn about 100 miles south-east and across the Rhine. Here he commanded a squadron in an Engineer Regiment under command of John Stibbon, who eventually became an Army Board member and Chief Royal Engineer three after me. A splendid family story comes from my daughter Celia, her husband Deane and my son Robin. The latter was studying civil engineering at King's College

London. One day in 1970, they set out in Deane's car to cross the channel and drive up to Rheindahlen through France, Belgium and Germany. On reaching Dover, Robin found that he had left his passport in London. Not a bit abashed, Deane said he was to conceal himself under a mackintosh in the back of his station wagon while the party passed through customs before boarding the ferry. Robin did so and got through immigration undetected. The same procedure was followed in France, Belgium and at the German border late in the evening. Here, Deane found that he had put his passport in the back. A hand came out from under the mackintosh to pass him the passport. Fortunately this hand was undetected in the darkness. The party arrived at Rheindahlen in triumph. The hard part was left in my hands next day – to explain the case to the Embassy consular staff in Bonn and arrange for temporary passport cover to get my son back to London at the end of their holiday.

On another occasion, my son came on holiday with his fiancée, to whom he had got engaged in London. Betty and I were convinced that she was totally unsuitable for him. We worked him over and over, both there and on his return to London, and eventually he broke off his engagement. To round off the story, he only got a third-class honours degree in civil engineering at King's College and decided in consequence to seek his fortune in Australia by going out on an immigrant ship for the subsidised sum of £10. He set off in 1971 for Australia to lodge with my first second-in-command of 38 Engineer Regiment who had retired to a civil engineering job in Perth, Western Australia. On the ship Robin was recruited by a talent scout from the Seventh Day Adventist Church and scarcely saw my contact in Perth before taking a job in the crushing plant of a huge copper mine in the northern part of Western Australia. Ever since, he has continued in this faith, becoming a pastor after a year's course at St Andrew's University across the great lake from Chicago.

Life in Rheindahlen was good value. Despite running two staffs and participating in a couple of exercises on the ground with HQ Northern Army Group, my workload was less demanding than in London. I got on very well with Desmond Fitzpatrick, whom I used to brief each week on the intelligence picture, particularly that pertaining to the Soviet group of Armies in East Germany numbering twenty divisions. Both Chiefs of Staff, British and German, were most congenial, as were my colleagues in HQ and my two staffs. Desmond was a commander of the old school, a cavalryman, stern on the outside but kindly when one got to know him. After retirement he remained as Colonel of the Blues and Royals for many years, accompanying the Queen to her Birthday Parade on Horseguards on horseback.

Exercises with Northern Army Group could be amusing. On one occasion everyone got all packed up and ready to load into vehicles supplied by a Dutch transport company over the border in Holland, when a message came in that most of the vehicles had been sabotaged, by putting sand in petrol tanks, possibly by their Dutch drivers: Dutch loyalty to NATO and, with it, their determination to resist Russian aggression were at that time equally suspect. Eventually German army trucks were sent up from Düsseldorf so that the Headquarters could take the field.

Family life continued with my daughter Janet, her husband Andrew and a dog of indeterminate pedigree. One of our favourite areas to visit from Rheindahlen was the Moselle Valley, then part of the French Zone of occupation of Germany. We arranged for Janet and her dog to meet us there and to spend a night at the French Club in Trier. During the first afternoon we explored the river valley of the Moselle. On the banks of the river we saw the dog rolling in the grass. Little did we know until we got back into the car that the dog had been rolling in some nasty smelly muck. On arrival that evening at the French Club in Trier we dared not take the dog, now christened Moselle Reeker by me, into the Club. Having been allotted rooms, we smuggled Moselle Reeker up to my daughter's room where we had to wash the dog in the bath – an unpleasant task. Still undetected, we managed to get the dog back into the car for the night, as dogs were not allowed in the Club. Next day, after an excellent dinner and night, we departed for another day's exploration of this lovely grape-growing valley.

Another fascinating aspect of my job was that I controlled the policy for BRIXMIS, the British Mission accredited to the Soviet Zone of Occupation of Eastern Germany. They were empowered to proceed anywhere in that zone, subject only to being stopped by Russian troops from entering military areas or Soviet exercises. The East German police, the ubiquitous VOPOs, harassed them wherever they could, but were unable to arrest them. By taking risks it was amazing what pictures they could and did take of Russian troops, for example crossing the River Elbe on their latest bridges and ferries. Their information was grist to the mill of my old organisation, the Defence Intelligence Staff in London, and was sent on to both Paris and Washington. American and French teams operated in a similar manner in East Germany and divided the territory into three parts. BRIXMIS were based in Berlin together with a station from GCHQ, largely manned by service people. Various other intelligence-gathering activities were mounted from Berlin. One of these I had taken part in during 1956/57.

BRIXMIS, commanded by a British brigadier, operated in the southern part of East Germany including the Meissen showrooms just north of that city. On my first visit to Berlin to talk to them I was told that their team occasionally visited these showrooms and could buy me some Meissen porcelain pieces. The exchange rate was at that time five East marks for one West German mark, so payment in West marks paid off handsomely, and I commissioned several purchases. I still have these beautiful objets d'art, my favourite being an otter. On the bottom of each is the famous blue Meissen logo.

Another adjunct to being BGS (Int) was that I had access to the Russian Military Mission that operated in the British sector of West Germany in a similar way to BRIXMIS. On one occasion I notified them that I wished to visit, and was received by the Russian General then commanding them and his staff. The guessing game was to decide which of these were GRU full-time intelligence agents, and which were seconded serving officers. All were kept under surveillance as best we could, but they operated under the same rules as BRIXMIS, so they enjoyed considerable freedom of movement throughout the British sector of West Germany. On occasion they had been arrested and cautioned but they at least did not get shot at, as did BRIXMIS. What they made of my visit I have no idea.

Rheindahlen was a remarkable place for getting around West Germany. Not only did I get away into the French sector but I also visited the American part of southern Germany by visiting their headquarters in Heidelberg. For our summer holidays Betty and I put our car onto a car train at Cologne and travelled through the night to Italy. We booked a room in a hotel at Lido de Iesolo near Venice. This allowed us to go by the day into Venice itself using the ferry a few miles west of our hotel. The lagoon and the canals, the buildings and bridges, the art galleries and the gondoliers all became well-known to us. What a gem Venice is; it is a tragedy that the place is slowly sinking and becomes ever more prone to flooding. Remedial action to build barrages to protect the city from sea encroachment seems very slow to get started even now.

Within West Germany two other ports of call needed regular visitations. These were the British Corps HQ at Bielefeld, that was responsible for tactical command of the British divisions facing the Russians, and similar headquarters for the Belgian forces east of the Rhine. Contact in intelligence terms had also to be made with German Army headquarters commanding German territorial units in the British sector. The Dutch did not have a headquarters in the British sector, as troops from North Holland were to move forward in the event of

Russian attack. All of these needed to know the British assessment of Russian plans in the event of Moscow ordering an assault. They also wanted to hear our views on the success of deterrence and our best guess at likelihood.

Shooting with the Rheindahlen shoot was great fun. We covered a lot of ground and shot a lot of birds, often with local landowners and farmers. The Germans were great ones for shooting etiquette and were always immaculately turned out, sometimes putting us Brits to shame. Betty used to come beating on fine days.

That autumn I heard from the Military Secretary in London that I had been selected to become a major-general the following February and in that rank would be returning again to the Defence Intelligence Staff as Director of Service Intelligence. Betty and I made our preparations to take back our house in Guildford from the American tenants. After celebrating Christmas with our family in the quarter in Rheindahlen, a house that we had much enjoyed, we said farewell to a lot of new friends there and set off home for England in late January 1971, in a car packed to the roof with household effects, including the contents of our drink cupboard. We reached Dover in the early hours of the morning and were subjected to the usual customs ordeal. I declared a quarter-bottle of this liqueur and a half-bottle of that. Customs, in their usual bloody-minded fashion, insisted on charging me on each and every bottle from my drink cupboard. Sadder, though not wiser, we drove on to Guildford for breakfast in our own house. A year spent serving in West Germany meant nothing to the British customs!

CHAPTER 9

London (1971–1975) DS (Int) then Deputy Chief of Defence Staff (Intelligence)

When I returned to London from Germany, the sixties were well over. I had had to sell our cottage in Charlton near Andover because of the announcement that a new town to house East Enders from London was to be built north of Andover. Examination of the detailed plans showed that new building was proposed right down to the back fence of the cottage, swallowing up green and scrubby fields. I put Appletree Cottage on the market at once. To my surprise, I sold it quickly, albeit at a low price that was still the going rate at that time. I decided to put the money into Betty's name and to buy a small flat in London. Betty became the proud owner of a first-floor flat in Marsham Court, Marsham Street, Westminster that was only fifteen minutes' walk from the Ministry of Defence in London via Parliament Square. This flat was let when I returned to London for duty with the Defence Intelligence Staff (DIS) once again, at the enhanced level of Major-General, Director of Service Intelligence; I began to commute to my work in London from Guildford, where we had reoccupied our house.

Organisation in the DIS was unchanged since my long stint as BGS (Int), though personalities were changing by rotation between the Services at the top levels. During my time in Germany, Lieutenant General Sir Dick Fyffe had been replaced by Air Marshal 'Mac' MacGuire, who was earmarked by the Air Force to become Director General later in 1971. Mac was a delightful Irishman who had graduated from Trinity College, Dublin, just before the war. He joined the Air Force and as a wing commander was taken prisoner by the Japanese in Java. He became senior officer in the camp for prisoners outside Batavia, now Jakarta. After an escape by some prisoners from this camp, he was punished by the Japanese commandant by being buried in the parade-ground up to his neck for three days. He survived and, post-war, rose through the Air Force ranks to become an air marshal. I saw much of both him and his delightful wife over the next few years. The more I saw of him, the more I liked him. As an ex-prisoner of war of the

Japanese, he was less affected by imprisonment than any POW that I ever came across. As DGI, he was asked by the Japanese Government to visit their intelligence machinery in Tokyo. After some heart-searching and consultation amongst his staff, including me, he decided to accept: all credit to him for doing so. In 1971, he took over as Director General and, as it was the Navy's turn, his replacement was Vice Admiral Sir Louis Le Bailly, a naval engineer. Lou was a man of firm convictions. Amongst other attributes, he enjoyed writing to *The Times* and being published in their 'Letters' columns. Some years before he had commanded Manadon, the naval technical college at Plymouth. He came to the DIS with a high reputation for brains but lacked any previous experience in intelligence analysis and staff work. He therefore relied much on me for support. This was to prove to my advantage, as this narrative will illustrate.

In my new directorate, I controlled the work of four area staffs covering the entire world. The largest of these were the three single service staff branches covering Soviet forces threatening NATO Europe. Their heads at colonel level were directly responsible to me. The other three covered the rest of the world, each under a colonel level staff officer. Our most important product was frequent assessment of Soviet capabilities and intentions. Northern Ireland also figured high on the list of targets for assessment. Crises in the Arab world, tension between India and Pakistan, troubles in Rhodesia, now Zimbabwe, all these and more figured in our daily briefings to the Director General and weekly offerings to the Joint Intelligence Committee in the Cabinet Office. Here I rejoined the mess for Cabinet Office, Foreign Office, and other civil servants plus Ministry of Defence officers and civil servants. As ever, conversations and contacts over the lunch table were of great value to me.

Late that summer, as anticipated, 'Mac' MacGuire was promoted to Director General and in his place came Lou Le Bailly. He allowed me full rein in handling those cases with which he found himself unfamiliar. In the autumn tension between India and Pakistan grew and grew. Assessment Staff products were ever more regularly produced for the Joint Intelligence Committee to discuss and promulgate to Ministers, senior civil servants, Chiefs of Staff, and so on. Lord Peter Carrington was at that time Minister of Defence under Edward Heath as Prime Minister. He began to send for the DCDS (I) regularly. I also went to act as spokesman for the DIS staff view. Based on what I said, Lord Carrington then went off to cabinet meetings.

An attack duly took place. Lord Carrington was called to Number Ten for a Cabinet Meeting. He insisted that I should accompany him to

Number Ten and said that he had cleared with the Prime Minister that I should speak first at the Cabinet Meeting. Frantic telephoning took place to the Joint Intelligence Committee chairman, the Co-ordinator of Intelligence and to the Foreign Office, to ensure that what I should say was in keeping with JIC assessments. I duly appeared in the Cabinet Room and said my piece. One or two questions were thrown at me that suggested divergence of view on which country would win. I stuck to the DIS and JIC line. The Prime Minister thanked me and I withdrew.

So ended the first of a number of appearances at the side of Lord Carrington until the upshot of the Indian attack was plain for all to see. In addition, I was called on two occasions to brief the Prime Minister and his Private Secretary in his office in Number Ten on the progress of the war. These briefings were late in the evening; despite this the door of Number Ten opened as I approached. I was escorted upstairs to give my account. After questions from the Prime Minister, he nodded to show that I could go. This I did with no offer of a glass of something to sustain me that late in the evening. Such is the life of those serving in Whitehall. Quite a different atmosphere pertained when, soon after, the Head of the Assessments Staff and I were summoned to Chequers at a weekend to report on the latest scene in Pakistan as seen by the JIC. We were received by Edward Heath with courtesy and a drink while introductions were made for those of his colleagues present. We said our piece to the assembled company and drove back to London in good order. I must stress that all these top-level briefings were based on the excellent analysis and judgement by the staff of DI2 that dealt with the Far East. Their reading of the India–Pakistan War was very good indeed.

As it turned out, contact direct with Mr Heath paid off handsomely. Lou Le Bailly was due to move up to Director General from DCDS (I) in the late summer of 1972. It was the turn of the Royal Air Force to provide his replacement. That spring, I believe, a submission went from the Ministry of Defence to Number Ten, giving an Air Force name to replace Lou. I never heard who this was but I believe he had no previous intelligence experience. Back came the Prime Minister's comments. As told to me subsequently by Lou, these were that the Defence Ministry already had a suitable candidate, one Willison by name, and the PM could not understand why he had not been appointed. This really put the cat amongst the Whitehall pigeons, as the question of Buggins's turn was at issue. After much dispute, of which I was blissfully unaware at the time, the Air Force conceded and the Army accepted that I should fill the post in the rank of lieutenant general, even though I had only been a major-general for about twenty months. This was a fantastic stroke of luck for me as I had hitherto expected to be retired after the one job as a major-general. Career prospects up to that rank only ran to fifty-five years of age, whereas lieutenant generals and above could be employed until aged sixty.

I have gone way beyond a proper account of my time as Major-General, Director of Service Intelligence. This was a most satisfying job. The main thrust as always was towards reading out the nature of the threat to NATO from Soviet Russia and the states of Eastern Europe subservient to Moscow. This culminated each summer in a large conference in Brussels. Americans, British, Canadians, French, Germans, Dutch, Belgians, Turks, Greeks – all were there to redraft annually what was called MC161, the threat to NATO. The intelligence staff of SHAPE were there, headed by a British major-general; altogether it was a huge gathering of intelligence experts. They all met for the best part of two weeks each year to draft a new paper that would provide the basis of all levels of planning throughout NATO, Europe and North America, for the following year. The end product was classified at a level of security below that which extended amongst Canada/UK/US-eyes-only products. However, cells existed in every NATO headquarters to hold this product for use in time of war, where further intelligence existed beyond that releasable to national and international staffs in peace.

As can be expected, much time had to be expended in argument with other national staffs over details of the contents of the MC161. This had to be produced in various drafts for submission to Heads of National Intelligence before being promulgated. DCDS (I) and his opposite number in the Defense Intelligence Agency (DIA) in Washington normally attended in person for much of the conference, as did many other national chiefs of intelligence. The staffs of DI3 (Navy, Army and Air Force) were strongly engaged throughout these proceedings.

Nations vied with one another to stage evening entertainment for the assembled company. In addition, dinner parties in that excellent street of restaurants behind the Grand Platz in Brussels were also staged. Each year, my consumption of mussels was prodigious. Brussels is rightly renowned for the quality of these shellfish and indeed for the overall quality of dinners on offer. One needed to get into training for the annual MC161 conference in that city!

Preparation for Brussels meant visiting Washington and Ottawa beforehand to locate points of disagreement that naturally cropped up. Intelligence analysis is not an exact science; examination of some of the raw material would, and did, lead to disagreement on findings, and these had to be argued out in detail. In Washington itself the CIA, DIA and

NSA (National Security Agency) disagreed on occasion on the weight that could be attached to a source. Thankfully in London the work of the Cabinet Office normally ironed out contrary views between collectors, the DIS and the Foreign Office. But all this took a lot of staff work; DS (Int) was embedded in all this argument in a big way. All this is pertinent to the furore following the issue of the Hutton Report in 2004. Intelligence analysis must rely at least in part on human judgement, and is never a wholly mechanical process.

The Defence Intelligence Staff covered the whole world. Events in the Arab World, throughout Africa and the Far East, in Central and South America and in Europe, including those at sea and in the air, were ours to record and analyse. I have already mentioned the Indo/Pakistan war. Vietnam continued to be headline news throughout the period that I filled the post of DS (Int). The JIC weekly assessments, based upon our military assessment of the progress of the war, were often contentious. My visit there in 1968 was still a help in 1971/1972 in appreciating the finer points of what went on. The argument continued over in America as DIA, NSA and CIA all had slightly divergent views, not least on the value of air bombardment against the Ho Chi Minh trails through Cambodia. I have a vivid memory of air photography of a moon-like landscape churned up by repeated bombing; yet visible through it all were Viet Cong bulldozers clearing a path for trucks and men to move. This convinced me, if not the American audience, that supplies would always get through whatever the Americans might throw at them. Events through to a ceasefire showed that this had in fact happened.

Washington remained a crucial place to cultivate for many reasons. As a major-general I was able to penetrate the fastnesses of the large American intelligence network. I enjoyed successive visits to the DIA where Danny Graham, whom I had first met in Vietnam, was now a two-star officer. The CIA at Langley opened their doors to me and I enjoyed many fruitful discussions with their analytical staff, though not with their operational chiefs. NSA were very kind in showing me what they got up to and in discussing with me the topics of the day. Danny Graham was a tower of strength. Down the years, I stayed with him and got to know him and his wife very well. In due course he became head of the DIA as a three-star general, while I had become the three-star DCDS (I) in London.

I did not neglect to go eastward as well as across the Atlantic. I went as far as both Australia and New Zealand for talks with their respective defence intelligence staffs. One diversion was to visit Jakarta in Indonesia to talk to their equivalent of the Institute of Strategic Studies. I gave them a carefully edited dissertation on how we in London saw their part of the world. Question time lasted for more than an hour. Judging by the questions asked, the Indonesian military were well served by some good brains amongst their numbers. I managed to get driven up to the Poentjak Pass where in 1946 1 Seaforth had been stationed. The major change to the landscape was the clearance of much secondary jungle and the planting of tea bushes in serried ranks. I bought some thoroughly drinkable tea that Betty and I enjoyed back home.

I kept no papers from this time, not even a diary, so I find it difficult to put events in order, as I subsequently served three full years as DCDS (I), followed by almost three years as Director General of Intelligence (DGI), all in London with the DIS. I continued to belong to the Cabinet and Defence Staff Mess in the Cabinet Office throughout.

At this point, it may help the reader if I present a summary of the posts I held from 1971 to 1978.

From to January 1971 to August 1972, I was Director of Service Intelligence, as a major-general.

In September 1972, I was appointed to be Deputy Chief of Defence Staff (Intelligence) as a lieutenant general.

In September 1975, I was appointed to be Director General of Intelligence, as a civil servant, a Deputy Under-Secretary, retiring in August 1975 from the Army.

I remember vividly the characters of the political masters that had to be served throughout this period. In 1970, while I was away in Germany, the Conservatives under Mr Heath came to power. After the winter of discontent, Mr Heath went to the country in 1974 and was defeated by Labour. Mr Harold Wilson took over as Prime Minister and remained until he unexpectedly resigned in favour of Mr Callaghan towards the end of my time as DGI. I had retired by the time that Margaret Thatcher came to power. This meant that for my latter years in Whitehall, Labour Ministers were in office. I shall expand on them as this narrative progresses.

Within the Ministry of Defence I got to know the Minister of State, Edward Gilmour. Curiously enough, when I got married, for the second time, to Trisha Clitherow in 1994, I discovered that she had bought her house in the heart of Lymington from Gilmour's mother back in 1977 soon after her first husband, a naval commander, died of a heart attack. Gilmour dealt, amongst other things, with weapon development, so on occasion I had to brief him on what was the latest information about Russian technical developments in the Soviet Armed Forces. I formed the view that he did not have the intellectual capacity of his boss, the Secretary of Defence.

Deputy Chief of Defence Staff (Intelligence), 1972–75

As 1972 drew on, the announcement was made publicly that Lou Le Bailly was to be appointed Director General in September and I would replace him as Deputy Chief of Defence Staff (Intelligence), so that my days as DS (Int) were drawing to a close, although with no diminution of workload, as a number of parts of the world continued to see strife and mayhem. Relations with Lou continued to deepen as his knowledge of defence intelligence analysis and staff work developed fast. We made a good team, both within the Ministry of Defence and across the road in the Cabinet Office. In view of his promotion, I continued to act as spokesman in many situations. These included cultivation of Foreign Office contacts. Through so many tours down the years, I had already met many Ambassadors who occasionally returned to the Foreign Office as heads of departments, usually at Under-Secretary level: and the previous contact proved useful.

In Guildford, Betty and I continued to extend our range of local friends. One of these was general manager of the Mirror Group of Newspapers, who lived in a house on a parallel road to ours further up Guildford Hill. He persuaded me to buy a joint share in a 28-footer of French origin that was to be kept up the Hamble River at Moody's yard. I therefore resumed yachting in the summer of 1972, this time in a much larger boat than the dinghies I had been used to for so many years. Perforce I had to learn deep-sea navigation, an art that he understood but which was new to me. We made several joint cruises that year, including one across the Channel to Cherbourg and on to the Channel Islands at Guernsey. This voyage really whetted my appetite for a larger boat and, after one more season, I bought him out, as I was allowed to do under the terms of the written agreement that we had signed before the original purchase had taken place. This had been drawn up by a solicitor at my partner's insistence and covered every eventuality, a wise precaution in both our interests. Every summer thereafter, Betty and I spent afloat as I progressively honed my skill as captain and navigator. I found sailing a marvellous antidote to the rigours of life in Whitehall. Most of August 1972 was spent at sea in the Channel during my leave between jobs.

For the next three years Lou and I formed a strong team. As DGI he concentrated on management of civilian employees, organisation and public relations, whilst I took on intelligence judgement at the highest level. Both of us were full members of the JIC in the Cabinet Office. He advised ministers in the Ministry of Defence, while I was a member of the Chiefs of Staff Committee, answerable to the Chief of Defence Staff and to Service Chiefs of Staff. He concentrated on the large number of civilians in the DIS whilst I did the same for serving officers and men on that staff. He had to retire from the Navy to become a Deputy Under-Secretary in the Civil Service, following the precedent set by Kenneth Strong, the first DGI back in 1964.

The DCDS (I) office consisted of a serving major level officer as Military Assistant and a Civil Service PA of middle rank, with a chief clerk presiding over a supporting staff of typists and filing clerks. Soon after my arrival I wrote to the Engineer-in-Chief, head of my own Corps of Royal Engineers, to ask for a sapper as my military assistant. He wrote

Cruising with Betty, 1980

back to say that suitable staff officers recently qualified at the Staff College at Camberley were in short supply, and therefore it was not possible to meet my request. I sent for him and explained that any young sapper, with a lieutenant general for his first reporting officer, was made for life if he did well. (I should add that the Engineer-in-Chief was a major-general.) He still refused to produce anyone on the grounds that the Corps was suffering from a shortage of young majors. Foiled in this way, I unburdened my soul to John Gibbon, Vice Chief of the Defence Staff, whom I had got to know well. As a gunner officer he told me to leave it in his hands. Twenty-four hours later he was on the phone to say that he had found a young gunner recently out of Camberley who answered my requirements. This turned out to be Alex Harley, who suited me admirably. Much later he became an Army Board member as Adjutant General and is now Master Gunner of St James's Park.

My experience with the Corps of Royal Engineers deepened in 1973 when Charles Richardson, Chief Royal Engineer, asked me to lunch. He had succeeded my old enemy, 'Splosh' Jones, as Chief Royal Engineer a year or so before. After lunch he asked me if I would like to become a Colonel Commandant of the Royal Engineers. I said I would and in October 1973 I was so appointed. The Corps has twelve colonels commandant, including the Chief Royal Engineer, who, in other parlance, is really colonel of the regiment, an honorary position. He farms out duties to the remainder and initially I was asked to oversee Corps shooting. To my chagrin I was too busy in Whitehall to do much to follow this up, as I should have done. But the appointment allowed me to regain contact with the Corps that lasted until the end of 1982 on my final retirement as Chief Royal Engineer.

I well remember my first appearance at a meeting of the Chiefs of Staff in the Ministry of Defence. The three Chiefs of Staff were grouped round the Chief of Defence Staff at the head of the long conference table. Further down sat the Vice Chief of Defence Staff (John Gibbon) and the two Deputies, myself for intelligence and the other for equipment, with the Chiefs of Staff Secretariat, headed by a one-star officer, at the foot to take notes that were later edited and issued as the rulings of the great men. Sir Peter Hill Norton was in the chair as Chief of Defence Staff, with Admiral Le Fanu as Chief of Naval Staff, General Sir Michael Carver as Chief of the General Staff, and Air Chief Marshal Sir John Grandy, the Chief of Air Staff. I had to give tongue in due course to brief on the hot topics of the day, notably the scene in Moscow and the latest on the war in Vietnam. I felt a bit nervous to begin with but soon warmed to my task. Then the services business of the day was discussed; at that time the prolonged Navy versus Air Force argument over carriers versus fixed wing aircraft kept cropping up.

Each week for the next three years I attended Chiefs of Staff meetings when I was in London. Each week also I took my seat in the Cabinet Office conference room for meetings of the JIC. This was normally presided over by a Foreign Office Chairman at Deputy Under-Secretary level, flanked by the Coordinator for Intelligence in the Cabinet Office. This post was normally filled by a retired Chief of MI5, MI6 or GCHQ. Members of the JIC were the current heads of these three organisations, the DGI and myself from the Ministry of Defence, the head of the Assessments Staff, normally Foreign Office, the various heads of geographic assessments staff teams for current intelligence, and the JIC secretariat headed by a one-star level officer seconded from one of the agencies represented round the table.

Briefings for these meetings took much time and effort from the Defence Intelligence Staff. In addition, we had briefings each morning from the staff of DS (Int) and the Directorate of Scientific and Technical Intelligence as appropriate. Within this framework of meetings the normal activities of the day were interwoven. These included numerous other meetings, both staff and visitors from elsewhere in Whitehall, and, never to be forgotten, the reading of endless reports and snippets of intelligence material. No wonder it was necessary to arrive daily in the office at an early hour and to leave late.

This load was increased by social duties which included numerous invitations from embassies and to other MoD functions. I found myself courted by the editor of *The Diplomatist*, the magazine of the mass of foreign embassies accredited to the Court of St James. His staff insisted on taking my picture at embassy functions, and it appeared regularly in the magazine. His deputy was a beautiful Irish girl who attended most of these functions. It had so happened that after some months of living in London during the week in our flat in Marsham Street, Betty decided that it was better to stay most of the time in the house in Guildford, so I had to go to many of these parties on my own. The Irish girl was always there, and we got to know each other well. I progressed to the stage of asking her to lunch with me on several occasions and even to dinner at a restaurant in Holland Park on one occasion. Afterwards she drove me home in her car and dropped me outside Marsham Court. I told Betty about these events and unfortunately she got the scorecard wrong. On her next visit to London she went to the Irish girl's office and had a bit of a to-do with her. Needless to say, this was the end of my friendship with the girl.

My creature comforts were better looked after as a Lieutenant General. I was allotted a car from the MoD pool and an excellent civilian driver, who lived with his parents in the East End of London. George Mattocks drove me not only in England but even over to Belgium for yearly MC161 sessions in Brussels. I was fortunate enough to get him to drive for me once again as DGI, and so our relationship therefore lasted for six full years. Even thereafter as chief Royal Engineer until the end of 1982, he always got to hear of my occasional requests for an MoD staff car and was there to drive me as usual. I still hear from him to this day. Added to this luxury, I had both a flat in London and a house in Guildford. George Mattocks drove me to work each day, took me to receptions of an evening, and generally made life a lot easier by virtue of my not having to rely any more upon public transport or even Shanks's pony.

In the Birthday Honours of June 1973 my name appeared under the list of appointments by the Queen as KCB. Added to an OBE awarded in 1959 and MC dating from 1945, this meant quite a useful array of gongs and other ribbons. I received a confidential letter several weeks beforehand that the Queen had honoured me with being created a Knight. From the date of the list being published I could call myself Sir David. Better still, Betty could also benefit and henceforth would be known as Lady Betty. The final stage was to present myself for an investiture at Buckingham Palace. Both daughters attended, and new hats and dresses had to be provided. (My son was away in Australia.) The great day dawned, and George Mattocks appeared to take us to the Palace. There my family was escorted to the spectators' gallery in the Throne Room. I was led away for briefing on procedure, before joining the line awaiting the investiture itself. One by one we came forward, bowed to the Queen, went down on one knee on a cushion, were duly dubbed on both shoulders with the Queen's sword, and after a few words could move on to join the family. Afterwards came photographs and away to my club – the In and Out – for a celebratory lunch. This was indeed a special day.

As DCDS (I), I got a substantial entertainment allowance from the DGI. I joined the Royal Thames Yacht Club. Here I ran functions for the diplomatic community of defence attachés. The DIS included a section for looking after defence attachés with officers of all three services represented. This staff set up drinks parties and occasional dinners. Once a year the attachés en masse, plus their wives, were invited to watch the Queen's Birthday Parade on Horseguards and to lunch thereafter. The DGI and I were there to greet them, aided by the Attaché Liaison Section. Seats were allotted on the corner stand outside the drab slab of the wartime Admiralty Building, where the Queen's procession from the Mall turned right from Buckingham Palace Road and then left onto Horseguards. Her Majesty always waved to us as she came past the stand.

I had a call from the Defence Services Secretary to ask if I could find a job for Prince Michael of Kent. I thought of the Attaché Liaison Staff where a vacancy for an army officer was coming up. Prince Michael duly reported for duty and very good he was in cultivating the mass of army attachés serving in London.

Amongst many others, I got to know the Indian Defence Adviser, a Sikh major-general. He invited me to call in on Delhi during my forthcoming tours of the world. These usually occurred in winter, starting in the autumn of 1972. Another acquaintance was the Japanese defence attaché. One day in 1973 he told me that the Japanese Ministry of Defence would be delighted if I could visit Tokyo. Delhi therefore became an annual visit and, in late 1973, I visited Tokyo, as this narrative will show.

In the autumn of 1972, I carried out my first visit to Washington and Ottawa as DCDS (I). I went round the houses in Washington to call on all the various agencies that constituted the American intelligence community. I was based on the DIS liaison staff that lived with the DIA and much of my time was spent talking with their experts on various parts of the world, notably Vietnam. Here a ceasefire was already in sight. This came to fruition in 1973. With the CIA, I discussed the latest developments in Russian weapon development. One topic of some fascination was the curious craft seen on the Caspian Sea, colloquially known as the Caspian Sea monster. Much speculation took place as to whether this puzzling craft was making use of the surface tension of the lake water. In fact nothing ever came of this trial vessel, though at the time naval interest was intense. I also went round the US Navy, Army and Air Force intelligence staffs to discuss their technical intelligence programmes. NSA remained a most important agency for discussion of many topics.

Ottawa was also good value. Canadian intelligence was organised much as was ours, without Naval, Army and Air counterparts. I valued discussions with various elements of analytical effort and had a talk with their equivalent of Chief of Defence Staff. Later that autumn I set out eastward on a further tour starting in Cyprus, where the British continued to base collection facilities, notably the army- and air-manned MOD stations. I then moved on to Delhi. Scotty, godfather to my daughter Janet, had become a major-general as Defence Adviser to the High Commissioner to India. I stayed with him in a delightful house provided by the Foreign Office not far from Army HQ in Delhi. I went to this imposing structure for several days for discussions with the chiefs of Army, Navy and Air Force intelligence that were still autonomous in the Indian set-up, as we had been until 1964. They were understandably reticent about Russian developments because of their reliance on Brezhnev's Soviet Russia for equipment and doctrine. I flew on next to Singapore for liaison talks with the local JIC, the Service Commanders and their intelligence staffs. From Singapore I flew BOAC back to the UK to resume the normal run of meetings, briefings, reading and so on that characterised my existence in Whitehall. My tour report went out to all and sundry in the Whitehall community.

In the summer of 1973, Betty and I started to go down to the Hamble at weekends to put to sea in our newly-acquired jointly-owned boat. This, as I have already recorded, was immensely relaxing, a most necessary function after the rigours of each week in Whitehall. On occasion, even then, meetings were required on Saturdays and Sundays. This was a pretty rigorous existence, mitigated by sailing at some weekends and a longer break for the summer holidays.

1973 was the year of the last serious war between Israel and Egypt. By this time briefing of Ministers, Chiefs of Staff and top-level civil servants had been modernised. Closed-circuit television had been installed for all recipients of JIC reports. In the event of a serious military clash, the JIC written word went out to all entitled recipients, followed by a briefing conference at which questions could be asked by ministers from the Prime Minister downwards and answers given by spokesmen from the Foreign Office, Ministry of Defence and other relevant collecting agencies responsible for reports quoted in the JIC assessment. Because of the war, I selected our spokesman from my old branch of DI4, whose work dealt directly with Middle East affairs, to answer any questions. Feverish discussion in-house occurred as to the line that he should follow in the initial briefing as to how we saw the war developing and what questions should be anticipated, together with proposed answers. This meant rapid reading of relevant material from all collection agencies, leading to a decision on what line to adopt.

The 1973 war started with an Egyptian assault across the Suez Canal that surprised the thin Israel defences. Soon their reserves took to the field in hard fighting in the Sinai Desert to stem the Egyptian advance. By this time Ari Sharon had retired from full-time service, but he was instantly recalled as a reserve general. He was appointed to a reserve force of tanks and infantry that rapidly managed to cross the Suez Canal at the north end of the Great Bitter Lake – a typical example of his leadership. Through the bridgehead that he established on the Egyptian bank poured a mass of Israeli armour. When the Egyptians asked for peace, Israeli tanks were well on their way to Cairo on the desert road that I knew so well. Naturally, I played a leading part in reading out the military situation day by day, as the war progressed up to the Egyptian decision to sue for peace. I think our read-out of what was happening in practice on the ground was reasonably accurate. Our spokesman did brilliantly in answering questions daily.

The next major event for me was news that my application for an MoD VIP Comet to fly me to Australia via Tokyo in November had been approved by the Permanent Under-Secretary MoD. This machine, operated by the RAF, was one of several converted for use by VIPs. The Comet, it will be remembered, was the first jet airliner of its kind. It was built for use by British Airways but the prototype had a window blown out on trial. It was back to the drawing board for the designers, and British Airways refused to put the refurbished aircraft into service, so the Government authorised only a very small number to be completed after modification. I was allowed to take my wife and my military assistant, plus any officers, men and women awaiting air transport, on each leg of my proposed course to India, Japan and Australia. If at any time during the journey a Minister required the aircraft, my MA and I could fly on by civil aircraft, whilst I should have to pay for my wife to fly home. I accepted this gamble. The first leg of our great journey was to join the aircraft at Lyneham with a view to flying to RAF Akrotiri in Cyprus. Betty and Alex Harley were thrilled as George Mattocks drove us to spend the night with Lou Le Bailly at their house in Wiltshire near Swindon. Next morning George drove us on to Lyneham. We took off at 0800 hours with a full complement of those awaiting a flight to Cyprus, plus Pam Aitken, wife of the Air Commander-in-Chief, who joined us in the VIP suite of the Comet. After a stunning flight, looked after so well by the RAF staff, we reached Akrotiri to spend the night with the General Officer Commanding Cyprus, Hugh Butler, and his wife Joanne. Early next day we re-embarked to fly to Bahrain by the normal route over Turkey and Iran for lunch with the Ambassador. That evening we reached Delhi to stay with the Scott Bowdens, Defence Adviser to the British High Commissioner.

Next day, Alex and I started work in GHQ Delhi after preliminary briefings in the High Commission. Jos Scott-Bowden, meanwhile, took Betty out to see the sights of Delhi. That afternoon we drove down to Agra, some four hours in all along the Grand Trunk Road. We put up in Clark's Shiraz Hotel and that evening walked down to see the Taj Mahal by moonlight – a magical sight. Looked at down the reflecting pool, the design is so skilful that the façade looks flat – an optical illusion. We returned to the hotel by bicycle trishaw for supper and bed. Up early, we drove down to the Taj Mahal before the crowds arrived by coach. We really appreciated the intricate beauty of the decoration and of the inset jewels, above looters' reach, that glinted in the sun. Next step was Fatipur Sikri, Akhbar's abandoned capital city, built of rose-red stone quarried locally. Conservation was started at British instigation in 1876. Judging by the mass of Indian tourists in their bright colours, preservation had proved a success. We motored on to the nature reserve of Bharatpur to meet Scotty and his family and see the birds, from six-foot high painted storks to tiny honey-eaters. Finally, we drove back to Delhi via the great ruined fort at Digne.

Monday meant back to the grindstone for me in GHQ Delhi, culminating in dinner given by General Chandoorka after a drinks party for senior Indian officers in the Scott-Bowden establishment. Our old Indian friends from IDC days in Belgrave Square were included. On 6 November the faithful RAF Comet that had waited for us at Palam airport took off for Bangkok. En route we could see the pink and gold peaks of the Himalayas shining through the distant blue mist at the horizon, the highest being Everest. After only a little over four hours we landed in Bangkok to be met by the military attaché and taken to a delicious lunch party, while he briefed Alex and me on the local picture. After lunch we flew on to Hong Kong, passing over Cambodia and the Vietnamese coast. Landing in Hong Kong by night is always magical; the lights from skyscraper blocks, the hillsides and from ships in the harbour are a wonderful sight as the aircraft swoops down low over the rocky ridges of the New Territories to land. That night we spent with the GOC and his wife in the old residence on the island, a house of great comfort and ease.

On 7 November, Alex and I spent the day talking with the intelligence community. In the evening beating retreat took place in the garden of King's House followed by a reception for the notables of Hong Kong, mostly Chinese. Dinner with the Caters was great fun. He had been at the IDC with me and was now Deputy Governor. 8 November was equally interesting. A visit to the radar station on Mount Tai Mo Shan, the highest mountain in the New Territories, was great value. 9 November found us in the air once more heading for Japan. Betty rested after her strenuous programme in Hong Kong while Alex and I worked on my tour report plus preparation for the forthcoming visit to the Japanese Ministry of Defence in Tokyo. At Nagoya, a Japanese air force base, the aircraft refuelled. We were looked after by a Japanese Air Force general and encountered the Japanese custom of bowing. In Tokyo we were met by our Japanese host and his wife; a Vice Admiral, he was chairman of their joint planning staffs. Fortunately, they both spoke good English as they had served in London. Nevertheless, we had to go through the customary ceremonies of welcome, including bouquets given to Betty with many deep bows. An hours drive followed, to the Palace Hotel in Tokyo opposite the Imperial Palace. Dinner was with the defence attaché, Brigadier Hefill, and his wife to meet the other British attachés.

Next day was Saturday. After lunch we struggled through the dense Tokyo traffic to the Central Station to catch the 'Bullet Train' to Kyoto. Grand Central Station was so busy that it had to be seen to be believed. Japanese columns, led by cheerleader boards held aloft, snaked through the station foyer in what seemed to be hundreds. Led by the naval attaché with his arm held aloft, our small party threaded its way to the requisite platform where we had to stand on a marked spot shown on our ticket. The train drew up with the marked door exactly opposite our position. A couple of hours later, after reaching 140 miles per hour en route, the train arrived dead on time. Opposite the exit door stood the British

Council man for Kyoto, who drove us for drinks at his lovely apartment. We were slightly startled to hear that next door was the HQ of the local Red Guard – a notorious terrorist organisation. The party was then driven by our host to the International Hotel for western style dinner and bed.

Next day we awoke to find our window looked out onto Nijo Castle, which we went round after breakfast. A British Consul driver then took us to see the sights. At the Nanzen-ji temple complex we admired the Japanese-style gardens of boulders, small trees and pale gravel beautifully raked. Next stop was the Shisendo temple, where we were struck by the Japanese girls dressed in kimonos as well as by marvellously colourful gardens. Lunch in the hotel Japanese-style restaurant was tempura – a fish dish. We went on to the Kyoto crafts centre to buy family presents, then visited a last temple with lovely geisha girls about and finally took the train back to Tokyo.

On Monday, Alex and I got down to work, while Betty first had a two-hour manicure followed by a madly social day. Admiral Inoue received us. We saw in succession his staff, the intelligence staff headed by a rear admiral, the chairman of the Joint Chiefs of Staff, who made me a present that I still have, and the head of Defence Intelligence, who spoke no English but was clearly powerful in his own right. To my surprise, he had a police background. During the day I learned just how powerful in Japan was the Civil Service who provided the second tier of ministers under the elected politicians. I formed the impression that real power lay with them. That evening Admiral Inoue entertained our party to dinner at the Naval Club in Tokyo. On arrival we had to pay our respects to Admiral Togo's shrine in the gardens of the Club, a reconstruction since the war. Betty and I had to take position opposite the shrine itself, flanked by two sailors dressed in samurai regalia. To the sound of a gong the Admiral's spirit was invoked. We were handed green bouquets to present as we climbed up eight steps to the altar. Glasses of saki had to be knocked back in one. Finally we were escorted into the main anteroom of the Club. This had a tapestry round all four walls depicting the Battle of Tsushima Straits in 1905 when the Japanese Navy totally defeated the Russian Far East fleet. There was Admiral Togo on the bridge of his battleship and opposite him Russian warships sinking. Togo had returned to Japan from Portsmouth some months before the battle. A seven-course dinner followed plus speeches by Admiral Inoue and myself. He referred to the oil crisis hitting Japan as elsewhere following the recent Arab/Israeli war that had occupied my attention in London for so long. Presents were exchanged and we departed in accordance with the time set out on the invitation – a sensible arrangement.

13 November found us back on the faithful Comet bound for Manila and then Jakarta in Indonesia. The Comet had moved round to Haneda airport, the main civil airfield for Tokyo. On the way out we saw the monorail trains now operating from central Tokyo. We flew over Okinawa, the Coral Sea, and so to Luzon and Manila for refuelling. The defence attaché, an airman, met us and drove us along the coast road while he briefed me on local Filipino affairs. That evening we arrived at Jakarta airport – hot and humid – to stay with Ambassador Coombs in his lovely house surrounded by gardens and a swimming pool. In the morning I departed for the Indonesian Ministry of Defence for talks with all and sundry. Betty as usual had a madly social day, meeting all the wives of the head men. We met for lunch with the British service attachés and their wives. That evening the Ambassador staged a large reception, in honour of Princess Anne's wedding, that many Indonesians and my party attended. The Indonesian General Subud gave dinner for us and the Indonesian joint staff chiefs. Next day was also spent by Alex and me visiting many parts of the Indonesian establishment, while Betty went south to Bogor and Sukarno's palace and up to the Poentjak Pass of 1 Seaforth's fame. That night we staged a party in an embassy staff house put at our disposal for the occasion of entertaining our RAF Comet crew. There followed dinner with the Ambassador and his wife and Indonesian guests, and so to bed.

16 November saw us in the air once again. This time the Comet was bound for Darwin with one additional passenger, the wife of the Air Attaché Jakarta. In Darwin the aircraft was re-fuelled while we had a quick tour by road of the city of Darwin, accompanied by the Australian station commander. After lunch we flew to Canberra, still 1,850 nautical miles away across the Australian continent. En route, as on every flight, Alex and I worked on tour reports, setting out views on the country visited and comments on personalities encountered. At Canberra we were met by Ann and Maurice Callender, the DIS man accredited to the Australian intelligence community. He had for many years served in London. Both looked after us well for the weekend, including a trip to a nature reserve at Tidbinbilla.

A very busy week followed in Canberra. After talks with the High Commissioner and his staff, I went to the Australian Department of Defence for long discussions with the Australian intelligence staff, both the equivalent of our Assessment Staff in the Cabinet Office and with the Defence intelligence people, inter-service much like our own. I saw the

Permanent Under-Secretary for Defence, a formidable figure with a fierce reputation. He and I got on well after a bit of preliminary skirmishing to assess relative abilities. I had a session with the Australian joint chiefs of staff, much like our own chiefs of staff committee.

Whilst visiting the Australians, I received a message from London to say that a Minister wanted to use the Comet, so it was being withdrawn to the UK, leaving me to paddle my own canoe thereafter. Alex was very busy in consequence arranging for Betty to fly home by civil flights at my expense, while he and I were to fly on to New Zealand before returning civil to London. On Friday, Betty and I flew down to Sydney for a night in a circular hotel in King's Cross, an area of the city renowned as the red light district. That evening we walked down through the botanical gardens to see the Opera House. This was and remains a thrilling and remarkable building. Next day we flew by Ansett to Mackay in central Queensland. Robin, our son, and his fiancée Heather met us and took us to a hotel in Mackay for the night. Robin and Heather were to be married on the Sunday in a Seventh Day Adventist ceremony. On Saturday we met Heather's family and the pastor who would marry them. The wedding day dawned and in no time we were seated in the church, which was a simple structure with windows open along each side. The ceremony was in most aspects similar to an Anglican wedding except spoken in colloquial language. The reception was in the local sports club not far away; delicious eats but no alcohol made life a bit more difficult. When honour was satisfied, we retired to our hotel for a rest before Dr Ian Chenowith, bless him, arrived to take us out to their lovely home on a hill outside the town looking over the sea. After a swim in their excellent swimming pool, we were bidden to a barbecue with many of their friends. At last we would rejoice in not one but a number of drinks. I can recall the pleasure still. I am in touch with the Chenowiths even now.

On Monday it was back to the grindstone for me. Betty departed for the UK by civil flight. I rejoined Alex and flew to Wellington. Their set-up is a scaled down version of the Australian pattern. I had a session with their Chiefs of Staff as well as with their intelligence staff whom I found well-versed in world developments. Finally came the long flight home, albeit tired but triumphant in achieving all objectives set for a trip of 33,000 miles lasting nearly four weeks in my case. First-class travel eased my burden back to Whitehall and the weekly routine that I have set out earlier in this narrative.

Attendance at Robin's wedding in Australia had completed the programme for marrying off my three children. Already grandchildren were beginning to proliferate. Celia and Janet maintained their rivalry, with Adam being born to Celia in early 1969, and Lucy to Janet in September of that year. In March 1971, Thomas and Simon arrived in their respective families within weeks of one another. Catherine and Peter were yet to come some years later. Betty and I were kept busy enjoying these additions to the family. Robin and Heather in due course of time added James, Becky and David to the list.

In London, 1974 proved to be a turbulent political year. That spring, Mr Heath went to the country and lost to Labour. The Civil Service rapidly organised briefings for the incoming ministers under Harold Wilson as Prime Minister. This was clearly a well-known drill that had been used many times in the past. At an early stage, Defence Intelligence was instructed by the Chiefs of Staff to give a briefing to the new Minister of Defence. As a ministerial briefing, this was clearly one for the Director General himself to give. After much rehearsing and changing of visual aids, this went ahead. It was well received by the new Secretary for Defence. The briefing was of course at the highest level of security; new ministers in some cases needed positive vetting before receiving such a briefing, though this was unusual except for junior ministers on first appointment.

Later in 1974 I made my annual trip to Washington to go round the intelligence agencies. As always, the DIS liaison team had set up a programme, starting with the DIA. They were the US equivalent of our own Defence Intelligence Staff, except that they did some direct collection through agents. My old friend Danny Graham had earlier become the head of the DIA in the same rank as myself. It was therefore a great pleasure to start discussions with his staff. Betty came with me on an indulgence flight, and we stayed with her sister in Georgetown, as I had done earlier. Bridget's husband had remarried her after parting company for a number of years. As a lawyer he had a job in Congress with the Committee of Un-American Activities, and one afternoon he showed me round the Capitol building. I was struck by the size of the staffs serving each senator, unlike our members of parliament.

Danny had arranged for me to see Mr Schlesinger, the incumbent Secretary of Defence in the American administration. The pair of us arrived at his outer office for a meeting at 12 o'clock. His Secretary said he was busy, so would we sit down and have a cup of coffee? It came to 12.30 and there was still no movement. We were both due at the British Embassy for a lunch party at 1300 hours. We telephoned to say we might be late. One o'clock came. We telephoned once again, asking that the lunch party start. 1330 hours passed and we still sat there. At a quarter to two the bell rang and we were summoned to the presence. Schlesinger was a big burly man whom I had not met before. We were bidden to sit down and as we did so, the Secretary for Defence looked me up and down and said:

'Waal, General, I reckon you Brits screwed it up at Suez!'

I thought quickly and decided to take the offensive.

'Secretary of State, I reckon you Americans leant on us Brits unmercifully.' He looked me in the eye, abandoned that topic and without more ado we got down to substantive business. After a full half-hour, we excused ourselves and departed rapidly for the British Embassy. We arrived as the guests were leaving the lunch party. Thank heavens a bit was left over for the two of us, while we recounted to our hosts what had happened. They seemed to me to be unsurprised.

That Friday afternoon I had booked a hire car in a garage in Chevy Chase. I was confronted with a compact car that was automatic. I had never driven an automatic before. I was asked if I knew the controls. I asked to be reminded. I got into the car and started up a ramp with many right angle turns. With my heart in my mouth I eventually reached ground level, two floors above, without hitting anything. Taking my courage in both hands, I launched out into the traffic and headed off for Georgetown. My brother-in-law asked if I enjoyed driving an automatic. 'A piece of cake,' I replied. Next morning Betty and I set off for Fort Monroe opposite Newport News via Richmond. We spent a splendid few days in the Norfolk, Virginia, area. We visited the Chesapeake Bridge Tunnel across the mouth of the Chesapeake Estuary, some fourteen miles long, the botanical gardens and Virginia Beach amongst other sights, while living most comfortably at Fort Monroe. Finally it was back to Washington, return the car – still intact – and fly back home. My next car in the UK was an automatic. I have continued to enjoy driving one ever since.

1975 continued the same pattern with tours east and west, meetings and briefings in London, short sharp trips to Belgium and Western Germany, entertaining visitors to London and so on. I also took a last trip out east as DCDS (I). My first port of call was Muscat. I flew on to Dhofar, where rebel elements were still holding out east of the border with Aden, now under strong Soviet influence. Russian arms were supplied regularly to the dissident forces, whilst on the other side there were British armoured cars and SAS elements supporting the Sultan of Muscat's Armed Forces. In my honour they had decided to fire every weapon they possessed at the rebel stronghold. I got out of my helicopter and was conducted to an observation post overlooking the enemy position. Fire was opened, I suspect doing a lot of harm to the local rocks but not worrying the enemy unduly. After talking with many people I moved off to rejoin the helicopter. As we did so, the unmistakable sound of a Katushka multi-barrelled mortar was heard firing from the hills below at our concentration. Luckily, the bursts were along the ridge a bit from my position. This, I think, was the last time in my career that I came under fire.

From Muscat I flew on to Delhi to call on the Indian authorities. Scotty was coming to the end of his tour of duty. I had to stay elsewhere as he and his wife were up in Simla. In GHQ Delhi I was met as usual by the intelligence staff at the door. My host led me by an unusually circuitous route to the offices of his superiors. I asked the reason. Marshal Malinovsky, Defence Minister of Soviet Russia, was in the building that day. His masters did not want us to meet in the corridor.

At the weekend I flew up to Chandrigar. After a hair-raising ride by taxi, I was delivered to my hotel in Kasouli, at over 7,000 feet up in the mountains, about thirty miles from Simla. I was met by a charming Colonel from GHQ in Delhi whom I did not know: he was in Kasouli to take out his son from boarding school. That afternoon, the Colonel took me round the cantonment on foot. We visited his club, which seemed exactly as it had been under the British Raj, and called in at the cottage of his old sergeant-major. Around the walls of the cottage were pictures of British officers going back to the founding of his Sikh regiment, as well as of the Indian officers who had succeeded them after independence in 1947. No wonder goodwill towards the British remains at so high a level, in some sections of Indian society! That evening, the Scott-Bowdens returned, and we had a very delightful evening with both them and the Colonel's family. Next day we explored Kasouli. From vantage points one could see right down the mountain to Chandrigar. In the evening we drove down the mountain and flew back to Delhi. To my sorrow I had to leave Delhi next day and fly on to Hong Kong. A highlight there was to visit the hill road section that formed the border with Red China, then proving obstreperous towards the Colony. A drive along the border track facing the Chinese road opposite was fascinating. And so back to London where life remained busy as ever.

That spring, Lou Le Bailly's replacement in September became an issue. Lou kindly nominated me to succeed him. My grapevine yielded much argument behind the scenes. I suspect that the RAF were quibbling because I had moved up to DCDS (I) in place of an RAF officer. Word also got around that I was tough with handling staff. Eventually I was told that I had been appointed DGI for a two-year term with option to fill a third year if all agreed that I should do so. An RAF officer, then AOC Scotland, was to replace me as DCDS (I). He did not have previous intelligence experience within the DIS. I felt I had no option but to accept these terms. So the die was cast for my retirement from the Army in August and after a month's leave to assume the appointment as Deputy Under Secretary in the Civil Service as DGI. The following month I duly handed over to Air Marshal Dickie Wakeford and prepared to assume the top slot in a month's time.

Betty and I were much exercised as to how to arrange housing for my last job in London. We had tried commuting from Guildford; my spending the working week in the Marsham Street flat; my wife spending most of her time in the London flat during the week; or her staying largely at our house in Guildford. None seemed totally satisfactory. We therefore resolved to sell up in Guildford and find a house in London from which to organise our life in the capital. In favour of this solution were several factors. They included the need to entertain DIS staff in our own home and the constant calls to attend receptions and parties in the city, commensurate with the appointment of DGI. Wear and tear on us both would seem to be less with coiling up our tail into London, despite the turmoil of moving after nine years in Guildford.

By now we had replaced our original yacht with a Moody 30 that, though slower in the water than our original boat, had more space aboard. So in summer we would have a lifeline. The Royal Thames Yacht Club still had premises at the entrance to the Hamble River. We could stay there while putting the boat to bed in the autumn and getting her ready for sea each spring.

The flat in Marsham Street was already let once again. We therefore set about house-hunting that summer through London agents. We were much attracted by a mews house in Eaton Mews South that backed on to houses in Eaton Square. This was owned by a couple younger than us, the husband working for Consolidated Goldfields in South Africa. Their marriage was on the rocks, so this house suddenly came on the market, at £70,000 if I remember rightly. (Prices began to rise at this time, as it transpired). At that price a mews house situated where it was and with a built-in garage, parking space in the mews and three bedrooms, seemed ideal.

Parallel negotiations had been occurring to sell the Guildford house, and not one but two couples were determined to have it. We heard from our agents that both had started bidding each other up. I determined to put an end to this by asking each to put in sealed bids, and we sold for £43,000. By selling some shares I could meet the asking price in

London. We therefore agreed to buy the mews house off Eaton Square and to take possession in late August. Our leave was spent partly on cruise and mostly in packing up and moving to London. Fortunately, the mews house was in excellent decorative order and came complete with carpets and curtains, so that all was accomplished in time for me to start taking over from Lou Le Bailly in my new role as Director General of Intelligence – my first post as a civilian.

CHAPTER 10

MoD London (1975–1978) Director General Intelligence

Returning to the MoD as a civilian was a curious sensation. Though Director General of Intelligence and a Deputy Under-Secretary, the atmosphere was still a bit odd. No longer did the interests and loyalty of the Services staff, Army, Navy and Air Force, come within one's bailiwick. This was now the domain of my successor as DCDS(I), Dickie Wakeford, with whom, until he relieved me, I had not had contact. He had come from Air Officer Commanding in Scotland. My particular responsibility was for the large civilian component of the DIS, ranging from under-secretary equivalents, such as the Director of Scientific and Technical Intelligence, to newly-joined entrants to the civil service who found themselves in defence intelligence. I resolved to visit every single one of the civilian staff under my direction. This took me the first eighteen months of my appointment. I found it most rewarding. In the original Joint Intelligence Bureau dealing with facts and figures about roads, railways, ports, airfields and so on worldwide, I met many retired officers who possessed a wealth of knowledge of their subjects. Supporting technical intelligence was a pool of linguists that included some Russian women.

One of the quirks of Russian Soviet existence was the need to find some outlet to publish research and development projects. These were most strictly controlled by the KGB in Moscow and the big cities of European Russia. But elsewhere it was remarkable how lax security was under a communist regime. Our attachés in Russia were constantly on tour right through to the Pacific at Vladivostok. Their briefs included looking at local bookstalls. Lucky finds came back to our translation staff, who on occasion found real nuggets amongst such publications. At the other end of the scale were fast-stream civil servants serving a tour of duty in the DIS in general, scientific and economic subjects. It was a joy to talk with them.

One of this fast stream was the DIS convenor for the Civil Service Union. He kept on at me to join the union myself. I eventually agreed, so for the period that I remained a civil servant, I joined. I may say that I only once attended a local union meeting. At that time the union was largely non-political. Its main aims were to keep a beady eye on working hours and conditions of service, particularly pay rates. As these were in many cases superior to those of servicemen and women, I found difficulty in sympathising. Nevertheless, I did my duty as I saw it.

I came directly under the Permanent Under-Secretary himself. He usually ran a weekly staff meeting that I attended. The members consisted of the second permanent under-secretary, the heads of research and development and procurement, the various deputy under-secretaries including the DUS Policy and myself. Hearing them each give tongue on what was going on in their parts of the ship was an education. On one occasion Mike Carver, who was still Chief of Defence Staff, called in at a weekly meeting for a quick word with the PUS. The first person he saw sitting round the table was me. He did a double take at the sight, as he had been used to seeing me at Chiefs of Staff meetings.

PUS, when I first took over, was a charming and cultivated man. In his own time at home he made violins. We got on like a house on fire. To my sorrow within the year he died suddenly while still in office. He was succeeded by Sir Frank Cooper who had spent much of his civil service life in the Air Department. We eyed each other with some scepticism to start with in the light of past history of the Air Department pressing for an air marshal to fill my job, but we soon became firm friends. Our relationship remained friendly until I retired. His conferences weekly were great fun. One of his favourite sayings was, 'I will give the Secretary of State a good going over.' I was reminded of the BBC programme then in vogue – *Yes, Minister.*

Within the DIS the daily briefing on matters of intelligence substance continued at full bore. Having been there so long, I am afraid I soon got down to interrogating the witnesses on the spot. When I retired, a Naval Officer provided a splendid piece of doggerel that I still have; it is at the end of this chapter. This took off my daily interrogation of speakers beautifully. I hold the view that such questioning sharpened up the minds of those with something to say that those present would benefit from.

I had to brief the Secretary of Defence on occasion. We developed a good relationship that I found stimulating. When he was moved on to Northern Ireland he gave a farewell party that I was invited to attend in the Defence Council Suite. I arrived pretty late and found myself one of the last to leave. The Secretary of State took me aside and confided that he had received his orders from the Prime Minister that would lead him to take certain actions in Belfast of which I might not approve. I was to understand that he did so in accordance with his instructions. I was to come and see him personally in Belfast whenever I was over in Northern

Ireland. Bless him, I did in fact avail myself of this promise on several occasions thereafter. In fact I never did disagree profoundly with his efforts to bring about peace between Catholics and Protestants, a task not even solved at the time of writing this narrative – despite an officially declared ceasefire in recent years.

Northern Ireland remained one of the prime subjects for weekly discussion in the Joint Intelligence Committee meeting in the Cabinet Office across Whitehall from the Ministry of Defence. I was deputy chairman of this committee as well as senior MoD member. Briefings for each item on the agenda were pretty detailed. Here again I tended to be asking the most questions of both military and civilian DIS briefers. This came from so many years of experience with the DIS. Newer members found this a bit tough, I know; interrogations are never easy when you are comparatively new to the job.

The Russian threat was the main subject, as always, for briefing within the MoD and for frequent assessment in the JIC. The staffs of DI3 and of the DSTI dealing with Soviet technical and scientific development bore the brunt of such briefing. I personally took the view that Communist military strength could be overplayed, though I fear that many elements in the American intelligence community took the opposite view. This put me at odds with certain staff members of DI3 Army that led to curious side effects. I had for some years been a member of the 'Senior' Club in the Mall. This was convenient to walk to for lunch. An announcement came that this club was to close. I applied for membership to join the Army and Navy in St James's Square. To my surprise, I heard from the Secretary that my application had been refused. I discovered that my case had been blackballed. Surprise, surprise: but DI3 Army staff were members, I found. I rejoined my original club, the In and Out, at 96 Piccadilly, and remain a member to this day.

Mr Archie Potts, DSTI, retired soon after I took over. His replacement was a very high-grade scientist from Defence Science. I was told that he would only be in this post for a few years before being upgraded to Deputy Secretary level. He and I got on famously. Together we bearded the American establishment at intervals. With such support I was able to ask for highly technical subjects to be discussed. Some of these were with CIA scientists and analysts, some even with single service staffs that handled the more esoteric subjects that had not been handed over to the DIA. Sessions in both CIA and with the US Navy were invaluable. Our travels took us to Omaha, Nebraska, to see Strategic Air Command. Fortunately I had got to know the Commander-in-Chief from his previous job in Europe as Deputy SACEUR. In his presence, the briefing on the capabilities of Strategic Air Command were breathtaking. Particularly striking was the growth of defences against Soviet Bombers in the event of attack over the North Pole.

We then flew on to Monterey where the US Navy University was established. We had some fascinating talks with their experts. I gave a talk to the assembled faculty and students on the world scene. The first afternoon I had spare time and opted for a walk. Americans rejoice in a car civilisation. As I walked down to the gate, any number of cars stopped and offered me a lift. The drivers were amazed when I refused and said I was going for a walk. I came to the main gate and had a slight problem in convincing the sentries that I wanted to walk on the beach across the main road and that I wanted to come back through the gate in due course. The beach was delightful; across the sea I could see the main city of Monterey, capital of Spanish California in days long gone. I heard a sound that was familiar but I thought out of place. It came again and I identified it as coming from a sea lion lying on a rock. I had no idea that sea lions existed on that coast; I had only heard them in zoos in the UK. The next day we were driven round the promontory sticking out into the Pacific south of Monterey. This was delightful as many famous golf courses have been developed in this area and the beaches looked gorgeous. Sea lions were numerous, I was glad to see. Lunch in Monterey city was equally enjoyable before the long flight back to Washington, a continent away as it seemed.

Back in London, life remained as hectic as before. Problems were compounded by what Betty and I called 'the great flood'. In the spring of 1976 we went away for a weekend with friends. Betty decided to stay on an additional day. On my own, therefore, I returned to our Mews House in London. As I opened the front door I was greeted by rushing waters down the stairs. I rapidly found the stopcock to turn the water supply off. Soon the flow stopped and I was able to make my way upstairs to survey the damage to all three floors of the house. On the top floor our bedroom was undamaged; the flow of water had clearly come down from the roof through the ceiling of the second bedroom. It had soaked the sitting room on the middle floor and carried on downstairs to the ground floor. I telephoned Betty to give her the dire news.

Next morning early, I rang the house insurers. Their representative arrived late morning to survey the damage to the structure, the expensive carpets that we had bought with the house, plus some furniture. The cause of the flood was the cold-water tank on the roof that had suddenly overflowed as a result of what the Water Company described as a base surge of water pressure. As the tank served both my house and the one next door this flood was substantial. To give him his due the insurance representative agreed on the spot that repairs should proceed. The great problem was to get the floors and stairs to dry out. Carpets had to be stripped off to expose ceilings, floors and stairs to the air. In one of the hottest summers on record, this still took many months. Betty arrived home in the middle of all this consultation. We decided to camp out in the ruins while the house was stripped off to dry. Kind friends offered much assistance. My DMSI, a Guards major-general called Jack Younger, cousin to my school friend Malcolm, kindly offered us his house in Cadogan Square. He was off to Italy for three weeks' holiday with his Italian wife, a *principessa*. This we gladly accepted. For much of that summer, however, we camped out in the ruins from Monday to Friday, while weekends were mostly spent on our yacht on the Hamble. It was not until September that the house dried out and could be reconstituted in toto. This additional stress certainly added to my problems at work, although fortunately our bedroom and bathroom survived throughout.

The disaster on the home front gave me cause for reflection on the lifestyle of an intelligence analyst at the top level in Whitehall. Intelligence very rarely produced sufficient raw material on any given subject to permit absolute certainty of judgement. The art of assessment that I had learnt in many years of service at various levels was essentially one of selection of material on which one could place reliance. The JIC pronouncements were the culmination of effort by a great number of people, starting at desk level. It was at this level that collation took place, the recording of the history day-by-day of what had occurred hitherto on any given subject. In those days the DIS still relied upon files of papers accumulated in many cases for years, indeed decades past. However, the electronic age was now upon us. During my three years many meetings were held under my chairmanship to plot the way ahead for getting all the vast store of knowledge onto computer files. Pilot schemes were put in hand to build up computer files. Factual information was comparatively easy to automate, for example data on ports, airfields, and even hardware development. Judgement information on fragmentary information was more difficult to record with precision commensurate with the complexity of the issue. Arguments were prolonged and difficult to resolve. However, steady progress was made in the whole process of automating the database across the wide spread of DIS responsibilities for reading out judgements on strategic, Navy, Army and Air Force subjects. A particular difficulty was coping with terrorists, notably the IRA at that time. Equally complex was how best to handle scientific and technical subjects where raw intelligence was fragmentary.

JIC discussions and products covered a wide range of topics: the mix of political, military and economic facts required thorough sifting by many keen minds. Northern Ireland remained a major subject. So did developments in the turbulent Middle East. The Indian sub-continent figured quite often, as did Africa. Ian Smith's Rhodesia needed to be interpreted. China and Korea needed regular treatment. Above all lay the threat from the Soviet world to NATO. Brezhnev's Politburo remained an enigma on which little hard evidence was forthcoming. As I write this, the difficulties surrounding the second Iraq war are argued endlessly in the media. The spotlight has turned on the intelligence community in London and in Washington. What did they report at the time of the outbreak of war on Iraqi holdings of weapons of mass destruction? We all live in the aftermath of the Hutton Report into the death of Mr Kelly, seconded to the MoD from the Foreign Office for duties not directly intelligence orientated. From what I have outlined above, intelligence produces the best judgement at the time on the issues of the day. It is up to policy makers to decide if these judgements are sound and to take action accordingly. I am more than glad that I handed over responsibility in 1978. I sympathise enormously with all those now in charge of world affairs. The media have become more and more obtrusive as the years go by. Dare I say it, but their understanding of the issues involved does not, in my view, keep pace with their obtrusiveness. Another pressure point on the intelligence machinery in Whitehall is now political influence. In my time this factor did not exist; our view was that we made intelligence judgements without fear or favour. It was up to policy makers to accept them as a basis for action or to set them on one side after noting them.

Intelligence appointments within Defence Intelligence were very much part of my job still, though the DCDS(I) now handled serving officer appointments. A key figure was the head of the DIS Liaison Staff in Washington. I came in strongly on this appointment when the time came for renewal. An air force officer who had headed DI3 Air had been filling the post when I took over as DGI. I was instrumental in influencing the selection of Jonathan Hall-Tipping to fill this post. He had served under me in DI4 and again as a half colonel. So his appointment to Washington was most welcome. Very well did he do in this post. I should add that after I retired he decided to do the same in America. He has subsequently taken up stockbroking after qualifying in Wall Street and remains one of my oldest friends.

From the personal angle, the reign of Denis Healey as Chancellor of the Exchequer was an unmitigated disaster. He raised taxes to an unprecedented level. I well remember receiving a bank statement for my own personal income over and above my pay as a retired Lieutenant General and as a Deputy Under-Secretary. I was paying 92 pence in every pound on the top slice of my own private income. The statement showed £400 remaining from my personal income for the year, if I remember rightly. Inflation rose and rose during the last years of Harold Wilson as Prime Minister, as it continued to do under his successor Jim Callaghan. Harold Wilson's resignation was a slight surprise; but stories had been rampant at the Cabinet Office mess at lunchtime. One concerned Lady Falkender, as she had been created by Harold Wilson. By this time she had adopted other boyfriends. She went on holiday to Gibraltar. A frantic message reached the MoD duty officer one night from Marcia saying that the Admiral at Gibraltar had refused her demand for his barge for the following day, for a trip by her and her latest boyfriend. She asked for the Prime Minister's assistance. The duty officer referred it to the duty officer at 10 Downing Street. Back came the reply – the Prime Minister authorised the trip. The duty officer had to relay this information to the unfortunate Admiral. Both the DIS and the JIC dealt only with overseas matters plus threats to the realm inside the UK; officially, therefore, we paid no attention to the home political scene. Needless to say, we all had our private views on concession after concession to trades union pressure.

About this time a rumour was started by the left wing of the Labour Party that received wide publicity in the media and has continued to do so occasionally ever since. This was to the effect that MI5 was involved in intrigue to unseat the Government of Harold Wilson. I happened to have got to know Mike Hanley, the Director of MI5, well. We had lunch together several times and on each occasion he raised the issue of the rumour as causing him much discomfort. He denied it absolutely and I believed him. Nevertheless this tittle-tattle continued to plague him even after he retired.

By autumn 1976 our house in Eaton Mews South was fully dried out and repaired. Betty and I resumed entertaining. Many members of our staff plus friends in and around London were invited to our house.

In August 1977 I set off on another visit to Washington. By this time a charming US Army general, who had been interpreter to several Presidents when meeting Soviet leaders, had taken over as Deputy Head of CIA. He lived with his sister in a most convenient house overlooking the Potomac River, where he kept a motorboat. He invited the Hall-Tippings and myself to come out in their boat for a Sunday picnic. We motored rapidly down river to opposite George Washington's house and estate at Mount Vernon where we anchored and ate a delicious picnic. It was quite a day to remember. Next day he invited me to see his boss, who was one George Bush, later President for the first Iraqi war. George Bush was most affable and knowledgeable. He had recently seen service in China. Later that winter he came to London on a visit to MI6. He asked to see me. I took him out to lunch at Simpson's in the Strand. He obviously enjoyed English dishes, including the roast beef of old England.

I found mayhem reigning in the DIS on my return from Washington. In my absence Dickie Wakeford and the Air Force had tried to unseat me at the end of my initial two-year contract. This had not been raised with me before my departure by anyone. I had assumed that as no one had objected, my third year was a certainty. I suppose I should have taken heed of a chance remark by Mike Carver, who was Chief of Defence Staff, to the effect that, 'should I need support he was always there to provide it'. I missed the significance: he already knew of the move to limit my tour of duty to two years. Clearly both he and Frank Cooper, the PUS, had sided with me. I was greeted by the news that Dickie Wakeford was to retire from the post of DCDS(I) almost immediately. After a day or two I heard that Gus Halliday had been appointed to succeed him on promotion to vice admiral. I was told by the PUS that Gus would succeed me the following August as the Navy had exerted their right to the post. So in short order I had to accept reduction of my tenure of duty by a month, lose my deputy, and welcome another DCDS(I) – fortunately not new to intelligence staff work, as he had been Commodore Intelligence some years earlier.

In addition I had to preside over a farewell dinner arranged by the DMSI, by then a rear admiral, for Dickie Wakeford, and to give the main speech of thanks. Knowing what I did of the background that no one else on the DIS had cognisance of, I found this a difficult task. I gather my speech did not fully please the organiser of the occasion, but such is life at the top. I welcomed the arrival of Vice Admiral Gus Halliday and got down to the task of working him in to the DIS at a more senior level. In August 1978 he duly succeeded me as DGI, a month short of my tenure of this post for three years.

Back-tracking chronologically to 1976, the next task that befell me was to brief the new Secretary of State, Fred Mulley. His appointment came about as a result of a Cabinet reshuffle by Harold Wilson that resulted in our existing Secretary of State being transferred to Northern Ireland. I duly prepared a high-grade picture show for Fred Mulley, interspersed with the DIS view on the issues of the day, notably the threat to NATO from the Soviet Bloc. Because of the high security content of the briefing this was scheduled to take place in one of the subterranean levels below the MoD main building. The timing was after lunch and the audience consisted of the Chiefs of Staff and their Secretariat. The Chief of Defence Staff was away that day, so the Chief of Naval Staff stood in for him. At 2.30 in the afternoon Fred Mulley appeared and I started. After ten minutes it was clear to me that the new Secretary of State had gone to sleep. I thought rapidly while continuing to speak and show slides. I decided to speed up my delivery, ending with a thunderous 'Secretary of State – have you any questions?' Fred woke up at this request, and lamely produced two questions. I answered both by observing, 'S of S, you will remember I said in my address so and so – do you have something more in mind?' He rapidly murmured something and stood up to go. The First Sea Lord looked at me fixedly as the door closed.

'David,' he said. 'I nearly risked the future of the Navy by kicking his shin, but decided not to.' A few days later Fred Mulley went to sleep on the Queen with the media present. The resulting tumult lasted several days! My experience remained unknown.

In the winter of 1976 I undertook another tour of the Far East. This time I went straight to Hong Kong for several days before flying on to Australia and New Zealand. Hong Kong as usual was fascinating; the New Territories were a particularly fruitful source of looking, from close to, at Communist China. Talking to the Hong Kong Police Commissioner and the Head of Special Branch complemented updating by the local representatives of MI5, MI6 and GCHQ. Australia was equally worthwhile. I had an excellent session with the Australian Chiefs of Staff as well as with their equivalents in New Zealand. I stayed with the British High Commissioner, and was introduced to croquet on the lawn of his residence in Wellington. I managed to fit in a visit to cousins of my wife who lived about seventy miles north-west of Wellington. The matriarch of the family had married the organist of Wellington Cathedral in the late nineteenth century. It was quite a wrench to have to face the long air journey back to the UK.

In 1977 my biggest surprise was to be asked by the Corps of Royal Engineers to become Chief Royal Engineer in place of Charles Richardson. John Reid, whom I had known well, was scheduled to succeed him. He had risen to the rank of lieutenant general, his last job being Director of the International Military Staff of NATO in Brussels. I had visited him in this capacity on more than one occasion. Soon after retirement he became seriously ill and had to say that he could not take on the task. I was the only other lieutenant general available on the list of Colonels Commandant. The only full general was Bill Jackson, who

As Chief Royal Engineer at Old Comrades Parade at Chatham, 1980

was Quarter Master General of the Army. He felt that he could not take on Chief Royal Engineer in addition to his new function. I therefore found myself in the post with a year still to serve as DGI. On overseas visits, in particular, I managed to fit in visits to engineer units of Commonwealth Forces as well as attending to the respective intelligence communities. The same was true of Germany that led to visiting engineer units in the British Zone as well as to visiting Rheindalen and Bonn. In addition I presided over meetings of the Chief Royal Engineers Committee in London, over Corps guest nights in Chatham and the annual garden party for families at Minley given by the Colonels Commandant. This brought me into wide contact with the Corps family, a facility that was expanded after my retirement from full-time work in Whitehall.

A well worthwhile event in the autumn of 1977 was a presentation by Prince Michael of Kent of a research project that he had spent the previous year in preparing. I had been approached by the Military Secretary for a second time on behalf of Prince Michael for a real intelligence job, after completing his tour of duty as a member of the Army Attaché Liaison team in London. He was allotted an intelligence corps sergeant as his assistant. For a year they laboured away in a high security environment in a floor below ground under the MoD building. His presentation was a great success. The DIS were engaged across the board in detailed analysis of data as resources in manpower permitted. I use manpower in the sense of both men and women employed within DIS staff.

1978 dawned, my last year in office. I planned a large number of visits worldwide. Gus Halliday was a tower of strength and would stand in for me as I went off on successive visits. Each of these required much briefing and preparation, over and above the weekly grind of life in London. Being both DGI and Chief Royal Engineer added to my task. After the disaster of 1976 to my Mews House and the events of 1977 leading to the departure of Dickie Wakeford, I had really begun to feel the strains of office. My memories of those final visits is blurred and, in consequence, I can only record those highlights remaining in my mind. My tour of the Middle and Far East lasted several weeks. Australia is imprinted on my mind because my wife flew out to join me. After the usual official visits in Canberra, I took a week's leave. Betty's ankle was still in plaster after a nasty fall while skiing the previous winter. However, she was determined to see our son and bravely overcame the hazards of travelling out to Australia with a leg in plaster, on her own, to meet me in Canberra. Her accident had occurred in Italy where we went for a short run in deep wet snow, as the snow was thin where we were staying in Austria. At the bottom of the Italian slope, Betty failed to appear. John Sharp and I went back up in the ski lift to find her. Not far below the top we found her sitting in snow with an ankle twisted right round. She had bravely got her skis off and was awaiting rescue. Agonisingly slowly we got her down the slope between us, had a hot meal and drove the long haul back into Austria. Having reached our hotel, I took Betty to the local hospital. There I was grateful for prompt and efficient treatment in resetting the ankle. After a few days in hospital she was able to fly back with me to England. The ankle took a full year to heal completely.

After the usual profitable sessions with the intelligence community and the Australian Chiefs of Staff, I visited the chief engineer of the Australian Army and his staff. He very kindly arranged for us to visit the Snowy Mountains Authority and to tour this large project for two days in one of their cars. Robin joined us for the journey down in a hire car. The headquarters of the Authority were most informative and helpful. After lunch we drove deep into the mountains to a village built by them near one of the hydraulic power stations that had been built underground harnessing the head waters of the Murray River to flow eastward through the mountains instead of westward in the Murray River valley. We were put in the same bungalow that the Queen had occupied when she opened this power station a few years earlier. Next day we went round the cavernous structure hacked out of solid rock, before driving on round much of the remaining project back to the headquarters. A lovely drive followed down to the sea coast near the border with the state of Victoria. We spent several days driving slowly back up this attractive coast to Sydney. Nights were spent in beach hotels where Betty and I enjoyed Sydney rock oysters while Robin had his vegan fare. He had adopted vegan dieting after converting to the Seventh Day Adventist Church. Betty flew back to the UK from Sydney. Robin returned to Brisbane, while I flew on to New Zealand.

Here I had fixed with my New Zealand opposite number to meet me with a government car in Auckland. After a night there, we set out for Rotorua. The sights and smells of the geysers were well worth the time spent in those parts. On the run south we passed through country that much resembled the English countryside. It had been settled by English farmers in the 1840s. They brought their own seeds from home and recreated this home environment. After a night in Rotorua, we drove southward to a GCHQ-style site manned by knowledgeable New Zealand servicemen from all three services. Further south we reached the area of the great volcanoes of North Island where the New Zealand Army had a large tract of country as a training area. Here the New Zealand Division was deployed on an exercise that allowed their territorial forces to flesh out the full strength of this division. I called on the divisional commander after meeting the CRE. Then, together, we helicoptered round several Field Squadrons – largely territorials doing their annual training. I was struck by the comfort of their camps. Tents all had hard wooden bases that I doubt would be seen at similar camps in the UK. But enthusiasm was apparent, as were basic engineer skills. Evening came and we set out on the long run to Wellington. By this time a New Zealand captain RNZ who had been on my IDC course in London was Chief of their Naval Staff. I stayed with him and on my final day had the usual discussions with their intelligence staffs and with my friend's colleagues as Chiefs of Staff. I also had a talk with their Defence Secretary and with the senior Engineer Officer. It was good to be able to visit in both my capacities.

Back home my next preoccupation was to present the DIS budget to the Secretary of the Cabinet, supported by the PUS of the Treasury. The Coordinator of Intelligence in the Cabinet Office was also present. This was an annual function that I had become accustomed to. On the first occasion I was worried that I should not be able to answer searching questions; it remained a testing ordeal requiring much preparation. Somehow I managed to survive intact, though the pressure was on to cut the size of the DIS. Each year, after much discussion inside the DIS, I had to offer up a number of posts, both civilian and military. Fortunately civilian posts could mostly be met by retirements; service posts were more easily handled by the respective personnel branches. By my third budgetary session, total DIS strength was down to about 800. I should add that pressure to reduce came from the MoD rather than from the intelligence community.

Yet another memory from those times relates to the preparation of the annual White Paper. This was masterminded by the DUS (Policy) of the day, with whom I had cultivated close relations. He asked me to draft the threat section of the annual Defence White Paper that was issued by the government. I did so without fear or favour, subject only to security considerations. I set out in particular the bare bones of the Soviet threat to NATO as the centrepiece. This passed through the DUS (P)'s scrutiny and that of the Secretary of State. The draft had finally to be cleared by 10 Downing Street. DUS (P) rang me one day to say that it was back to the drawing board, as the Prime Minister, Jim Callaghan, had returned the draft for revision. Privately he told me that the Prime Minister had written over the threat section of the paper, 'If this draft is published, the Government will fall.' We had to water down the content substantially before Number Ten would approve publication.

Farewell tours in Western Europe were fun. Of all places, I received an invitation to visit my Swiss counterpart in Berne. This included my wife for a weekend visit. We flew over to Berne and were met by the defence attaché, a sapper whom I knew. Friday was spent in talks with the Swiss general in charge of intelligence, his masters in the Swiss Ministry of Defence and with his staff. That evening we were driven out to a skiing resort where my Swiss hosts had a chalet. We spent the weekend langlauf skiing, a sport requiring much more effort than the downhill skiing that we were accustomed to. We enjoyed the exercise and were invited to take our loaned skis back to the UK with us. Our hostess was a Turkish lady of great beauty that her husband had married while serving as Swiss Defence Attaché in Ankara. During the weekend much discussion took place over evening dinner. I took away an impression of just how fiercely Swiss conscripts and mobilisation would oppose any threat to their national independence. I reflected privately on just how far this would get them in the nuclear age.

We moved on to Bonn to visit the Germans. During the last three years I had got to know well the head of German military intelligence in their Ministry of Defence. His career had been unusual. At the end of the Second World War he commanded a German submarine operating from Bulgaria in the Black Sea. When he received the news that Germany had surrendered after the death of Hitler in Berlin, he wondered where to surrender his ship. The consensus amongst his crew was to do so in a Turkish port. Turkey had remained neutral throughout the war, so this seemed the best course of action. He and his crew were interned for some months and then repatriated to Germany. (His mother was in fact English and had survived the war.) After some years in civilian life, he heard that the German Navy were being resuscitated in common with the German Armed Forces. He volunteered at once and was accepted back. He worked his way up through the system to Rear Admiral in charge of Defence Intelligence. He was most welcoming and took me round his Ministry that I had entered on several occasions.

We moved on to Brussels to visit SHAPE where MC161 – the threat to NATO – had brought me on numerous occasions. I saw all the top brass including SACEUR himself – an American officer whose predecessors included Al Haig, of political fame in America, whom I had got to know well. The head of SHAPE intelligence was a British major general, and a number of the staff were old friends. They included a fellow sapper, Mike Lewis, who had been on the IDC course in Belgrave Square with me. This visit, as so many, was a great pleasure.

London remained as busy as ever, but I was soon off again on a visit to Paris at the invitation of the French. Here I stayed with the defence attaché. In the morning we were invited to lunch at the famous British Embassy that was staging a function for the current IDC course from

London. To my surprise, the Ambassador introduced me to General Gerard, who turned out to be Chief of French Intelligence and my host for my afternoon session with French Intelligence. I found that he spoke good English. During the war he had been posted to Dakar in West Africa as a young officer. When the British Navy attacked their Vichy French counterparts in the past, he was able to make his escape to South Africa. He then moved up to Mombasa and joined the Free French movement under Charles de Gaulle. He took part in the campaign up into Ethiopia against the Italians and was present at the key battle of Keren. Once the campaign was won, he joined the French forces in the Western Desert under General Koenig and then participated in the invasion of Sicily and the subsequent series of battles up to the Italian peninsula.

We got on famously and at the end of lunch he said he was looking forward to our afternoon session. Accompanied by a fluent French speaker from our Embassy, I duly reported to the outer offices of the French President, where the heads of French Intelligence were located. I was received by the general in his office and greeted in English. He pressed a bell on his desk and in came his directors, both civilian and military, for the main discussion of the day. The general announced that the session would be conducted in the English language. Jaws dropped widely round the table. In the event only two of the company had a slight language problem but all coped well. I am sure that English had not been heard in the outer offices of the President of France for many a long day. The face of my French interpreter, a first secretary from the Embassy, was a study!

Another visitation was to Denmark and Norway, both of which I had visited a number of times in past years. Copenhagen remains one of the most delightful cities in Europe. Erik Fournais had his office in the fort not far from the Royal Palace. He had escaped by boat from Denmark during the war. He served with MI6 and had much to do with the growth of Danish resistance against the German occupation. After the war he graduated upward to become Head of Danish Intelligence. He did a stint as a major-general heading intelligence at NATO Headquarters in Brussels, where I also had dealings with him. On return to his own country, his authorities could only give him a Colonel's job again. On this occasion I stayed with the British Lady Ambassador to Denmark in her charming residence. She could not have been more helpful, as were the Service attachés on her staff.

I flew on to Oslo to visit Headquarters, AFNORTH, commanded by a British officer of four-star rank. I also called on the Norwegian Ministry of Defence that housed their intelligence staffs. On earlier visits I had stayed with Tony and Diana Younger, with whom Betty and I had once shared a house in Camberley in 1945 while Tony and I were both students at the Staff College. He was Chief of Staff of AFNORTH as a major-general and a fellow sapper as well. I well remember an earlier visit to AFNORTH while General Walter Walker was in command. He invited me to a reception at his palatial residence. On arrival I was surprised to see Gurkha soldiers with drawn kukris standing at each corner of the main staircase. Most of their guests were Norwegian civilians. The look on their faces spoke volumes.

The Norwegian military were kindness itself in their offices in the heart of Oslo. It was sad to think that this was my last visit in an official capacity. At the weekend the Norwegian Naval captain commanding their intelligence machinery insisted on taking Betty and me out sailing on the Oslo fjord. We had a splendid time and fetched up on a small island in the afternoon where his family had a substantial house. There we enjoyed a barbecue of gargantuan proportions. He took us back afterwards to the defence attaché's house where we were staying.

This kindness reminds me of earlier occasions when I had experienced Norwegian hospitality. One year Betty and I took our car across the Channel and proceeded via Belgium and Germany up to the car ferry from North Germany to Denmark. We reached Copenhagen for talks with Erik Fournais and his staff. Overnight we caught a ferry from Copenhagen to Oslo. There I had the usual talks with Norwegians and attended an intelligence conference at AFNORTH, while Betty stayed with the Youngers. The Norwegians had organised a party for those attending the conference in the evening. We duly set out for this party and drove to a lake running east and west where an excellent barbecue was being staged. As the sun went down at the west end of the lake in a blaze of colour, the full moon rose at the east end. This was a memorable sight that lives still in my mind.

My last major farewell trip was to Washington and Ottawa. Both trips were fun and I was able to include visits as Chief Royal Engineer and as DGI. In Washington I had got to know well Danny Graham's successor, an Air Force Lieutenent General. His comment to me as we said goodbye was 'Thank you, David, for your annual teach-in.' This, I thought, was more than kind. It was borne out by Frank Cooper some years later when he remarked to me at a party after we had both retired, 'David, I never realised while I was PUS just how influential you had been on the Washington intelligence scene.' This was another kind thought that I am not sure was altogether merited.

Farewell visit to Washington as Director General Intelligence MOD with Director of DIA, 1978

While in the Pentagon I saw the Chief of the US Corps of Engineers. US Engineers are different to our own, as they also have responsibility for works services on inland waterways throughout continental USA. But despite this they also run the full gamut of engineer support for the US Army worldwide. It was a great pleasure to visit the home of their Corps at Fort Belvoir where an RE officer was posted as liaison officer.

I flew up to Ottawa. There I had a nostalgic visit to their senior Engineer Officer as well as to the intelligence community and Chief of Staff. I had a delightful visit to a Canadian field squadron that formed part of a brigade to the west of Ottawa. The officer commanding had no engineer-in-chief plus supporting staff to provide guidance. Such are the effects of too severe a pruning of military resources, as the Canadian forces had suffered.

Back home, Betty and I were much exercised in mind about where to settle on retirement from the London scene. We were determined to keep sailing, so we quartered the area west of Southampton at weekends. Lymington seemed to answer our requirements, not least in permitting both house and yacht to be based close to one another. We registered with Jackson's, the estate agent, to buy a house. After several false starts he rang us in London one Friday to say that a house that might suit us was just coming on the market. We dashed down by car to Lymington on the Saturday. We liked the house, but were told that it was due to come on the open market on the following Monday if we did not accept the asking price. Without time even to stage a survey, we argued fiercely over the rest of the weekend and, first thing Monday, we rang Paul Jackson to say that we would buy the house at the asking price. Completion was demanded within a month. This, too, we swallowed and by early summer the house was ours. Fortunately, sale of our mews house in Eaton Mews South was simple, as demand was high. We made more than enough to buy the new house, down Lower Pennington Lane about a mile or more from the local High Street. We moved in to Long Barton during the summer, and I prepared to hand over my job to Vice Admiral Gus Halliday.

The final weeks in office had seen a series of farewell parties and visits, both within the MoD and also the diplomatic community. I even had a dinner with the Chinese Ambassador. This was memorable for the table layout with a large rotating centre that was constantly refilled with succulent dishes. The Chinese red wine was also potable. The Russians were less forthcoming. I had attended their annual drinks party in the Ambassador's residence in the diplomatic quarter of Kensington on a number of occasions. One always felt under surveillance there, despite the very good red caviar to go with the drinks that one consumed with care. The Americans were more than kind. I had been to their Ambassador's residence in Regent's Park on several occasions. The CIA representative in London was an old friend, as were the liaison team from DIA working within the midst of the DIS. I said farewell to the Ministers in our building; to the JIC members in the Cabinet Office; to the many friends in the Foreign Office. It was particularly tough to have to say goodbye to so many old friends in the DIS whose support had for so long been essential to my own efforts. Betty and I left for Lymington in a daze of kindness and hospitality. I felt most tired and in need of a long rest to recapture energy. What happened subsequently is the subject in bare outline of my last chapter.

I end this chapter by giving verbatim a copy of my final briefing in the MoD.

Final DIS Briefing For DGI 18 August 1978

1   We represent five Colonels,
    Though I'm in Navy Blue

And I fly aeroplanes, of course
Dressed in a lighter hue.
On matters of intelligence
We've briefed from day to day
But now it is to DGI
Farewell, we've come to say.
2 For views across the ocean blue
Both long term and ephemeral,
No living being knows as much
As our Director-General;
His knowledge is exhaustive
And his mind is analytical,
His patience soon expended
If the argument's political:
He can tell the subtle diff'rence
Twixt the Lebedev and Vaviloff,
Recite the Afric' ports of call
Where Soviet sailors have it off,
And even if he cannot gauge
The Red Fleet's capability,
He'll always put a briefer right
On Aden's visibility!
3 His knowledge of the Warsaw Pact
Is practic'ly impeccable,
He quotes you every army's strength
And all of them are checkable,
He knows their tank's performance well
And whether they are used enough,
He's counted all the medals on
The chest of Marshal Ustinov;
He does not like to listen to
The milit'ry mi-nu-ti-ae
Of movements in GSFG
Or routine vodka resupply,
But woe betide a briefer
If he fails to spot and emphasize
A trend that needs analysis
And watching with two hawkish eyes!
4 On aerial intelligence
Of CRUSTY CRATE and KUTAKHOV
He often wants more detail

Than the briefer plans to tell him of
You cannot play a BLINDER, boys
And Flannel it right through
It pays not to be CARELESS, lads,
Or he'll have a go at you.
On FLAGONS he's an expert
Whilst on FOXBAT he's unbeatable
And if you think he's dozing
When the lights' out at the back
Beware the fearsome gimlet eye
You might just get the sack.

5   He knows the Cypriot bishops
Who exert a secret influence,
And which Icelandic skippers
Might produce another crisis tense;
He can name the Spanish generals
Who might launch a sudden coup d'état,
And as to Baader-Meinhof's gang
Why, yes, he knows just who they are;
He knows the virtues and the faults
Of every NATO Nation too,
Assesses situations from
The Skagerak to Kyprianu,
And if you need an expert
On the secrets of the Vatican
I don't know if he'll tell you
But I feel quite certain that he can!

6   If he has a favourite subject
T'is the Middle-East Affair,
From Masira to Mount Hermon
He tells us that he's been there.
Although the PLO intrigues
Are positively Byzantine,
He seldom gets no feel for those
Mysterious matters Levantine;
He can quote the latest casualties,
Of ZANU and of ZAPU too,
If you don't know the answer
He will very quickly have at you.
He seldom hands out bouquets
But on Scorpions is very keen

We hear he's left as parting gift
The latest mark of guillotine.
7 And so we join to bid him
A tender last farewell
From the Briefers' prickly rostrum
Which, at times, he's made a hell
But, by and large, we've pleased him
Tho' we've supped with a long spoon
As we've tried to keep our powder dry
Lest we use it up too soon
So off at last he's going
Doubtless to pastures new
But he takes the best of wishes
From all the Briefing crew.
8 And now at last you must retire
We wait on your relief
We leave you with the Statement
This completes the morning brief.

CHAPTER 11

Lymington: 1978 onwards

IT IS NOT POSSIBLE, or desirable, to record all that occurred to me since my retirement in August 1978. All that I propose to do is to set out the main events of what now amounts to over twenty-five years of so-called retirement. Until the end of 1982, I was still Chief Royal Engineer and needed to fulfil a number of engagements in this capacity. In 1980, Robin Leigh-Pemberton, who was chairman of Nat West Bank, as well as Lord Lieutenant of Kent, invited me to work two days a week with the headquarters of Nat West. This started a second career as a political consultant to the Board of Nat West for five years. I then joined County Nat West, their merchant bank subsidiary, and finally Pareto Partners into the nineties, when this strand of my life finally ended. I was invited to be vice-president of the New Forest Area of St John's Ambulance in the mid eighties with a view to succeeding Dick Lloyd, who lived in Lymington, as president. I enjoyed a number of years in this latter capacity. Sailing remained an abiding interest until the turn of the century when I reverted to a motorboat to keep me in touch with salt water. Betty died after a heart attack aboard our boat in 1989. I married Trisha in 1994 after five years coping on my own at Long Barton. Each of these events I will set out in outline in this, the last chapter of an eventful life.

Being Chief Royal Engineer kept my nose to the grindstone soon after my retirement in late August. A ten-day tour of British Engineer Headquarters and units in Germany started in mid October. Betty and I first drove to Rheindahlen where we stayed a night with the Chief Engineer BAOR, Barry Pollard and his wife. Next day I called on the various elements of the Corps in Headquarters BAOR; combat engineers, Survey, Postal; then off to Düsseldorf to call on HQ Rhine Area and finally to Oerlinghausen for a night with the Commander of 1 British Corps Engineers. Oerlinghausen was where I had come to rest with 246 Field Company in 1945. On the following morning, I called on the Corps Headquarters in Bielefeld before driving on to Osnabruck to see 2 Armoured Division Engineer Regiment. 16 Field Squadron, that I had commanded in Egypt in 1950/51, provided the Guard of Honour. I subsequently went round their portion of the barracks before going on

Freedom of Nienburg Procession, 1979

to drinks at the regimental WOs and Sergeants Mess and lunch with the officers. After lunch I toured an independent squadron in Osnabruck and motored off to Verden to stay with CRE 1 Armoured Division, Richard Peck commanding. Next morning I went round the regiment in Nienburg. In the afternoon we set off for Hanover to visit a postal unit and then on to Hameln to stay with 28 Amphibious Engineer Regiment. It was a delight next day to see their equipment in action as ferries on the River Weser before moving on to Iserlohn to stay with my daughter Janet and her husband Andrew, who was commanding a squadron in 26 Armoured Engineer Regiment. 23 October saw visits to 14 Topo Squadron, a survey unit at Ratingen; on to Willich to go round a CRE Works establishment, plus engineer base workshops, stores depot and plant park; and finally back to Rheindahlen for a last night with Chief Engineer BAOR. Formal dinner parties took place each night with Betty resplendent as always. It was no wonder that, after a return via the Zeebrugge to Dover ferry and the long run through to Lymington, we needed several days to recover.

I have given this tour detailed treatment as it became the norm for successive tours in every year up to 1982 inclusive. I covered Germany on each occasion, leaving the Engineer-in-Chief to visit UK based units. For special occasions I took part in UK events, not least the Minley Garden Party for officers and their wives, both serving and retired, given annually by the Colonels Commandant Royal Engineers. Germany remained my largest commitment, both strenuous and rewarding. At Nienburg I took the freedom of the town on behalf of 21 Engineer Regiment who were based there for many years. I did the same at Hameln, home to 28 Amphibious Engineer Regiment. In 1981, I visited my old unit in Berlin, staying at the Villa Lemm with the GOC and his wife, who was the daughter of Margaret Wellesley.

In the UK, special events also occurred at which I presided. One of these was a visit to Chard in Devon to receive relicts of Lt. Chard VC, who took command at the Battle of Rorke's Drift in South Africa against an onslaught by many thousands of Zulus. The family had decided to make a presentation of his sword and bust to the RE Museum to follow up his VC medal. The actual centenary of Rorke's Drift took place on 21 January 1979. On this date at Hatch Beauchamp, Donald Phillips, direct descendant of Chard himself, made the presentation, after which we all attended a service in the local church. Lucky members subsequently went to the Phillips' household for lunch. The Royal Engineers Band from Aldershot provided the music. Troops on parade were from 100 Field Squadron Royal Monmouth Royal Engineers, Royal Engineers Association and Royal British Legion and the Corps of Drums of 100 Squadron.

Yet another happy occasion was the annual Corps weekend at the Royal School of Military Engineering at Chatham. Betty and I usually stayed with Unity Baines, widowed mother of my son-in-law, Andrew, who had a house in Rochester near King's College School and the Cathedral. Saturday was devoted to social occasions, notably a smoke-filled party in the Garrison Warrant Officers and Sergeants Mess in the evening. Sunday saw a large Royal Engineers Association parade on the square at Brompton Barracks, where I had first paraded as a young officer in 1939. After my inspection of the parade and standards from all over the country, we moved to Rochester Cathedral for a church service attended by the Lord Lieutenant of Kent, Robin Leigh-Pemberton, local MPs, Mayors of Rochester, Chatham, and Gillingham conurbation and families of sappers, past and present. Next came a march past outside the Mayor's parlour of Rochester at which the Mayor, the Lord Lieutenant and I took the salute. The party adjourned for lunch at the Royal Engineers Mess in Chatham. An irritant at this function year after year was the uninvited presence of my old enemy, General 'Splosh' Jones, who had retired to Kent. He insisted in marching in the procession of old comrades and attending the lunch. He did it, I suppose, out of nostalgia for the Corps. Even at the Minley Garden Party, my first garden

Chard presentation, Hatch Beauchamp, 1981

party acting as principal host, he intercepted me on my way to thank the Director of Music for the concert before tea, to comment that 'did I know that part of my duties was to thank the Corps Band for their performance?' Old animosities die hard, I fear.

I paid a visit to sapper units in Northern Ireland in April 1981. Jeremy Rougier was Chief Engineer before becoming Engineer-in-Chief, once my troop commander in Aden back in 1960. 33 Independent Field

Squadron was the resident squadron on a full tour of duty, reinforced by 33 Field Squadron operating in unpleasing places like Crossmaglen near the Irish border. I presented Long Service and Good Conduct medals that had been richly deserved.

An unexpected invitation from America appeared in my post one day in the spring of 1980. This was an invitation to give the 'Threat to NATO' address as a lead in to an American Army symposium on Barrier/counter-Barrier Warfare in Washington from 5–7 June. The cover letter said that I would need to be fully updated at Top Secret level, as the conference was at that level of security. In Washington, many retired folk retained their security clearances as members of 'Think Tanks' surrounding the Pentagon. In the UK, all clearances are removed on the day of retirement – officially no one wants to know you. I therefore wrote to my successor, asking for restoration of security clearances with a view to briefing before attending the symposium. Back came the reply that no exceptions could be made in the UK to my request. I told Washington accordingly. They replied saying that, of course, they would restore my clearances and could I come a day earlier for suitable briefing? I said I would do just that. In the event, both pre-briefing and the symposium went off smoothly. I think my address sold well to the assembled company.

Another remarkable occasion was the visit of the Chief Minister of Gibraltar to Minley to celebrate the long period in which the Royal Engineers, notably Fortress Tunnelling Companies, had served on the Rock. Gibraltar Barracks, Minley, was looking immaculate as General Sir William Jackson, Governor of Gibraltar at the time, stood ready to receive the Chief Minister. The proceedings passed off without a hitch of any kind, followed by lunch in Minley Officers Mess.

An additional Corps event was the annual AGM and dinner for the Royal Engineers Association. This took place each year in London and was attended by delegates from all over the country. One year I had the temerity to invite questions from the floor before closing the meeting. Inevitably this led to local grievances being aired, for which I had no answer. Nevertheless I still feel deeply about the need to encourage each element of the Corps family to feel integrated. About this time I began to produce an annual Christmas Message in the appropriate edition of *The Sapper*. This was focused on endeavouring to encourage the Corps family, be they serving, Territorial Army, or retired, to feel at one with other elements. This policy has been pursued by my successors with excellent results. At intervals, the Corps Committee met under my chairmanship to consider Corps affairs. One of the most important

Visit by Prime Minister Gibraltar to Gibraltar Barracks Minley with Governor General Sir William Jackson GCB, KBE, MC (late RE), 1981

decisions was to proceed with a new Corps museum at Chatham. The cramped premises inside Brompton Barracks were most inadequate, and it was decided to proceed with taking over the Pavilion building as the new museum. I always maintained that, once the central courtyard was roofed over and large exhibits of equipment could be displayed under it, the Museum would succeed. My successors were clever in devising fund-raising means so that this work could be undertaken. At intervals I have myself been back to Chatham to see progress. Now the Royal Engineers Museum is one of the best in the country.

Finally, I should record two Royal visitations to the Corps, one to the Surveyors at Hermitage and one to the Postal Headquarters at Mill Hill. Survey Branch laid on a splendid visit. Hermitage, near Newbury, was looking its best. Her Majesty as Colonel-in-Chief of the Corps was most interested in the various elements that go towards map making, printing, and distribution. Lunch in the mess was first rate and I found Her Majesty ready to discuss almost anything, despite prior warning not to raise subjects unless she did. Mill Hill was equally good as a visit to another hard-working element of the Corps, now removed from the Corps family as a result of Army reorganisation. Once again the day was beautiful, the displays of handling Army post of great interest and the lunch first-rate. A noted painter produced a picture of the Queen inspecting the main sorting office. I have a photocopy still.

In the Autumn of 1982, I needed to select my successor after five years as Chief Royal Engineer. General Sir Hugh Beech had become a member of the Army Board and was the obvious choice as an officer younger than myself and therefore still in touch with contemporary Army problems. I forwarded the name to the Palace and received the Royal assent through Sir Philip Moore, Her Majesty's Private Secretary. We were bidden for an interview with Her Majesty. She had always shown a wide interest in Corps matters and kept us both answering numerous questions in her private study in the Palace. As we departed I was fascinated to see the Permanent Secretary of the Ministry of Defence sitting patiently waiting for his audience.

The Nat West experience was most interesting. Robin Leigh-Pemberton invited me to lunch at the Bank HQ in Lothbury, just behind the Bank of England: this followed the annual Corps function at Chatham where I had been host and Robin the principal guest as Lord Lieutenant. At lunch, Betty suggested that I was getting bored in Lymington and needed something additional to do. At the lunch in London, I was surprised to find the entire Board of Nat West assembled. I was asked a number of questions and answered as best I could after two years away from Whitehall. The following week I got a letter from Robin, inviting me to join the bank as an adviser for two days a week with access to the Board dining room for lunch. I accepted and in early autumn 1980 reported for duty.

I was allotted an office and use of a secretary. I was asked initially to go through the bank intelligence staff, headed by the excellent David Kern, to see if I could suggest any changes. David and I got on at once, as did his staff who were largely divided into desk officers keeping files on the many parts of the world in which the bank operated. The main clients were the International Bank that operated in the Nat West tower that had recently been completed as the tallest building in the City of London. I became a Freeman of the City in 1981, having been recommended by Lord Mais, a war-time sapper who had recently been Lord Mayor. Induction at Guildhall had been a great occasion; his successor presided and both he and Lord Mais signed my application to become a Freeman. Gus Sinclair, the newly-appointed Engineer-in-Chief, and my wife attended the ceremony at Guildhall that Betty and I much enjoyed.

The bank invited me to carry out tours on their behalf, accompanied by a banker from the International Bank, to various parts of the world. The first of these took me to North and South America in October

With David Kern at Nat West, 1982

1981. Washington and New York offered briefings on South America. This I gladly accepted before going on to Mexico, Columbia, Argentina and Brazil. Washington allowed me to make contact once again with old friends now retired into 'Think Tanks' surrounding the Pentagon. One briefing from the Heritage Foundation given in eastern Washington in a largely black neighbourhood sticks in the mind. New York was useful, not least in calling on the World Bank. Mexico came next; a Cuban was the Nat West representative in Mexico City, an extraordinary place. The Cuban was highly intelligent and well informed. He had laid on an elaborate programme for the two of us. Christopher Tickell, then Ambassador, was most helpful as were the embassies of the US and Canada. We met Mexican bankers, businessmen, and journalists and enjoyed a number of social engagements. My report to the bank's chairman, directors and head men concluded that Mexico would remain on course to develop the resources for the decade or so, though the going looked like being a little rough for the next year or two.

Columbia was utterly different. My report concluded that one cannot visit this country without carrying away a sense of unease as to how society will evolve in future – prophetic words as it turned out. Bogota memories include the Gold Museum, an exquisite experience in lighting and gold Inca artefacts, a mugging in the streets that failed to get my

Freedom of the City of London, 1979

wallet, and a presidential palace where the incumbent had for many years come and gone by helicopter, never by car.

Argentina was quite different again. Neither the defence attaché, ex DIS in my time, nor his ambassador had any foreboding that the Argentine military would invade the Falklands three months later, though admitting that the capability existed. Buenos Aires already looked a run-down city that had reached its zenith before the First World War. The great mass of Italian settlers in and around the capital city had to be seen to be believed.

Brazil was a world apart, given its Portuguese background. I went in turn to Sao Paulo, Brasilia and Rio de Janeiro before flying home. Sao Paulo was a sea of people and skyscraper blocks and the car factories on the outskirts were huge. Brasilia, the seat of government in a new capital city, boasted buildings by world-famous architects including Le Corbusier. Rio boasts the Copacabana beach; we were lucky to be taken out to sea on a yacht owned by a British entrepreneur. Brazilian bankers were most informative.

In all these countries, as much was learned through social contacts at lunches and dinners as from formal office visits. I arrived home with my written report to all and sundry ready for typing. Robin Leigh-Pemberton kindly arranged for me to give an oral presentation to the Nat West Board of Directors. He did this each time I went on tour.

After I was established at Lothbury, I wrote to the permanent under-secretaries at the MoD and the Foreign Office, asking for permission to contact top-level officials in both ministries should I need briefing in the event of a fast-moving situation that warranted my masters being given the latest facts. Both agreed, as old friends of the past. I used the Foreign Office contacts to check what was happening in a number of situations that ensued. I was therefore in a good position to handle events in the Falklands early in 1982 after the Argentinian invasion and subsequent dispatch of a task force from the UK to rectify occupation of a British colonial territory. With my other hat on as Chief Royal Engineer, I went down to Southampton to wish bon voyage to the sappers loading onto the *Canberra*. The departure of the ship was a highly emotional time for the families involved. I produced regular notes for distribution within Lothbury and the Nat West tower, giving my views on the developing situation once a lodgement on the Falklands was secured on the long, hard slog to Port Stanley. Once the crisis over the survival of our Carrier to Argentinian air attack was resolved, I came down heavily in favour of a British victory. The Group Chief Executive told me how useful he had found these notes, not least in saving the bank large sums of money, regrettably unspecified.

1982 saw a further tour on behalf of the bank, this time eastward in October/November of that year. My peregrinations took me to Thailand, Indonesia, Philippines, South Korea and Hong Kong. Bangkok, as always, is a fascinating city. Politically there seemed hope that the series of military coups had come to an end. Economically, Thailand at that time seemed determined to press ahead with development on Western lines. A return to Jakarta was most welcome in my new civilian capacity. As ever, the regime was underpinned by the military as they provided so much of the infrastructure in the outer islands. At that time, Islamic fundamentalism had as yet shown no sign of development; Indonesians seemed to profess an attachment to Islam that was benign. The Philippines, as viewed from Manila, seemed peaceful, though banditry onshore and piracy offshore occurred away from population centres. Mindanao remained a sore point with its Muslim population still at odds with Manila. Things move slowly in all these countries.

Korea was the most ebullient society that I visited, after a short stop for refuelling in Taiwan. The population of South Korea seemed determined to overtake their erstwhile Japanese masters in economic growth and productivity. Seoul was an exciting city to stay in, despite proximity to the border with North Korea and the resulting provision of shelters against air attack throughout the built-up area. An interlude to strictly Nat West business was a day with the American and South Korean Army. As Chief Royal Engineer, I had been in touch beforehand with the defence attaché. He arranged for the three of us to visit Panmunjon in the centre of the demilitarised zone. Under American auspices, I stood with one foot in South Korea and one in the North, watched by stern communist North Korean guards. The DMZ was itself a bird sanctuary for much of the Far East as the shore-to-shore strip across Korea was heavily mined. That afternoon the South Koreans took us down into the bowels of the earth where they had uncovered a major North Korean tunnel leading under the border into South Korea. A single sentry facing into North Korea seemed to have a lonely vigil. Hong Kong, too, shows just how far the entrepreneurial spirit can grow an economy. I felt that the basic issue remained how to kowtow to the 'Emperor' in Peking while continuing to operate a free economy in Hong Kong. I fear this issue still bedevils Hong Kong after reabsorption into China.

1983 saw Robin Leigh-Pemberton appointed as Governor of the Bank of England. He kindly invited me to dine in the Lothbury offices with other Directors of the Bank to greet his predecessor as Governor. Conversation between the two men over the dinner table was worth a guinea a minute. Robin's successor at Nat West was Lord Boardman who had hitherto presided over the Midland's section of the Nat West empire. He proved not to be as interested in the world scene as was his predecessor. Progressively our personal relations fell apart, leading to my departure from advising Nat West in late 1984 to support only their merchant bank, County Nat West.

In 1993 I did a tour of the Middle East and in 1994 a tour of Iraq and Turkey. The tour of the Middle East started in Muscat and led to Amman in Jordan. Abiding memories are of the British Embassy in Iraq dwarfed by horrible skyscraper blocks erected in the desert around its ancient compound, and of a pause at traffic lights in Amman enlivened by a large car going in the opposite direction. It too stopped at the lights; out poured guards, guns at the ready; even King Abdullah was constrained to halt at the lights, unlike more tyrannical rulers in the region. I found Turkey attractive, though much of my time was spent in and around the shores of the Bosporus. Ankara had its points, not least around the British Embassy. Smyrna was well worth a visit, not least to the international NATO headquarters located there.

Each year back in London I issued to the top management of Nat West a series of notes on topics of the day, ranging from the Far East through Russia to the Middle East, Africa and South America. In this, my access to under-secretaries in the MoD and the Foreign Office proved to be most helpful. Top management, particularly under Robin Leigh-Pemberton, was concerned as to what they could do in the national interest. I also lectured at their instructional establishment at Heythrop Park in Oxfordshire.

County Nat West, as a merchant bank, had a very different atmosphere to that of its parent institution. I had got to know its chairman well and several of the main characters in the bank. I was invited to address audiences in their City offices about once a month, to advise as necessary on the merit of events politically and to tour America annually to talk to big company clients and address audiences, based on the marketing team in New York. This I did, despite a deteriorating relationship within the bank as years went by. Nat West did not fully understand the difference between a parent clearing bank and a merchant bank that was dependent upon an entrepreneurial system. Scandals surfaced; the chairman had eventually to face charges in the courts; new executives came in who fell out with others longer in post. Two senior people I had great respect for resigned in consequence. Two more were sacked in curious circumstances. Meanwhile, I carried on with my responsibilities that included several trips round North America. The time came when I received an approach from four senior executives who had left County Nat West. They asked me to join a new bank they were forming that was underwritten by Mellon Bank of America. This bank provided premises in the City of London. I decided to accept, resigned from County Nat West and started work with the new bank, later to be named Pareto Partners, a purely investment bank. The complete marketing team in New York resigned en bloc and came over to the new bank. I resumed a similar function to that I had held with County Nat West. This lasted into the middle nineties, when we parted by mutual consent, as I had reached seventy-five years of age and felt the load of touring audiences in America was increasing, although these visits always remained fun. Accompanied by one of the New York team, and on occasion one of the four partners from London, I penetrated into large tracts of America. Sacramento, capital of California State, was particularly interesting. There I confronted an audience drawn from Calpers, one of the richest State pension funds in America. Atlanta in the State of Georgia was equally rewarding, as was Los Angeles. Chicago provided another field for calling on big American businesses. Back in London I was invited to address audiences and advise bank executives as Pareto Partners grew. It really felt like the end of the road when I had to give up participation in this successful venture.

1984 was a red letter year for me. Going up in the train to London one day I found myself in the same compartment as the Principal Private Secretary to the Queen. He and I had got on very well during my years as Chief Royal Engineer. On parting he said he had enjoyed our talk and would be in touch. He was indeed, and with his letter came an invitation to join the Royal party on *Britannia* for the forthcoming celebration of the 40th anniversary of D-Day in Normandy. On his advice, no doubt, Her Majesty had decided to take one three-star officer from each Service as part of her entourage. On 5 June therefore, in early afternoon, I found myself at Buckingham Palace, driven by my old driver from the MoD. I went to the official side of the Palace and there met the other members of the party to accompany the Queen. Mid-afternoon we drove to Waterloo Station to join the Royal Train. This delivered us to a station close to the Portsdown Hill House that had housed Eisenhower and his staff forty years before. Behind the Queen, we all trooped into the Operations Room, where maps of the beaches were displayed and explained by the briefing staff. By car we proceeded down into Portsmouth. The Queen's car was met by a large and enthusiastic crowd, as we threaded our way onto the quayside where *Britannia* lay alongside. Soon we sailed, preceded by the Trinity House flagship with their dignitaries in full panoply on the foredeck. The guard destroyer followed *Britannia*. That night we had drinks before dinner with the Queen and the Duke of Edinburgh. The Queen, as always, had about five minutes' talk to me about Royal Engineer affairs.

I was up at the crack of dawn next morning to see the ship enter the Caen Canal at Ouistreham and proceed to Pegasus Bridge on her way to Caen. Pegasus Bridge was of course open, the Café Gondrée plainly visible. I was able to describe the scene in 1944 as I had seen it until I was wounded. Arrival in Caen was an anti-climax, with no welcoming crowds or dignitaries. Mitterand had ruled that initially the Queen was a guest of the City of Caen. No recognition of her presence could be laid on till after she had called on the Mayor of Caen and seen the Cathedral, before returning to the ship to host a lunch party, including a French minister. We duly disembarked in the timber yard designated by the French as the ship's berth outside Caen. As we drove into the City, crowds appeared and many Frenchmen cheered the Queen on her way to the Mairie. Here she was met by the Mayor and corporation, speeches were made and we were all conducted round the Cathedral.

We returned to the ship; guards of honour appeared, and soon the crowned heads of Europe, presidents and ministers from France arrived. A drinks party took place before lunch on board. I spoke to a number of crowned heads from Europe including the Queens of Holland and Denmark and the King of Norway. After lunch we boarded cars for the cemetery at Bayeux, where the main British ceremony was to take place. We took station to receive President Mitterand. He was late and eventually appeared in a small new Citroën car – a sales gimmick, I suspect, for French cars. After the Church of England service of memorial, the Queen entered the waiting helicopter, with the entourage in a following RAF flight. We headed west for the American beaches at the southern end of the Cherbourg peninsula. Suddenly our helicopter started circling, an unpleasing manoeuvre. A written note appeared from the pilot saying that both helicopters had been ordered to halt as there was congestion at the landing site. We knew that the Queen hated helicopter flights, so this was most unfortunate. However, the delay was soon over.

We landed and were met by minibuses, including one for the Queen, laid on by the French. We drove to the beach where stands had been erected at the back of the beach. Our stand was slightly back from that of the Heads of State. Our seats were in the middle of the rows and we had to climb over a number of uniformed Allied officers to reach them. The ceremony then got underway on the sand where small waves were lapping the high water mark. A member of our party who had been present at the dress rehearsal whispered to me that waves were coming right over the colour party's boots on that occasion. Fortunately, this did not happen on our day, though some of the national marching contingents got their feet wet. The Heads of State left their seats and trooped round the Services contingents in a form of inspection. At the conclusion of the ceremony, people surged onto the beach from our stands. We British were not to be outdone and climbed over many seats to see the fun. The Admiral in the party and I were rapidly walking to the exit when we felt ourselves prodded in the back. We turned and confronted American Secret Service agents escorting Mrs Reagan off the beach, her husband having escaped with other Heads of State before the crush started. We gave way and soon reached our mini bus for the flight back to Arromanches, where the Queen was to take the salute at a march past of veterans. This went well and we followed the Queen once again by helicopter to Caen airport and the flight back to the UK in an aircraft of the Queen's flight. I found myself in a compartment with the Duke of Edinburgh. Conversation was desultory en route as we were all tired. The faithful George Mattocks collected me at Northolt and drove me home to Lymington.

In 1994, Scotty Scott-Bowden and I went to Normandy for the 50th Anniversary. I attended a civic dinner in Portsmouth at which the Queen was present. I sat next to the Chairman of the Joint Chiefs of Staff in Washington at the dinner. We had a lively discussion of world events. In Normandy we were looked after by 32 Armoured Engineer Regiment from Germany. They were responsible under the Commander of the British 3rd Division of today for much of the ceremonial functions to mark 6 June – D-Day fifty years on. The CRE, Peter Wall, is now a major-general; the commander of 3 Division has become Chief of the General Staff. We lived with the Regiment which provided a car for us. Celebrations on D-Day included a ceremony in 3rd Division War Cemetery in Hermanville and a visit to Pegasus Bridge. On the 7 June, I unveiled the Corps war memorial on the hill, east of Arromanches, by kind invitation of my successor but three as Chief Royal Engineer.

Going back in time, Dick Lloyd, who had settled east of the Lymington river on retirement, invited me to become vice-president of St John Ambulance for the New Forest area. His aim was that I should succeed him on his reaching the age of 80 and that I should get to know many volunteers who ran the various divisions in the Forest and provided leaders for adult members, cadets, and latterly Badgers, for those too young to become cadets initially. The area Commissioner, who was

Unveiling of Royal Engineers Memorial, Arromanches, 1994

based in Lymington with a small staff, ran the area professionally. There were five ambulances scattered amongst the divisions, which ran from Totton and Fawley in the east to New Milton, Ringwood, and Fordingbridge in the north of the New Forest, Brockenhurst in the centre, as well as Lymington itself. I attended annual inspections for each division, carried out by full-time staff from the County Headquarters in Winchester. There I got to know Mary Fagan as County Commissioner, now Lord Lieutenant of Hamp-shire. Highlights of the year were Cadet enrolment ceremonies for the aArea run in parish churches for the divisions in turn. I was horrified when County announced that aArea staff were so hard to come by that they had decided to abolish Area Headquarters; divisions were to come directly under County. I was out on my ear in consequence, to my sorrow. I still see friends from those days in the street on occasion to this day.

Family affairs went through crisis with the years, as well as much happiness. Betty and I cruised each summer to France and to the West Country as far as the Helford River beyond Falmouth. She had a heart attack in July 1989 when returning from our annual summer cruise. We were lying off Studland and decided to swim. I came back aboard to find her collapsed on board, having preceded me out of the water. I called up the coastguards and soon both a launch and a helicopter arrived. The launch crew cut my side rails to get her stretcher over the side. Soon she was winched up into the helicopter that flew her to Poole General Hospital. I followed and found her comfortable in bed with diagnoses that her treatment in hospital had been timely and successful. I rang a friend in Lymington to come over and help me take the boat back to Lymington. In the early hours my phone rang. Betty had had a further attack – could I come at once? I rang my two daughters and then drove rapidly to Poole. Betty was just alive. I held her hand until she died. Both daughters arrived just too late. Her funeral took place in Lymington, organised in part by the Corps of Royal Engineers Headquarters staff from Chatham. Cremation at Bournemouth followed, attended by family only, and then a reception at the Lymington Yacht Club. So ended a partnership that was already planning a 50th Anniversary party in 1991. As ever, we had our ups and downs, but it was a grave loss that took a long time to pass.

With the help of grandchildren of both my daughters' families, I continued to cruise in my Moody 29. Janet had to go to America to bring back Robin's three children. He and his family had got into a terrible tangle in Alabama and needed rescuing, at my expense, but Janet took on three more children just as the youngest of hers was leaving the nest. Robin came to live with me for the best part of a year, before leaving to paddle his own canoe. Trisha and I married after a splendid holiday in South America in a party of eight. I could go on and on about family adventures, but I feel I should leave it there.

On reflection, I have had a great life. God has been kind in granting me old age without major mishap, despite a heart bypass operation in 2002. In a new century I am not sure that I fit in. I continue as always to read myself in as best as I may on the developing situation at home and abroad. My telephone no longer rings with people seeking my views. I am so glad for this dispensation. Surrounded by my family, now Trisha, three children, ten grandchildren and four great-grandchildren, I am content. May similar good fortune attend my friends.

Index

Abdullah, King of Jordan 57, 191
Abraham, Iona 72
Abraham, Matt 65, 72
Abyssinia 107
Addis Ababa 81, 107, Aden 72–6, 82–4, 87, 94, 100, 104, 108–9, 156, 183
Africa 98–9, 103, 107, 122, 139, 164
Africa Corps 14
Africa, Horn of 50
African Unity, Organisation of 107
Ahmed 75, 95
Aitken, Lady Pam 149
Alamein 14
Alanbrooke, Viscount Lord 34
Alexander, Earl 34
Alexander, Sergeant 12
Algeria 16
America 114, 122, 184
Amman 56, 129, 191
Anderson, General 82
Andover 11, 15, 135
Ankara 172, 191
Anne, HRH Princess 152
Argentina 187, 189
Armagh 17
Army Education Corps 57
Army, Indian 2, 34
Arromanches 194
Arton, Bourne MP 88
Asher, John 18
Assad, Hafez 129
Astor, Jake 4
Astor, Lady Nancy 4
Athens 6, 45
Auchinleck, General 14
Auckland 170
Australia 100, 103, 117, 122, 131, 140, 149, 154, 167, 169
Austria 48, 61, 122, 169–70

Baath party 109
Bab el Mandeb Straits 83
Baghdad 53–4, 73–4, 100, 108
Baghdad Pact 47
Bahrain 6, 74–5, 78, 84, 108, 149
Bailey bridge(s) 15, 16, 28–9, 87
Bailey, Donald 15
Baines, Andrew 124, 131–2, 181–2
Baines, Lucy 154
Baines, Peter 124
Baines, Peter (grandson) 154
Baines, Unity 182
Baines, Simon 154
Baker, General George 109
Bali 38
Bandung 37, 39
Bangkok 150, 190
Bardia 14
Barnikel, Barny 15
Barnstaple 48, 67
Basrah 108
Basutoland 101, 106, 108
Batavia 36–7, 40–1
Bates, Air Vice Marshal Sir Leslie 110
Bates, Betty Vernon 7, 10, 11, 15, 17, 23–5, 30, 33–4, 43–4, 48, 51, 53, 55, 58, 61, 67–9, 71–6, 78, 83–5, 87, 90, 98, 109–113, 125, 131, 133–5, 140, 145–7, 149–55, 157, 162–3, 165, 167, 169–70, 172, 174–6, 180–1, 186, 196
Bates, Bridget 34, 125, 154
Bath, Royal School 58
Battalion 1 Royal Lincolns 50, 61
Battalion, 1 Seaforth 36, 41–3, 88, 117, 140, 152
Battalion, 3/5 Gurkha 39
Battalion, 4/8 Gurkha 39
Beach, General Sir Hugh 75, 186
Bechuanaland 101, 107–8
Beirut 56, 109, 129

Beit el Falaj 77
Belfast 127, 160
Belgium 2, 11, 145, 156, 174
Belize 90–2, 94–5
Benbecula 89
Benghazi 56
Benouville 18, 21, 22
Benyon-Tinker, Valerie 34
Berlin 57–8, 60–64, 68, 115, 172, 182
Berne 172
Bharatpur 149
Bicester 58
Bielefeld 31, 116, 134, 180
Binney, Lt Col. 11
Bir Hakim 14
Birdcage Walk 46
Birkbeck College 97
Bishops Monkton 85, 87
Bishopton Park 85
Blacker, General 47
Blake, George 63
Blücher Dormitory 4–6, 97, 109, 122,
  Blue Nile 81
Boardman, Lord 191
Bocock, Mr 62
Bogor 152
Bogota 187
Bombay 6, 36
Bomber Command 29
Bonn 131, 169, 172
Bosporus 191
Boston 67–8
Bovington Camp 2
Bracknell, RAF Staff College 68 69, 70
Brasilia 189
Bray, General Sir Bobby 83, 84
Brazil 187, 189
Bremen 28, 29, 30
Bremner, Richard 6
Brezhnev, Leonid 164
Brigade, 185 18
Brigade, 24 Infantry 75, 80
Brigade, 32 Army Tank 14
Brigade, 8 Infantry 26, 28
Brigade, Commando 22
Brigade, I Indian Infantry 34, 37–40
Brisbane 170
British India 4

British Somaliland 80
BRIXMIS 61, 63, 132–3
Brompton Barracks 182, 185
Brussels 109, 138–9, 167, 173
Buckingham Palace 146, 192
Buenos Aires 189
Buitenzorg 37
Bulawayo 107
Bulgaria 172
Burma 34
Burnett, Air Chief Marshal Sir Brian 47
Burntollet Bridge 115, 120–1
Bush, President George 166
Butler, Joanne 149
Butler, Major-General Hugh 149

Cabinda 105
Cabinet Office 46, 100–2, 109, 114, 117,
  120, 128 136, 139, 142, 144, 153, 171,
  176
Caen 20, 22, 193
Cairo 3, 51, 148
Calam, Sergeant Major 50
Calcutta 45
Caldwell, Brigadier 'Hindy' 10
Callaghan, Lord (James) 140, 165, 171
Callender, Ann 152
Callender, Maurice 152
Camberley 1, 2, 4, 64–73, 95, 97, 110,
  143, 174
Cambodia 118, 139, 150
Cambria House 7
Camranh Bay 118
Canada 114
Canberra 117, 152–3, 169
Cape of Good Hope 100
Cape Town 105
Cariappa, General 6
Carr, Brigadier Jim 85, 96
Carrington, Lord Peter 136–7
Carslake, General 4
Carter, Brigadier 75
Carter, President Jimmy 124
Carver, Field Marshal Sir Mike 127, 159,
  166 127, 159, 166
Cass, Brigadier 'Copper' 25, 32
Cassel 31
Castle, Nijo 151

Cater, Dep.Gov.Hong Kong 150
Caulfield, Toby 69, 72
Chandoorka, General 150
Chandrigar 156
Chard 182
Charlton 11, 15, 19, 25, 33, 45, 72, 111, 135, Charteris, Colonel Martin 46
Chatham 169, 182, 185–6, 196
Chenowith, Dr Ian 153
Chequers 137
Cherbourg 193
Chesapeake, River 155
Chetumal 94
Chicago 192
China 164, 166, 169
Christian Science 2, 3, 4, 67
Church, Seventh Day Adventist 131, 153, 170
Churchill, Randolph 71
Churchill, Sir Winston 15, 46, 71
CIA 103, 120, 124, 139, 161, 165
Civil Rights 120–1
Clark, Catherine 154
Clark, Deane 123
Clark, Thomas 154
Clark, Adam 154
Clitherow, Trisha 140, 180, 197
Clutterbuck, Major-General Richard 85, 109
Cochrane, Tommy 10, 72
Cold War 63, 73
College, Imperial Defence 109, 111, 113, 118, 171–3
College, Joint Services Staff 118
Cologne 133
Columbia 187
Company, 17 Field 18, 19
Company, 246 Field 18, 25, 28, 180
Company, 253 Field 18
Company, 59 Field 11, 12, 14
Company, 71 Field 22
Constant, Brigadier John 52, 99
Coombs, Ambassador 152
Cooper, Sir Frank 160, 166, 174
Cope, Diana 6
Copenhagen 173–4
Copper Belt 105
Cornwall, Duchy of 106

Corozal 94
Corps, 15, Field Park Plant Troop 86
County Nat West 180, 191–2
Coverdale, Miles 87
Cowie, Major 12, 13
Cowley, Captain John 4, 52
Cowtan, Major-General John 10 10
Cowtan, Rose 52
Coxwell-Rogers, Brigadier 12, 13, 16
Cranwell 6
Craven, Dacre 21, 23
Cross, Military 1, 14, 30, 44, 146
Crossmaglen 184
Cunningham, Lt General Sir Hugh 54, 100
Cyprus 56–7, 149
Cyrenaica 56

Dakar 173
Damascus 129
Danang 118
Dar es Salaam 100, 108
D'Arcy, Hyacinth 1–5, 33
Darling, Major-General Douglas 47
Darlow, Bob 26, 31
Darwin 152
DCRE Works 60, 62
D-Day 18, 20, 22, 24, 65, 192, 194
de Gaulle, General Charles 173
Deane Drummond, Major-General Tony 75, 77–8
Deccan 4, 6
Defence, Ministry of 45–6, 53, 70, 76, 103, 109, 112, 114, 117, 120, 124, 135, 137, 140, 142, 159, 161, 164–5, 167, 169, 171, 176, 179, 182
Defense Intelligence Agency 103, 107, 109, 120, 126, 138–9, 154, 161
Delhi 146–7, 149, 150, 156–7
Delmenhorst 28, 29
Dempsters 3
Denbigh, Mr 5
Denmark 173–4, 193
Denning, Vice 115
Devon 2, 48, 56, 58, 67, 85, 110–11, 182
Dhala 104
DI2 137

DI3 116, 138, 161, 164
DI4 102, 114, 148, 164
Digne 149
Dimbleby, Richard 29
Diredawa 81, 82
DIS 102–3, 113–4, 117, 120, 126, 128, 133–7, 140, 142, 145–7
DIS cont 154, 159–61, 163–6, 169, 171, 176, 189
Division, 21st Panzer 22
Division, 23rd Indian 34, 37–8, 40
Division, 3rd Engineers 18, 25, 26, 27, 28–9, 31, 33, 65, 129–30, 194
Division, 43rd 31
Division, 51st Highland 27
Division, 59th 17, 46
Division, 6th Airborne 20, 22, 65, 66
Division, 7th Armoured 14
Division, Japanese Guards 36
Division, Ninth Parachute 36
Djibouti 81
Dortmund Ems Canal 28
Dover 134
Downing Street, 10 (Number Ten) 137, 165, 171
Drake's Island 89
Dresden 61
DSO 1, 14, 33, 44, 78
Dublin 2, 6, 122
Dunkerque 11, 12, 13
Düsseldorf 130, 132, 180
Dutch East Indies 34, 38

Earle, Air Chief Marshal Sir Charles 109, 113–15
Eddy, Mary Baker 4
Eden, Sir Anthony 70
Edinburgh, HRH Duke of 193–4
Edwards, Chris Admiral 26
Edwards, David 50, 83
Egypt 3–4, 14, 48–9, 50, 52, 54, 56–7, 69–70, 83–4, 99, 100, 128, 148, 180
Eindhoven 25, 26
Eisenhower, General 34, 102, 192
El Ballah 50–1
Elbe, River 133
Elizabeth, HM Queen 145–6, 167, 170, 185, 192–4

Elizabethville 105
Elworthy, Air Marshal Sir Sam 94
Engineers, 4th Divisional 11
Engineers, Royal School of Military 122
Enschede 28
Episkopi 56
Ethiopia 77, 81, 173
Euphrates, River 107
Evill, Lt Col. Tom 32
Ewart Briggs, Christopher 122
Eyre, Major-General Jim 99

Fagan, Mary 196
Falkender, Baroness (Marcia) 165
Falklands 189
Falmouth 196
Far East 47, 99, 102, 114, 122, 137, 139, 167, 169
Farnborough Airport 11
Farnham 4, 33, 71
Farouk, King 50
Fatipur Sikri 149
Fawley 196
Fayid 54, 56, 58
Festing, General 'Frankie' 80
Fitzallan-Howard, Major Miles 115
Fitzgeorge-Balfour, General Sir 109
Fitzpatrick, General Sir Desmond 126, 132
Folding Boat Equipment (FBE) 18
Fontainebleau 130
Fordingbridge 196
Foreign Office 100, 103, 112, 118, 122, 136, 139, 142, 144, 148, 164, 176, 189, 191
Fort Belvoir 175
Fort Monroe 155
Foster, Captain 10
Foulkes, Major-General Tom 50, 53–4, 84 50, 53–4, 84
Fournais, Erik 173–4
Frensham Pond Sailing Club 68, 76
Fyffe, Lt Gen. Sir Dick 115, 135
Fyler, Virginia 107

Gaborones 108
Gatford, Jack 10, 48, 72
Gatow 58

GCHQ 100–1, 103, 114, 115, 120, 121, 124, 133, 144, 147, 150, 167
George VI, HM King 10
Georgetown 155
Gerard, General 173
Germany 122, 126, 130, 132–4, 135, 140, 156, 168, 172, 174, 181–2
Gibbon, General Sir John 143
Gibbs, Field Marshal Rowley 116 116
Gibraltar 165
Gibson, Dr 23, 25
Gillington, Colonel John 36
Gilmour, Edward 140–1
Glaser, Frau 58
Goch 27
Golan Heights 129
Gondrée, Café 22, 66, 193
Gondrée, Madame 22, 66
Gondrée, Monsieur 66
Goulson, Margaret 61
Graeme, Colonel & Mrs 72
Graham, Lt General Danny 139–40, 154–5
Gross, Mr 3
Guatemala 94
Guildford 110–12, 123–4, 130, 134–5, 142, 145, 157–8

Haig, General Al 172
Haile Selassie, Emperor 81
Hall-Tipping, Jonathan 99, 164–5
Halliday, Vice Admiral Gus 166, 169, 176
Hampshire Regiment 3, 6
Hanley, Sir Mike 165
Harby, Major George 15, 16
Harley, Alex 143, 149, 151–3
Harrison, Brigadier 16
Hawkins, Captain 11
Healey, Denis 164
Heath, Sir Edward 136–7, 154
Hefill, Brigadier 150
Hess, Rudolf 60
Hingston, Audrey 52
Hockey, Mr 3
Home Office 120, 127
Honduras, British 90, 94
Hong Kong 150, 157, 167, 190

Humphreys, Major-General Charles 55, 69
Hunt, Anne 44
Hunt, General Peter 44, 116
Hurricane Hattie 90
Hussars, 13th/18th 22
Hussein, King of Jordan 57
Hussein, Saddam 109
Hutton, Brigadier Mike 83

Imperial Services College 1
India 6, 12, 24, 31, 104, 136–7, 149
Indonesia 34, 190
Inoue, Admiral 152
IRA 17, 120–2, 126–7, 163
Iran 54, 149
Iraq 50, 53, 73, 100, 107, 124, 164, 191
Ireland 1, 5
Iremonger, Wing Commander Johnny 46
Italy 14, 133, 169

Jackson, General Sir William 116, 167 116, 167
Jackson, Paul 176
Jackson, Peter 96
Jakarta 37, 135, 140, 152, 190
Jamaica 90–2, 94
Japan 31, 149, 151–2
JARIC 114, 116, 124
Java 34, 37–9, 41, 88, 117
Jebel Akhdar 75, 77–8
Jeddah 83
Jerash 129
Jerusalem 129
Johannesburg 105
Joint Intelligence Bureau 102, 159
Joint Intelligence Committee 46, 99, 101, 120–1, 126, 136–7, 142, 144, 147–8, 161, 163–5, 176
Joint Planning Staff 46–8
Jones, General 'Splosh' 65, 67, 95–6, 98, 143, 182–3
Jordan 50–1, 57, 100, 129, 191

Kamaran Island 83
Karachi 6
Kasouli 156
Katanga 105

KCB 145
Kelly, David 164
Kent, Prince Michael of 146, 169
Kenya 50, 56, 83, 100, 104
Kenyatta, Jomo 83
Kern, David 186
KGB 159
Khama, Seretse 108
Khormaksar 75, 76
Khota Bahru 43
Kinshasa 104
Kipkabus 104
Kitson, Frank 77
Kloppa, General 14
Koenig, General 173
Kohat 4
Kommandantura 58, 60, 115
Korea 56, 164, 190
Kuala Lumpur 42–3, 116, 117
Kuwait 78, 79
Kyoto 150–1

Laing, Jamie 6
Lake, Great Bitter 50, 148
Lambeth 98, 99, 106
Langley 139
Lawless, Kathleen 6
Le Bailly, VA Sir Louis 136–7, 141–2, 149, 157–8
Le Corbusier 189
Le Fanu, Admiral 144
Lebanon 56, 129
Lebua, Chief Jonathan 106, 108
Leigh-Pemberton, Robin 180, 182, 186, 189–91
Lendrum, Harold 42, 63
Lewis, Mike 109, 172
Libya 50, 56, 100
Lingen 28
Lloyd, Major-General Dick 46, 98–9, 106, 180, 194
London 2, 47, 90, 92, 98–9, 109, 117, 120, 123–7, 131, 134–5, 145, 150, 153–4, 157–8, 164, 166, 169, 171, 173, 176, 184, 186, 191–2
London, King's College 111, 131
Long Barton 176, 180
Lossiemouth 18

Lothbury 186, 189–90
Lourenço Marques 106
Lovat, Lord 22
Lovell, Miles 47, 49
Luce, Sir William 84
Lusaka 105, 108
Luzon 152
Lymington 46, 73, 87, 141, 176, 180–1, 186, 194, 196
Lyneham 90, 149

MacDermott, Mr 5
MacGuire, Air Marshal 'Mac' 135–6
MacLagan, 'Chu' 43, 117
Mais, Lord 186
Makarios, Archbishop 57
Malaya 39, 42–4
Malaysia 36
Malim, Mr 5
Malinovsky, Marshal 156
Mallaby, Brigadier 38
Manning, Douglas 91, 94
Mary, HM Queen 47, 57
Mattocks, George 145, 149, 194
Mau Mau 74, 104
Maude, Rodney 18
McClure, John 46
McNamara, Aline 73
McNamara, Brian 73
McWilliam, Brigadier Maurice 80–2
McWilliam, Norah 81–2
Meares, Brigadier Ken 116
Medina 129
Meekin, Wally 74, 78
Merrill, Major Bob 63
Mexico 187
MI4 98, 99, 117
MI5 120–1, 144, 150, 165, 167
MI6 52, 120–1, 144, 150, 167
Middle East 47, 50, 52, 54, 56, 99, 103, 107, 114, 122, 148, 164, 169, 191
Mindanao 190
Minley 33, 34, 65, 77, 169, 181–2, 184
Mitla Pass, Battle of 69
Mitterand, President 193
Mobutu, President J.D. 104
Mogg, General Sir John 33

Montgomery, Field Marshal Viscount 24, 34, 71
Moore, Sir Philip 186
Moscow 62–3, 134, 138, 144, 159, Mosul 53
Mount Vernon 165
Mountbatten, Earl 38, 102
Mulley, Fred MP 166–7
Murmansk 15
Murray, River 170
Muscat 75, 77, 78, 100, 108, 156, 191
Museum, Royal Engineers 185

Nagasaki 31
Nagoya 150
Nairobi 75, 80
Nantes, Edict of 1
Nasser, Col. Gamal Abdel 50, 54
Nat West Bank 180, 186, 189–91
NATO 70, 114, 130, 132, 136, 138, 164, 166, 171–3
New York 187, 191–2
New Zealand 114, 117, 122, 126, 140, 153, 167, 170
Nicosia 56
Nienburg 181–2
Nittle, Jeremy 125
Normandy 17, 18, 19, 24, 65, 129–30, 192, 194
North West Frontier 4
Northern Army Group 132
Northern Ireland 114–6, 120–2, 126–7, 136, 160–1, 166
Norton, Admiral of the Fleet Sir Peter Hill 144
Norway 173, 193
Notley, Brigadier John 90–1
NSA 103, 139, 147
Nyerere, Julius 101, 108

OBE 78, 145
Oerlinghausen 180
O'Grady, Gerald 2
O'Grady, Phillip 2
Oldman, Hugh 36, 75
Omaha Beach 23
Omaha, Nebraska 161
Oman 36, 77, 84

Operation Overland 23
Operation Zipper 36
Oslo 174
Ottawa 100, 139, 147, 174–5
Ouistreham 18, 22, 193

Pakistan 136–7
Palestine 52
Panama Canal 7, 91
Pareto Partners 180, 192
Paris 130, 133, 173
Parracombe 2, 48, 111
Parsons, Mr and Mrs 72
Pasha, Glubb 56–7
Pattiala, Maharaja of 37, 39
Pegasus Bridge 21, 22, 65, 194
Peking 190
Penang 44, 45
Peng, Chin 47
Peng, Li 43
Persia 53
Philippines 190
Phillips, Donald 182
Pine-Coffin, Lt Col. 21, 22
Plymouth Sound 89
Poentjak Pass 37, 39, 140, 152
Poet, Brigadier Nigel 22, 67, 71, 73
Pollard, Major-General Barry 180
Port Stanley 189
Portsmouth 23, 70, 123, 152, 192–4
Potomac, River 165
Potsdam 63
Potts, Archie 161
Pretoria 100–1, 105–8
Price, First Minister George 92–4
Pritchett, V.S. 4, 5
PWD 91, 94

Radfan 95, 104, 109
Ramsden, James, MP 87, 98
Rawlins, Basil 50
Reagan, Mrs Nancy 194
Regiment, 1 Pattialas 37, 39
Regiment, 16/5 Royal Lancers 50
Regiment, 21 Engineer 182
Regiment, 26 Armoured Engineer 181
Regiment, 28 Amphibious Engineer 181–2

Regiment, 32 Armoured Engineer 194
Regiment, 35 Engineer 48, 50
Regiment, 38 Corps Engineer 67 67, 84, 85, 87, 89, 94, 98, 109, 131
Regiment, Blues and Royals 132
Regiment, King's African Rifles 104
Regiment, King's Own Yorkshire Light Infantry 115
Regiment, Royal Fusiliers 117
Regiment, Royal Hampshire 91
Reid, Lt Gen. John 167
Reisener, Dr 3
Rennie, General 18
Rheindalen 122, 126, 130, 132–4, 169, 180–1
Rhine, British Army of 62, 96, 126
Rhine, River 26, 27, 29, 131, 134
Rhio Islands 35
Rhodesia 107, 136, 164
Richardson, General Sir Charles 144, 167
Ridout, Carol 87
Ridout, Douglas 87
Ripon 33, 80, 84, 85, 87–8, 95, 97–8, 122
Robertson, General Sir Brian 55
Rommel, General 14
Rorke's Drift, Battle of 182
Rougier, Major-General Jeremy 94, 183
Royal Army Service Corps 22, 77
Royal Engineers 4, 9, 44, 48, 63, 98, 122, 144, 184, 193, 196
Royal Military Academy 2, 4, 5, 7, 65
Royal Tank Regiment 2, 7, 10–11
Royal Thames Yacht Club 146, 157
Royal Ulster Constabulary 121, 127
Russia 191

SACEUR 161, 172
Sandhurst 1, 5, 65, 107
Saudi Arabia 107
Scarman, Lord 127
Schleswig Holstein 1
Schumine(s) 25
Scott-Bowden, Major-General L. 10, 23, 25, 28, 31, 33–4, 52, 147, 149–50, 156, 194
Scott-Bowden, Jos 52, 149, 150, 156
Selassie, Emperor Haile 107
SHAPE 138, 172

Sharon, Ariel 69, 128–9, 148
Sharp, General Sir John 169–70
Sherwood Foresters 1, 3
Shinwell, Baron 34
Simpson, General Sir Frank 10, 97
Sinclair, Major-General Gus 186
Slim, Viscount 34
Smallwood, Air Chief Marshal Sir 'Splinters' 46
Smith, Ian 164
Sobuza, King, of the Swazis 105
Somaliland Scouts 80
South Africa 100, 158, 173, 182
South America 191, 197
South Korea 190
Soviet Bloc 102, 166
Spandau 60
Speller, Major-General Norman 68, 72
Squadron, 100 Field 182
Squadron, 12 Field 85, 90–2, 94
Squadron, 14 Topo 181
Squadron, 15 Corps Field Park 85
Squadron, 16 Field 180
Squadron, 30 Field 95–6
Squadron, 33 Independent Field 183–4
Squadron, 42 Field 50
Squadron, 48 Field 85, 96
St John's Ambulance 180, 194, 196
St Michael's School 58, 73 3, 58, 73, 97, 106
Stainforth, Graham 97
Stalin, Joseph 47
Stevens, Col. Mike 94, 96
Stewart, Pam 7
Stibbon, General Sir John 131
Strong, Major-General Kenneth 102–3, 143
Sudan 50, 100
Suez Canal 50, 68, 70, 128, 148, 155
Suez Town 50–1, 68
Sukarno 37, 152
Sumatra 36–8
Swaziland 101, 105, 108
Switzerland 122
Sword Beach 18, 20, 33
Sydney 153, 170
Syria 54, 129

Taiwan 190
Talbot, Rear Admiral 18
Tanganyika 101
Tangiers 2
Tanzania 101, 108
Tedder, Marshal of the RAF Lord 34
Terauchi, Field Marshal Hisaichi 37
Tet offensive 118, 120
Thailand 190
Thatcher, Baroness 140
The Diplomatist 145
The Sapper 184
Thesiger, Wilfred 107
Tickell, Sir Christopher 187
Tigris, River 107, 108
Timsah, Lake 52
Tjandjoer 37, 39
Tobruk 14
Togo, Admiral 151–2
Tokyo 37, 136, 146, 148, 150–2
Trench, Reggie 26
Trentishoe 47–8, 58, 67–8, 110–1
Tripolitania 56
Tsushima Straits, Battle of 152
Tunisia 16
Turkey 54, 149, 172, 191
Tutankhamen 3

Urquhart, Major-General Tiger 18, 20, 31, 32
Vickers, Brigadier Bill 115
Vietnam 114, 117–20, 139, 144, 147
Vigors, Ashmead 6
Vigors, Desmond 6, 107
Vigors, Edward 5, 6
Vigors, Evelyn 2, 4, 5, 33
Vigors, Hyacinth D'Arcy 1–4, 6, 10, 11, 15, 17, 23–5, 33, 48, 56, 67–8
Vigors, Major Phillip Urban 1, 3
Vigors, Mary 6
Vigors, Tim 6

Wade, Captain Jim 50
Wakeford, Air Marshal Dickie 157 157, 159, 166, 169
Walker, General Walter 174
Wall, Major-General Peter 194
War, First World 56, 189
War, Korean 118
War, Second World 6, 7, 10, 89, 122, 129
Washington 100, 103, 107, 124–5, 133, 138–9, 154–5, 162, 164, 166, 174, 184, 187, 194
Watkinson, Captain Watty 23
Waziristan 104
Wellesley, Margaret 182
Wellington College 2, 4–7, 15, 97, 109, 111, 122–3
Wellington, NZ 117, 153, 167, 171
Welsford, Deirdre 6, 7, 104
West Indies 91
Western Command 4
Whistler, Major-General 'Bolo' 31
White, Brigadier Neville 94
White, Sir Dick 114, 121
Whitehall 43, 55–6, 70, 73, 82, 88, 98–101, 106, 109, 114, 118, 127, 137–8, 140, 142, 144–5, 147–8, 154, 161, 163–4, 169, 186
Wilkinson, Sir Peter 118
Willison, Queenie 1, 2
Willison, Arthur Cecil 1–4, 10, 14, 15, 24, 31, 45, 48, 67, 110–1
Willison, Becky 154
Willison, Betty *see under* Bates
Willison, Celia Mary 17, 22, 24–5, 33, 43, 48, 57–8, 61, 63, 67, 73, 85, 97, 111, 123–4, 131, 154
Willison, David (grandson) 154
Willison, Heather 153
Willison, James 154
Willison, Janet Lesley 30, 33–4, 43, 48, 57–8, 61, 63, 67, 73, 97, 106, 109, 111, 123–4, 132, 147, 154, 181, 196
Willison, Mary 1
Willison, Robin David 46–8, 64, 68, 73, 97, 109, 111, 123, 130–1, 153–4, 169–70, 196–7
Willison, William 1, 2
Wilson, Baron (Harold) 140, 154, 165–6
Wilson, Jim 71–2
Wingrove, Brigadier 'Pooh' 37–8, 41
Winkfield, Major 13
Woods, Major-General Bill 90
Woolwich 7, 9, 53, 65, 72
Woolwich, 'The Shop' 7, 10, 47, 48

Works Services 60, 62–3, 84
Worsley, Francis 5

Yemen 104
Youde, Sir Teddy 106
Younger, Diana 33, 174
Younger, Major-General Jack 163

Younger, Malcolm 6, 163, 174
Younger, Major-General Tony 33–4, 56

Zambia 105, 108
Zanzibar 82, 101–2
Zimbabwe 163